THREE ESSAYS

by Albrecht Ritschl

Wipf & Stock
PUBLISHERS
Eugene, Oregon

D1261889

A. Ritschl.

Albrecht Ritschl

THREE ESSAYS

Theology and Metaphysics
"Prolegomena" to *The History of Pietism*
Instruction in the Christian Religion

Translated and with an Introduction by
PHILIP HEFNER

Wipf and Stock Publishers
199 W 8th Ave, Suite 3
Eugene, OR 97401

Three Essays
Theology and Metaphysics : Prolegomena to The History of Pietism :
Instruction in the Christian Religion
By Ritschl, Albrecht
Copyright©1972 Hefner, Philip
ISBN: 1-59752-034-9
Publication date 1/25/2005
Previously published by Fortress Press, 1972

Contents

Preface

This volume of essays has been almost a decade in its becoming, and therefore it is not surprising that the debts incurred in its appearance are many. It would not be possible to mention the names of every person who has assisted me in this work, but these persons should know not only that I appreciated their helpfulness, but also that this volume was dependent upon their efforts.

Certain persons and institutions dare not go unmentioned: Professor Jaroslav Pelikan, who first broached the idea, together with the Editorial Board of the Library of Protestant Thought and the Sealantic Foundation who supported this project when it seemed that the book would appear in that series. The Rev. Robert Hanson, who worked long hours to help make Ritschl speak idiomatic English; this translation owes a great deal to him and his diligence. The men who, as student assistants, helped with exasperating details: J. William Novak, Dennis Hartsook, and John Ruppenthal. Professors Robert Fischer, Paul Jersild, Darrell Jodock, Walter Kukkonen, and David Lotz, who made critical suggestions on the translations and introduction. The scholars who furnished me with copies of doctoral dissertations—their own and others I did not know about—which made the introductory survey possible. Librarians, especially in Chicago and Hamburg, who carry on a tradition of helpfulness and expertise that is simply indispensable. Finally, to two descendants of Albrecht Ritschl, who although they have not seen this work in manuscript were always ready to help, and who made possible the photograph that appears here, Professor Hans Ritschl and his son, Professor Dietrich Ritschl.

With so many helpers, it is sobering to recognize that I take full responsibility for the errors and misstatements that may appear herein. I would appreciate having them called to my attention.

Lutheran School of Theology at Chicago   P.H.
March 25, 1972
The 150th Anniversary of Albrecht Ritschl's Birth

Abbreviations

APOLOGY   Apology of the Augsburg Confession (1531)

      AS   The Smalcald Articles (1537)

      CA   The Augsburg Confession (1530)

      CR   *Corpus Reformatorum*

Fabricius   Cajus Fabricius, ed., *Die christliche Vollkommenheit und Unterricht in der christlichen Religion.* Critical edition in one volume. Leipzig: J. C. Hinrichsche Buchhandlung, 1924.

      LW   American Edition of *Luther's Works.* Helmut T. Lehmann and Jaroslav Pelikan, General Editors. Philadelphia: Fortress Press, and Saint Louis: Concordia Publishing House.

  R.u.V.   *Die christliche Lehre von der Rechtfertigung und Versöhnung.* 3 vols.; Bonn: Adolph Marcus, 1870–1874 and several later editions.

Tappert   Theodore Tappert, trans. and ed., *The Book of Concord.* Philadelphia: Fortress Press, 1959.

      ET   English Translation.

Materials and notes appearing within brackets [ ] are the editor's additions.

ALBRECHT RITSCHL:

AN INTRODUCTION

Albrecht Ritschl:

An Introduction

by Philip Hefner

I. THE MAN AND HIS SETTING

The theological achievement of Albrecht Ritschl is, like that of every man, closely bound to the world in which he lived. If not a product of the environment, at least it is understandable only as a part of that environment. This may pose problems, particularly for the American reader, because Ritschl's world of nineteenth century Germany is largely unknown and even unknowable for us. Furthermore, since the definitive comprehensive study of Ritschl and his place in history is yet to be written, we are still at the stage of putting bits and pieces together from the existing studies of the man, in an attempt to understand him.[1] In what follows, we will try to show how the religious, social class, political, intellectual, cultural, and even geographical factors of his life help us to unlock the truth of what he holds for us.

HOME AND FAMILY

Ritschl was an heir of what has been called the German protestant counterpart to the Roman Catholic hierarchical clerical succession: he was at least the third generation academically interested religious professional in his family. For several generations, the family home had been in Erfurt, a Saxon town where Martin Luther had attended the university. Albrecht Ritschl's grandfather, George Wilhelm Ritschl, was pastor at the St. John's Church in Erfurt and professor at the secondary school (Gymnasium) there. George's son and Albrecht's father, George Carl Benjamin (born 1783, died 1858) moved to Berlin where he was pastor of the prestigious St. Mary's Church, earned a doctorate in theology, and in 1827 became a bishop of the protestant church and general superintendent of the churches in Pomerania, which today is part of Poland, with his episcopal seat in Stettin (now Szezczin, on the border between Poland and East Germany). The bishop was apparently an extremely diligent member of the Prussian leading class, noted for his formality, hard work, and unwillingness to get involved in petty bickering between cliques. He enjoyed the respect of the emperors under whom he served, Friedrich Wilhelm IV and Wilhelm I. Without casting aspersions on the indisputable piety and theological earnestness of the bishop, we must remind ourselves that his office made him a member of the Prussian elite, what we would call today the Prussian "establishment." To be a bishop in this situation involved support for the decades-long policy of the Prussian government to unite the Lutheran and Calvinist churches into the Prussian Union Church. George Carl Ritschl was a bishop of this union church and noted for his vigorous and sincere support of the union. This made his work difficult inasmuch as Pomerania was a stronghold of "confessional" Lutherans who emphasized their particularity over against the Calvinists and the union church. Ultimately, the growing strength of these confessional Lutherans combined with the bishop's advanced age motivated his retirement in 1854, inasmuch as the opponents to the union had gained enough positions in the ruling council of the Pomeranian church to enable them to isolate their bishop.

Albrecht was the only surviving son of his father's second marriage (although five children survived from the first marriage) to Auguste Sebald, the daughter of the Commissioner of Justice in Berlin. His mother apparently set a lively, light-hearted tone in the home, balancing the father's gravity of disposition. She and her husband gave Ritschl a love for music which never waned. She was a member of the Berlin Singing Academy (her husband was at one time on its board of directors) in which the great theologian Friedrich Schleiermacher was also active. The anecdote survives that Schleiermacher once exclaimed after the choir practice that Auguste was a "gorgeous girl."

Albrecht Benjamin Ritschl was born into this family on March 25, 1822. What we can safely say about his early years is that he possessed a winning and flexible personality which enabled him to live easily in love and trust with all the members of a household whose personal relationships were complicated by the fact that the two brothers and three sisters from his father's first marriage were cared for more by an aunt than by the stepmother. Albrecht entered fully into the musical life of the family and also distinguished himself by his earnest studies, graduating with a superior record from the secondary school when he was seventeen years of age. In 1839 he began his studies at Bonn, which was also at that time a Prussian city and university, where the theological faculty, under the influence of Schleiermacher, was dominated by the dogmatician Karl Immanuel Nitzsch. The theological atmosphere was marked by a supernaturalistic piety of the traditional sort (thus matching the piety of his home), combined with a commitment to the serious pursuit of academic theology, including attention to new scientific developments. Among the father's admonitions to the young Ritschl were the words that he was as concerned with his son's spiritual development as with his intellectual growth, to which he added, "faith precedes understanding, understanding grows out of faith."

The significance of this home background cannot be overlooked if we are to understand Ritschl: (1) He grew up among the intellectual, cultural, political, and ecclesiastical elite of Berlin and Prussian Germany; he was accustomed to social and professional contacts with the elite, and his family appreciated and participated in the social, cultural, and professional activities of the elite. (2) From the earliest years, he had set before him the ideal of excellence and earnestness in vocational responsibilities, as the way to contribute to the maintenance of society. (3) Deep-seated piety and belief in what we would call traditional, supernatural Lutheran Christianity permeated his life. (4) Serious concern for the practical life of the church and its political administration was inseparable from his family's piety. (5) As proponents of and officeholders in the Prussian Union Church, his family communicated to Ritschl the sense that Lutheranism was best expressed in a Lutheran–Calvinist unity, and this sense included both an intellectual-theological and a personal opposition to the conservative Lutheran particularists who comprised the "confessional" or "orthodox" party; nevertheless, as bishop, his father set the example of trying to rise above the inevitable party bickerings between unionists, confessionalists, and pietists. Each of these five elements in his early background was prominent in Albrecht Ritschl's life, up to the time of his death in 1889.

STUDENT YEARS

Otto Ritschl, in his biography of his father, comments that Ritschl's theology, even at its most abstract, is the scientific elaboration and defense of his fundamental religious and ethical convictions.[2] This comment can serve as a principle for understanding Ritschl's development in his university studies. From his first semester at Bonn, through the time of his doctorate at Halle and his habilitation dissertation at Tübingen and Bonn, Ritschl was working out his destiny on two fronts: his religious-theological beliefs and his academic-scientific methodology. From the beginning of his university days, he lived in the atmosphere in which a supernatural approach to Christian belief was fighting for its life, partly over against an also supernatural Hegelian philosophy and partly against a scientific, materialistic world view that rejected both. As he progressed in his studies, he also witnessed the dissolution of Hegelianism into its so-called right and left wings, the former returning to a traditional supernaturalism, the latter becoming a radicalizing factor, both politically and theologically, tending in the direction of the avowedly atheistic Ludwig Feuerbach.[3] At Bonn, his professors presented a traditional Christian faith that was trying to take the scientific and philosophical demands of the modern world seriously, and among his personal friendships he counted members of the confessional Lutheran party with whom he carried on intense debates until he finally worked out in his mind a respectable theological opposition to that party, substantiating academically his personal predisposition for the Prussian union. At Halle, his professors continued to pose the supernaturalistic option, with a tinge of pietism. Ritschl was impressed, but could not give his burgeoning capabilities and desire for truth to their theological schemes. Here he began his love affair with the so-called Hegelians, notably Ferdinand Christian Baur, who taught at Tübingen, but whose books, specifically his work on reconciliation, caught Ritschl's attention. The philosopher Erdmann impressed Ritschl sufficiently to influence him to do his doctorate in that area, with a dissertation on Augustine. Ritschl was determined on an academic career, and he wanted to prove himself with Baur. His father resisted the son's turn to the philosophical and critical position of Baur and pressed him first to spend some months in Heidelberg, but finally consented to the study at Tübingen, where Ritschl began work in the summer of 1845.

Besides the importance of Baur for the young Ritschl and his development, this relationship and its rupture in 1856 goes down as one of the important friendships and breakups in modern theological history.[4] Baur was the first man who was able to develop a comprehensive historical theology, that is, he committed himself to the effort to understand Christianity through a critical historical investigation of its origins and development, with the intention to present it in its entirety and explain its essence and its significance. Ritschl turned to Baur because he found in him an impressive resource for pursuing rigorous scientific studies in concert with an unabashed Christian faith and piety. Baur was greatly influenced by Hegel, although it is erroneous to label him a "Hegelian." He insisted that historical study is not meaningful or "objective" unless it is carried on under a leading idea. For Baur this resided in an understanding of the *Geist* or Spirit revealing itself through the concrete manifestations of the historical process, mainly in the manifestations which embody the conflict and reconciliation of opposing tendencies, in a dialectic of thesis-antithesis-synthesis which is close to Hegel's. Ritschl sloughed off the theoretical, speculative scheme of Baur's, but he learned his historical-theological craft from him, and in dialogue and conflict with Baur he worked out ideas that would be of later importance for him. Ritschl harbored differences and misunderstandings of Baur from the beginning of their relationship which finally led to stormy clash, in which Ritschl's insensitivity to Baur was an important factor, making the episode one of the more regrettable in Ritschl's life.[5] Nevertheless, Ritschl considered himself a member of Baur's "Tübingen school" until as late as 1856.

Under Baur's influence, Ritschl pursued a meticulous study of the New Testament and the immediate postapostolic centuries. His habilitation dissertation (the German prerequisite to a teaching career) dealt with Marcion and the Gospel of Luke, concluding that the former was the original basis for the latter. This thesis won Baur's full approval, so that when Ritschl himself later abandoned it, the master was to become its ardent defender. This dissertation was accepted at Bonn, where Ritschl received the licentiate in 1846, qualifying as an unpaid lecturer in the same year, at age twenty-four.

CAREER AT BONN

Ritschl's teaching career spanned a period of just under forty-four years, at two universities—the first eighteen years, until 1864, were at Bonn, the last twenty-five in Göttingen. As a student, Ritschl had moved from a study of dogmatics, through the history of theology, to New Testament studies. At Bonn, he reversed that sequence, beginning as lecturer in New Testament until the end of the 1840s, then turning to history, with special concern for the reformation and the confessional positions of the various churches, until his appointment as extraordinary professor without tenure in 1853, when he began lecturing in dogmatics, which he was to continue until his death. From 1853 until the end, however, he continued to do research and to lecture in all three areas. Although his primary influence had been dogmatics, his last years were devoted to the history of the church and its theology, a field that he called his "youthful love," and his "escape" from the tempests of dogmatic controversy.[6]

A number of important episodes are to be noted in Ritschl's Bonn period, which ended when he was forty-two years old. (1) Ritschl entered into his first active political involvement, which turned out to be his last, also. In the wake of the February 1848 Paris uprising and because of his disillusionment with the Prussian Emperor Friedrich Wilhelm IV, Ritschl openly espoused constitutional democracy for Germany, joined the "Constitutional Union," and was elected to several offices in the Union, including that of being a delegate to a congress in Cologne in 1848. He was an observer at the famous Frankfurt Parliament, held in the Paulskirche in the same year. His was a moderate position, bitterly critical both of the radicals (the "Democratic Union") and the Prussian emperor. His disillusionment with the defeat of his party in 1849, together with the outbreak of violence in Bonn and the time-consuming demands which distracted him from his academic work, led to an early retirement from politics, although he remained active in efforts for university reform. This activity, in combination with union church sentiments and Baurian theological leanings, typed Ritschl as an activist, a critical spirit, and something of a liberal at Bonn. At this time he made a vow, which he never broke, to remain aloof from secular politics.

(2) Almost immediately after his arrival at Bonn, Ritschl began work on his book, *The Emergence of the Old Catholic Church,* which appeared in its first edition in 1850 and in its second in 1857.[7] This work, in its two editions, is significant for several reasons: (a) Whereas the first edition represents an attempt to apply Baur's method to the study of the development of New Testament Christianity into Catholicism, the second declares Ritschl's personal and academic independence from Baur and the Tübingen school, thus providing an alternative to that school for historical-theological studies which combined the same highly disciplined critical skills and concern for the overall historical significance of Christianity with a more conservative concern for the tradition and less reliance upon speculative schemes. (b) In the process of working out his differences with Baur, Ritschl solidified his fundamental interpretation of Jesus and the New Testament faith, which was to serve as a cornerstone for all of his later work. (c) The study of early Christianity laid down the basis for interpreting the emergence of the Christian church and the rise of Catholicism which was to be the kernel of the most important historical interpretation of Christianity up to our own day, that of the towering church historian, Adolf von Harnack, a later disciple of Ritschl.

Ritschl's differences from Baur did not take radical form until the second edition of the work, but they were latent from the outset. They can be summarized by saying that Ritschl on the one hand disagreed with Baur on a number of individual points of scholarly judgment, while on the other he rejected what he thought was Baur's tendency to sacrifice objectivity and the primacy of revelation to a theoretical philosophical bias, the conflict model of the dialectic of history. Although it appears that Ritschl misunderstood Baur's philosophical categories and underestimated how deeply they were rooted in Baur's historical studies, it is clear that Ritschl gave a priority to scripture which was in contrast to Baur and which constituted one of the elements of Ritschl's relative conservatism.[8] His individual scholarly disagreements with his teacher also appeared often to be conservative, since he tended to accept the authenticity of biblical documents where Baur often discredited their apostolic origins. Ritschl forsook the thesis of his habilitation dissertation, for example, only to have Baur take up the cudgels for it. In regard to the interpretation of early Christianity, on which Baur published a large work in 1853 and to which Ritschl's second edition responded, it may be said that whereas Baur had explained the movement of Christianity from the time after Jesus' crucifixion until the beginning of the third century as the struggle between Jewish-oriented Christians symbolized by Peter and Hellenistic–Gentile Christians under the aegis of Paul, culminating in the Johannine synthesis of the two represented in the Roman papacy, Ritschl to the contrary insisted that the Jewish and Gentile tendencies were more complex than Baur's conflict model allowed. Ritschl concluded that far from being a Jewish–Gentile synthesis, Catholicism was a wholly Gentile phenomenon, representing a deviation and estrangement from the Hebraic–Jewish heritage of earliest Christianity. This is the thesis that lives on in Harnack's history of dogma, where it is expanded and deepened.[9]

(3) Beginning in the 1850s, Ritschl gave increasing attention to church history and the history of theology, offering courses and writing a succession of articles on the nature of protestantism, the confessional documents, and opposing the confessionalist party. He did much basic research, which did not reach its fruition until some years later, when he had moved to Göttingen. These early efforts did help him, however, to solidify his understanding that the mainline reformation faith needed to be understood as an alternative to Roman Catholicism and that this reformation faith was best expressed by the unity of Lutherans and Calvinists, in opposition to the anti-union confessionalists. He also became even more convinced that the work of the reformation theologians was incomplete—a conviction that gave shape to his own professional vocation as a theologian.

As Ritschl probed more deeply into the reformation, he began to develop a discipline of reformation studies that were of considerable significance, even to the present time. Only recently has the work of

David Lotz[10] brought fully to light what earlier hints had suggested, namely, that Ritschl's concern for the reformation and specifically for the theology of Martin Luther was a crucial element of his own later dogmatic position and that both his concern and his specific scholarly interpretations of this period were greatly influential in the two generations after Ritschl. As a result of the studies that he undertook in the 1860s, Ritschl became one of the leading forces behind a "Luther Renaissance" which has been a major factor in twentieth century protestant and Roman Catholic theology. Even though Ritschl worked in a time before the great critical editions of Luther's works and other reformation documents were available, he established in a forceful way the thesis that Luther and the heart of the reformation faith differ from the authoritative portrayals of Luther's orthodox followers, including those of the confessionalists that opposed both Ritschl and his father in Pomerania. Ritschl established the now well-known (and in part discredited) disjunction between the theology of the "young Luther" and the mature Luther, as well as that between Luther and Melanchthon and the second generation of Lutheran dogmaticians. Ritschl's reformation studies must be placed in the context of his continuing animosities toward the confessionalists and the pietists, because these studies were used as polemical weapons against these parties. An example of how he turned this research to polemical purposes is evident in the "Prolegomena" to the *History of Pietism*, included in this volume.

(4) A vacancy in the department of systematic theology enabled Ritschl to begin lecturing in dogmatics in the winter semester, 1853–54. In the ten years that followed, until his departure for Göttingen, he developed a number of themes which became enduring characteristics for his thinking. Five of these themes deserve mention here: (a) He enunciated his position as a theologian *within* the Christian community of redeemed persons, insisting furthermore that the Christian faith must be considered a *corporate* expression of this community's faith prior to its individual expressions. (b) From this position, dogmatics deals solely with the *revelation* which is available in scripture and the tradition of scriptural interpretation. A preoccupation with revelation means that Jesus Christ is central to Christian theology and this in turn gives dogmatics its basic theme— that God's revealed will is the establishment of the kingdom of God.

(c) Preoccupation with revelation and Jesus Christ further suggests that the reconciled relationship of man with God is the arena within which theological thinking takes place. Through the sacrifice of the covenant, whose prototype is in the Old Testament, Jesus works forgiveness and justification for members of the covenant community; this justification is expressed in the community's reconciled life, which manifests itself through ethical work that builds up the kingdom of God. (d) Justification and reconciliation (the theme of the three-volume work which is Ritschl's magnum opus) appears very early, then, as a major concern for Ritschl's dogmatics. (e) From the first, Ritschl is intent upon being *systematic;* the various themes of the Christian faith must be unified in their presentation. Although his systematic penchant is the source for many of the distortions that mar his work, it was also to be his major strength as a dogmatician.

(5) Finally, we call attention to the opposition of the confessionalist Lutheran party which dogged Ritschl, even as it had his father. With the growing ascendancy of this party, which opposed both Ritschl's unionism and his Baurian background, in Prussian church affairs, the government officer in charge of university appointments and promotions consistently refused to consider Ritschl for advancement despite his growing reputation as a scholar and the recommendations of his faculty colleagues. Ritschl waited seven years to receive an appointment that would bring him a regular faculty position with salary and six more years until he was appointed to a tenured position in August 1859.

THE YEARS IN GÖTTINGEN

In the spring of 1864 Ritschl arrived in Göttingen to take over the senior chair in dogmatics, succeeding the right-wing Hegelian, I. A. Dorner. He had taken a wife five years earlier, his third child being born shortly before he left Bonn. Although his standing among his colleagues in Bonn was high, he chafed under the coolness of the government officials, and he interpreted their refusal to grant him adequate salary increases as an indication of their failure to appreciate him. Göttingen was in the province of Hannover, and Ritschl looked forward to exchanging the Prussian setting for a new one, with a new set of government and church officials.

Hannover was a "pure Lutheran" province, in the sense that it possessed no union church. The explicit program of the ecclesiastical officials was to pursue a policy of genuine confessional Lutheranism, purified of the rationalistic tendencies of an earlier generation and opposed to modernistic tendencies, yet alert to the modern world and incorporating healthy elements of pietism. Rationalist, pietist, and confessional Lutherans had all been a part of Hannover's recent past, as well as mediating theologians who attempted to synthesize orthodoxy and modern critical scholarly methods. The consequence of all these factors, however, was a situation which required Ritschl always to be wary of a resurgence of conservative confessionalism which formed a coalition with pietists, the difference here being that the ecclesiastical officials were not captive to the confessionalists. This situation was changed by the policies of Bismarck, who carried out campaigns of war with Austria, in 1866, continuing with the Franco-Prussian War of 1870. As the campaigns began, Ritschl retreated from the liberalism of the Bonn era, since he was of the opinion that Bismarck's policy was a realistic one. His status as a Prussian and as a supporter of Bismarck won him no affection in Göttingen, however, and when in August 1866, Hannover was annexed by Prussia, he felt himself severely ostracized by his colleagues. The confessionalist opposition took on added meaning, since orthodoxism now became a rallying point for Hannoverian opposition to Prussian hegemony politically as well as to Prussian unionism ecclesiastically.

Ironically, Ritschl seemed more attractive to the Prussian officials after the annexation, because he became a point of contact and a source of information for the Prussian ministers of culture and religion. In October 1869, he was appointed a delegate to the Hannoverian provincial synod, in connection with whose meetings he drew up a comprehensive report on the church-political situation in Hannover and northern Germany. This report was for the same minister who had snubbed him repeatedly in his later years at Bonn. His thesis was highly polemical: that the orthodox Lutherans in most of northern Germany were so implicated in the political situation that confessionalism was to be evaluated in political as well as in theological terms, as an expression of anti-Prussianism and "political particularism." He observed that ecclesiastical unionism and Prussian political expansionism seemed inseparable in the eyes of those who, within Prussia and without, could not share the dreams of the Prussian leaders. This report made a great impression on the minister, who called Ritschl to Berlin for further consultations, apparently even sharing the report with the Prussian king.

The unionism which Ritschl had shared by family tradition and which he undergirded with his academic studies in the nature of protestantism remained constant, even though the response it elicited from ecclesiastical and government circles varied from favorable to hostile. When this state of affairs is kept in mind, along with the ever-present pietist trends in the German church, against whom Ritschl expended as much polemical energy as he did against the orthodoxists, we can understand the existential and political circumstances in which Ritschl formed his identity as a theologian of the church. Not only his historical work, with its important emphasis upon Luther and the reformation, but also his philosophical and dogmatic work must be seen as a response, in part, to these circumstances.

At this same time, Ritschl was attempting to remain uninvolved in the specific party conflicts of the province and to avoid concrete participation in church affairs. He deliberately declined many speaking engagements and published relatively little between 1864 and 1869, on the grounds that anything he wrote or said would be used or abused by one or another of the parties. For the same reason, he discouraged his students from forming "Ritschlian" study groups among the parish pastors. He was beginning what he called his "life-work," the fruit of his vocation as an academic theologian, the three-volume *Justification and Reconciliation*. In these years, even though the temptation was great, he declined several calls to other universities, just as in the early seventies he was to decline the election as pro-rector of the university and four repeated offers of a joint position at the University of Berlin and a high post in the Prussian church administration. The concept of vocation, understood as a high ethical work related to the realization of the kingdom of God, which was so integral to his theological system, drove him to define himself more and more as an academic theologian, to the exclusion of other distractions. As a consequence, his interests and his personality became steadily narrower, to the discomfort of those who differed from him, but his life's purpose became more sharply focused and his theological contribution was progressively deepened and solidified.

In January 1869, after less than ten years of marriage, Ritschl's wife died, followed less than two years later by the death of his sister who had become his housekeeper and foster mother to his children. These deaths made a deep impression on Ritschl, whose grieving reached intense depths. We note a spirit of solemnity and even resignation entering at this time, never to leave him. For all his sternness and rigorous sense of vocation, Ritschl lived a life marked by many friendships, overcoming much of the anti-Prussian bias in Göttingen, and not by any means limited to theologians and clergy. He participated regularly in singing groups and was a party-giver of some note among his intimate circle of friends. This way of life did not disappear completely after his wife's death, but it did decline steadily. Although at the end of his life he lectured to large classes of over one hundred students, he seems to have been relatively ineffective as a classroom teacher, making much more impact with his writings than with his lectures. In the 1870s and '80s the influence of his theological thinking greatly increased—notably with the appearance of the magnum opus and his short summary of his theological system, *Instruction in the Christian Religion*. By 1879 he could write that his dogmatic position was expounded by disciples (many of whom had not studied with him, but were influenced by his writings) on every theological faculty in western Germany except for Heidelberg. But at the same time, Ritschl lamented all his life that his theology did not win the sort of positive reception that he thought it deserved. Many of his letters, at the height of his influence, speak with resignation of the "poor" hearing and negative response he was receiving. He was extraordinarily sensitive to those who became his disciples, rejoicing in their association, and at the same time equally sensitive to those who criticized him. In his later life, when controversy swirled around him, he responded only seldom to his critics and relied on his close friends to summarize the critiques, while he read only the most serious himself.

Ritschl's opposition was very hostile and vociferous, but its appearance in the late seventies and eighties was a tribute in itself to the immense impact Ritschl was making. Since, for all practical purposes, it may be said that his dogmatic achievement was complete

by the mid-seventies, it is not surprising that it is only after this time
that the opposition became intense, at first through the conventional
channels of periodicals and newspapers, but in the early 1880s
through the church-political means of seeking Ritschl's censure at
provincial synods. For the most part, it may be said that his disciples,
his colleagues, and the ecclesiastical officials defended Ritschl quite
well—some because they were enthusiastic adherents of the man,
others because they recognized that the seriousness of his achievement did not merit the kind of censure that some opponents were
demanding.

The climaxing decade of Ritschl's career, 1864–1874, was devoted
to the work on justification and reconciliation, in which Ritschl's
creative and systematic dogmatic gifts were brought to a sharply
focused expression. Roughly speaking, the next (and last) decade
of his life, 1876–1886, went into the three-volume *History of
Pietism*. During this time, Ritschl literally read every primary source
for Dutch, German, and Swiss pietism that the libraries of his time
could provide. His very last years were spent on the posthumously
published work on *Fides Implicita*, which dealt with questions of
faith and reason, from medieval times to the present. He had interrupted these studies to respond to critics in his essay on *Theology
and Metaphysics* and also to revise the work on justification and his
other books. He served two terms, in 1876 and 1886, as pro-rector
of the university; during the second term he presided over and
delivered the keynote address at the one hundred fiftieth anniversary
of the university. Toward the end, Ritschl suffered from a number
of ailments, aggravated by his feeling of loneliness at the deaths of
loved ones and friends and by the generally depressing effect of
controversy. In his last days, he was cared for by his son-in-law, the
New Testament scholar, Johannes Weiss, and his son, the church
historian, Otto. He died on March 20, 1889, five days before his
sixty-seventh birthday.

II. RITSCHL'S THEOLOGICAL CONTRIBUTION

We can best understand the popularity and the opposition evoked
by Ritschl's work if we turn our attention to the theological system
that stands at the center of that work. The appeal of Ritschl's
theology can be summarized by saying that *he presented a forceful*

contemporary statement of the Christian faith which resonated to the scene in which he lived, and he linked this statement positively to the tradition upon which his hearers wanted to rely, while also expressing himself in terms of a method that was scientifically significant. Let us look more closely at the elements of this summary: forceful contemporary statement of faith, positive link to tradition, and scientific method.

CONTEMPORARY STATEMENT OF FAITH

Ritschl's central statement of faith is a relatively simple, but original, linking of a few basic ideas. The Christian faith embodies Jesus' revelation, which is the message that God's will is to establish his kingdom. Correlative to God's objective will toward his kingdom is the relationship of man to God and that kingdom, a relationship that is spoken of in terms of the classical Christian doctrines of justification and reconciliation. Whether we speak of the kingdom of God or of man's relationship to God in justification and reconciliation, we meet a duality (Ritschl himself called it "an ellipse with two foci") comprised of that which man receives, as *gift,* which brings him near to God and the kingdom, and that which man must do, as *task,* to express his relationship to God and realize the kingdom. Forgiveness of sins, justification, adoption as sons of God— these are terms Ritschl uses to describe the gift, or the "religious" side of the duality, whereas reconciliation (as the evidence of justification), ethical vocation, love, are terms that spell out the task, or "ethical" side. The kingdom of God is the highest good—God's highest good in that in it he draws near to man and fulfills his own will, man's highest good in that the kingdom involves reconciliation and the ethical activity which fulfills man's own nature. The sacrifice of Christ for the covenant community, the church, forgives sins and thus brings man near to God, justifies him, and makes possible the life of love in the ethical vocation which fulfills man and the will of God in the kingdom.

This view of the Christian faith is first of all corporate, since it is only in the community of the believers that one receives the revelation of God in Jesus Christ, and the realization of the kingdom of God is a corporate reality embodied in the interrelation of justified and ethically responsible persons. But the individual is also challenged, since it is his fulfillment and his ethical vocation which the Christian faith speaks to most directly, just as it offers him a vision of his own reconciliation with God. The kingdom becomes God's highest good, in that his will is fulfilled in it. But the impact of the kingdom is knowable only as man's highest good, and as such it resolves the basic dilemma that confronts every man, namely, that he is a part of nature and seemingly subsumed within the gigantic system of the natural world, thus deprived of his distinctive spiritual value which tells him in his own mind that he is more than nature and therefore not to be subsumed under it. Ritschl's statement of the Christian faith, therefore, is focused on the fact of human life (later, we shall call this "a way of living," or *Lebensführung*), indeed a theology of *life,* which speaks not only of reconciliation with God but also with self and the world, not only of the religious dimension of life but also of the ethical. His theology is a theology of the inner, or spiritual, life, and the key to understanding this statement of faith is that it encourages man on the one hand by telling him that he is free to participate in the world through his vocation in society, which actually serves to build God's kingdom, while on the other hand it consoles him with the assertion that even if external conditions are unaffected by his vocational activity, God's providential working incorporates man within the system of God's kingdom, a system that does not subsume him under nature but rather relates him to nature in a way that preserves his spiritual distinctiveness and value.[11]

Positive Link to Tradition

Ritschl's statement of the Christian faith appealed to his hearers' religious and ethical needs; it showed them how to live with God and with the world and their fellowmen. But it did so in a way that gave special confidence to pastors and students of theology, because it based its premises on the tradition of religious faith which those pastors and students had been taught to respect and upon which they wanted to rely. First of all, Ritschl turned his hearers toward scripture and Jesus Christ. The message of justification and reconciliation in the kingdom of God is central to the preaching of Jesus, and the New Testament is a reliable resource for learning of that preaching, just as the Old Testament is a necessary presupposition for it. Furthermore, this message of the kingdom is central to the tradition of scriptural interpretation in which we have shared in the ongoing church of Christ. Although his thesis concerning the rise of catholicism held that the post-apostolic developments perverted the biblical faith in a Gentile environment, Ritschl nevertheless was able to document a continuous tradition of interpreting the message of Jesus which led through the Middle Ages, up to Luther's reformation and on to his own work as a successor to the reformers. He could document the deviations from this tradition, but he did so in a way that explained why the deviations took place, most often showing sympathy for the men who were compelled by circumstance to take a deviating position in spite of their own best intentions, while also very forcefully demonstrating why those deviations must be rejected in favor of a return to the authentic message. He led his readers through a continuous tradition which emphasized Jesus, the apostolic community, certain medieval figures including St. Bernard, Luther, and Calvin, to a certain extent Melanchthon, Kant, Schleiermacher, German Idealism, up to Albrecht Ritschl. It is no accident that he entitled his short systematic summary of Christian doctrine *Unterricht in der christlichen Religion,* which is the same phrase in German which entitles John Calvin's reformation summary of doctrine, *Institutes of the Christian Religion.*[12]

LIFE-STYLE AND HISTORICAL THINKING

In 1853, Ritschl himself laid down a principle of method that fairly represents his own work: "The principle of theological knowledge must be a synthesis of personal religious knowledge with the full understanding of the history of the reciprocal relations of piety with scripture and the understanding of the world."[13] His biographer restates the same principle thus: "The basic element in his teaching concerning Christianity is his biblical theology, which has been worked into dogmatics in terms of a certain shape of protestant piety, with theological concepts whose validity he had demonstrated in thorough investigations of the history of theology."[14] Two elements are described in these statements: (a) piety or life-style and (b) thinking through this life-style in historical perspective.

Life-Style

At the center of Ritschl's method was the conviction that religion
is first of all a "way of living" (*eine Weise des Lebens*), a "way of
conducting one's life" (*Lebensführung*). A way of living was what
Ritschl's historical studies examined, it was the focus around which
he organized his theological system, and it is that which he aimed
to influence in the church and society of his day. This is not to imply
that Ritschl reduced religion to ethics, because he put "way of living"
in a full context of religious and dogmatic considerations; but he
focused his study of religion on the existential moral, philosophical,
and psychic problems which attend the conduct of life. As we have
seen, this way of living was described in terms of the objective will of
God in his kingdom and the process of justification and reconciliation which takes place within man. Each of these two sets of concepts deals with the balance or equilibrium between that which man
receives, which sustains him and brings him near to God, and that
which man must *perform,* the imperative which commands his will
and flows from God's will. Although he did not develop this category
of "way of living" until relatively late with fullness and precision,
it was a concern which antedated his earliest work and in a less
refined way directed even the first edition of *The Emergence of the
Old Catholic Church.* The category is clearly determinative for the
work on pietism (included in this volume). Ritschl's presentation of
the "way of living" category made plain certain implications which
he presupposed, as well as certain consequences that followed from
it. For one thing, it incorporated within itself Jesus' theme of the
kingdom of God, a theme which Ritschl applied in a new and original
way for his time by using it as the primary interpretive key for understanding Jesus. At the same time, the category of "way of living"
belonged within the framework of the familiar justification concept
that was central for Luther. Finally, it also built upon the ethically
oriented kingdom of God concepts of two imposing figures in what
was then recent German intellectual history, Immanuel Kant and
Friedrich Schleiermacher, as well as the contemporary Richard
Rothe.[15] Thus, when Ritschl's readers dealt with his category of
"way of living," they sensed that they were dealing with familiar
strands of thought that had been dealt with prominently in their
intellectual and religious tradition, even though they also sensed

that they were witnessing an original reshaping of those familiar elements.

Justification and Reconciliation

When Ritschl spoke to his readers about justification, the central doctrine for Luther and Lutheranism, he confronted them with the sharply stated opinion that the Lutheran reformation, Luther included, had left unfinished theological business for their generation, in that justification had not been related adequately to regeneration and good works, and further that the older Luther and his followers had distorted the purity and power of the young Luther's insights into the nature of justification and reconciliation by increasing objectivism and metaphysicizing.[16] Justification is solely the act of God aimed at man; it involves no placating of God by Jesus Christ, since it is man alone who is estranged and needs reconciling, not God. Justification is a judgment by God that the sinner's transgressions no longer stand as a barrier to the nearness of God and the intimacy of man's relationships to God. Justification provides the answer to the sinner's question, "How can I stand before God in my imperfections?" The answer comes back, "Your sins are deprived of their alienating consequences by the God who has drawn near to you in Christ's sacrifice." Justification calms the conscience of the sinner who needs consolation in his guilt,[17] and reconciliation is the empirical evidence of that justification. To Ritschl's audience, this radical emphasis upon Luther and his central doctrine was something not shared by other dogmaticians of the day,[18] and it turned students and preachers directly to Luther rather than to orthodox dogmas, philosophical schemes, or pietistic spiritual processes. It also emphasized, in a new (and perhaps erroneous) way the consoling aspects of Luther's doctrine rather than the wrath toward sin and the consequent human inner torments, which were generally emphasized in treatments of Luther's thought.[19] This consolation of God's judgment freed man, in Ritschl's interpretation, for participation in the kingdom of God, and in this way the latter concept was the reverse side of the "way of living" category which incorporated justification.

The Kingdom of God

The kingdom of God is also a pure gift of God to men, consoling them in their situation, because it offers them adoption as God's sons and the possibility of participation in a system of meaning which preserves their spiritual status as human beings. In the process of offering this consolation, however, it is also a mandate for the ethical action which realizes this kingdom. The marks of Kant, Schleiermacher, and Rothe are clear. Kant's great contribution was his single-minded emphasis on the significance of will and ethical action as the chief character of man, opening up man's relationship to God and the total human community; in his own way, Kant linked this to the Christian concept of the kingdom of God. Schleiermacher added to this a more direct concern for the kingdom of God and spoke of the "highest good," which motivates man's action and which serves God's own highest good as expressed in the idea of the kingdom. Rothe underscored the developmental character of the kingdom as it stood as overarching key to the movement of history, progressively realized by man's ethical action.[20] As Norman Metzler points out, this prior thinking presented Ritschl with the clear concept of the kingdom of God as a duality—representing God's highest will for the world and man, thus an eschatological concept, and also offering to man his ethical mandate, which brings with it self-fulfillment.[21] But Ritschl, while taking over the thought of these predecessors, forcefully redirected it by arguing that this complex of thought was the key to interpreting the preaching of Jesus and that it is attested by the New Testament.[22] To Ritschl goes credit for having ensconced the idea of the kingdom so emphatically and irreversibly at the center of Christian dogmatics that it became determinative for his entire dogmatic system and unavoidable for his successors.[23] He also developed it more fully, calling attention to the dual character of the kingdom as gift and task, religious and ethical. Thus, Ritschl synthesized Kant and Schleiermacher—two of the towering intellectual influences in nineteenth century German culture, tempering Kant's ethical emphasis with Schleiermacher's concern for feeling and religion[24] and grounding them both in reformation and New Testament faith.

Life-Style and Method

The category of life-style or "way of living" belongs in a discussion of Ritschl's method, because he insisted on the one hand that the unity of his generation with Luther, with the prior Christian tradition, and with Jesus and the New Testament consists in the unity or agreement with this form of life-style.[25] On the other hand, as a matter of scientific principle Ritschl laid down the axiom that theology's task was not to describe God and his actions "from above," that is, as if the theologian stood in God's own mind, but rather in terms of the corresponding moral and religious actions which are stimulated or called forth by God. In other words, the only medium in which we can discern and describe God's action is in the style of life which the justified Christian lives; that style of life is both the substance of God's revelation in Jesus and the common link that Christians have with preceding generations of the church.[26] This represents a concentration upon man's life and particularly upon the psychic and spiritual dynamics that pertain to his religious and ethical choices, dynamics which have been of decisive significance for Christian theology.

Ritschl spelled out in detail the characteristics of this style of living. They consist of confidence in God's providence (this confidence is the expression of one's justification), which liberates man to enter into relationships of love, primarily through the faithful exercise of his vocation. Freedom to live in the world under God's providence is the hallmark of Ritschl's conception of Christianity. Humility and patience go along with this liberated life, as well as prayer and participation in corporate worship. Prayer and worship remind the Christian of Christ's revelation and example, and thus they are to consist chiefly of praise and thanksgiving for the gifts of forgiveness and freedom which God has given.

Historical Thinking

We have clarified the way in which Ritschl's method focused upon the Christian style of life, elaborated in philosophical and theological concepts which gave force and clarity to that style. But both Ritschl and his son Otto spoke also of the biblical and historical connections of this concept. We have already suggested how Ritschl drew upon historical and biblical sources for the materials of his concept of the Christian life, relating it specifically to Luther, the reformation, the New Testament witness to Jesus, as well as to Kant, Schleiermacher, and Rothe. But in terms of Ritschl's method, which was so compelling to a generation of theological students and pastors who adhered to his thought, there is more at stake than the fact *that* Ritschl appealed to history (including the Bible)—there is the question of *how* he approached history.

Baur

Ferdinand Christian Baur taught Ritschl two lessons that he never forgot. The first lesson was that the nature of Christianity is to be ascertained by subjecting it to critical historical inquiry in its total historical development from the beginning to the present; any single phenomenon in Christian history can be adequately assessed only by understanding the previous generations upon which it built, its own historical circumstances and the contribution it made to that situation and bequeathed to the next generation; and the whole of Christianity can be understood only by tracing these successive contributions under the interpretive guidance of a leading category which is appropriate to the study. Ritschl's leading idea was his category of Christian life-style. The second lesson was that the study of Christianity in terms of its history must be carried out by immersion in the concrete dynamics of the historical process by means of attention to the original sources; one must deal with as many of these sources as possible, and his interpretations must take intelligent account of all of them.

In part, Ritschl's break with Baur was due to his opinion that the teacher had not followed his own principle in this regard faithfully enough. With this twofold lesson firmly a part of him, Ritschl's corpus of works, especially (but not only) the magnum opus on justification and reconciliation, forms a whole.[27] He operated with his leading interpretive idea of "way of living," working through all of Christian history from the Old Testament backgrounds through the rise of catholicism, Middle Ages, reformation, and protestant developments up to his own time. He showed the twists and turns which the development of his leading idea had taken, always balancing the two factors, gift and task, within his discussion. He dealt both with the internal dynamics of the development (which Baur had emphasized) and the external factors affecting it (which Baur did not deal with so fully). Thus, he could explain not only *that* a Gentile deviation in understanding the Christian style of life had occurred, but also *why* and *how* it happened (due to pressures in the Roman Empire which alienated Gentile Christians from their origins), and he could sympathetically clarify how second and third century Christians were forced to their deviation, even though he emphatically rejected their deviation. In the same way, he could show how and why Melanchthon and the second generation of Lutherans were compelled to distort the reformation impulse through the objectivizing and legalizing pressures in their environment, and he could even understand how pietism, his *bête noire*, represented a sound reaction to his other bitter foe, objectivizing orthodoxy. He developed a theory of "vestigial leaves" (*Keimblättchen*) which antedated Harnack's "kernel and husk" theory, even though it achieved little prominence. According to this image, Ritschl judged that the second generation of a powerful movement was obliged to erect certain rigidities of thought and practice in order to preserve the truth of the movement, as a seedling develops hard vestigial leaves. From the plant, however, we learn that these early rigidities are to be sloughed off as soon as possible, when the plant is strong. The catholicizing trend in early Christianity and the dogmatizing trend of the reformation sustained the rigidities past their usefulness and turned them into deviation.[28] These reflections from his historical studies gave him a sense of being a new reformer which, although at times overbearing and exasperating, lent clarity and forcefulness to the alternative which he clearly posed to the deviations he had uncovered, past and present.

Interpreting the "Present Age"

Michael Ryan has probed deeply into Ritschl's use of historical method, relating it provocatively to Schleiermacher and to nineteenth century German historiography, particularly the theories of the secular historian, Leopold von Ranke.[29] Ryan believes that after his break with Baur, Ritschl became indebted to Schleiermacher more than to any other person. From Schleiermacher's method, Ritschl accepted the suggestion that dogmatics deals with the historical knowledge of the present moment "considered with a view to the future development of Christian doctrine," or, in other words, dogmatics builds on historical theology so as to develop an interpretation of the present, for the present.[30] Ritschl thus worked under the imperative of interpreting the "present age," which was determined for him by the movement from Kant through Schleiermacher in which was developed a category of the "religious-moral community" and in which Kant's emphasis upon the moral law and will was modified by Schleiermacher's concern for religion and feeling. To be sure, Ritschl also used Kant to criticize Schleiermacher. Ryan's analysis receives a corroborative counterpart in Norman Metzler's thesis describing a Kant-Schleiermacher-Rothe development in the concept of the kingdom of God and the highest good.[31]

The significance of Ritchl's attempt to interpret his present age must not be underestimated. The tendency is to underestimate the attempt, since Ritschl himself spoke misleadingly about his own theology as having no apologetic interests whatsoever and since he is also frequently characterized as self-assured and confident of the world in which he lived, the implication being that he was unaware that he was living in the last days of the modern era that began with the enlightenment and ended with World War I. Horst Stephan's remark that Ritschl's emphasis upon the church as the theologian's starting point led to theology's isolation from cultural matters has been influential.[32] It is not clear how conscious he was of the significance of his epoch and its imminent demise, but it is certain that the options he took for his work do represent a response to his times, and we dare not overlook the potential fruitfulness of those options. Several strands of thought must be brought into one focus in order to make this clear.

Ritschl was obviously aware, in the first place, that the scientific world view which was burgeoning in his time was crucial for the lives of all men. He understood the impact of this world view to reside in its tendency to include all of the world and man within a vast nexus of cause and effect which deprived man of his free will and which eliminated any qualitative differences between man and the rest of reality. He expressed this as the contradiction which man feels when he knows himself to be a part of this world and subject to its cause and effect system even as at the same time he knows himself to be created in God's image and different from, in a sense superior to, the world. Man's basic religious striving is toward wholeness, which means that he seeks to become a part of a whole which does not compromise his essential being. The scientific world view tells man that he is part of a whole which *does* compromise him by making him no more than any other constituent of nature. It is quite possible to interpret Ritschl's entire theology as an attempt to deal with this challenge of the scientific world view. Such interpretations have prompted some critics to charge that Ritschl's total presentation of the Christian faith is simply an effort to bend God to the task of meeting man's need for rescue from the cause and effect system of modern science.[33]

Ritschl also seemed to be well aware that the synthesis which Schleiermacher and Hegel had effected between speculative metaphysics and scientific modes of thought, or between Christian faith (metaphysically conceived) and the contemporary world views, was breaking down.[34] This breakdown was evident in his student days, and especially at Halle in the early 1840s when he was actively engaged in thinking through the Hegelian option and its development and dissolution in its right and left "wings." What Ritschl did was to reject metaphysics and speculation as constitutive for theology and faith (see the essay, "Theology and Metaphysics" in this volume). Paul Wrzecionko has described what Ritschl put in the place of metaphysics.[35] He took the epistemology of his Göttingen colleague, Hermann Lotze,[36] who explicitly attempted to construct a metaphysics that could harmonize with the scientific world view, and thus to open up a vast interpretation of human existence and God's relation to that existence, while "bracketing out" all metaphysical categories, including Lotze's own. Lotze's epistemology brought ontology and psychology together in its assertions that the separation between the knowing subject and the object it seeks to know is overcome when we recognize that in the temporal manifestations which occupy human processes of knowing the object is fully present through its effects— even that "object" which is the Ultimate. These effects, in form and operation *are* the object we seek to know, and thus it is mistaken to suppose that we must "get behind" or "above" or "below" these effects to another world where objects are "real." To this Ritschl linked Kant's and Schleiermacher's high regard for the ethical life of man and for the processes of his self-consciousness, and by means of Lotze's epistemology he could assert that a full and exclusive concentration upon this human spiritual life of ethical decision and religious self-consciousness would bring man knowledge of and participation in the "real." Of course, he centered on the religious self-consciousness and ethical decision that are expressed in the life of the Christian community of believers, in constant dialogue with the revelation of Jesus Christ in the New Testament and in later tradition. Encounter with this revelation, localized in the self-consciousness of the church, brought man into relationship with the ultimate reality of God, whose kingdom was the whole which preserved man's essential nature as spirit and related him to the rest of the world.

Little wonder that Ritschl could channel great energy into historical examination of the Christian sources of revelation! That was the place where the data of God were to be found, and he could challenge men to wrestle with this revelation in their own lives, since the impact of revelation upon their conscious lives was the impact of God. Ritschl's attention to Christian history was an alternative to metaphysics, whereas for Baur it had been the completion of metaphysics. Lotze further helped Ritschl to formulate his insight that the ethical response discernible in men's conscious lives is response to the activity of the real, God. This alternative to speculative metaphysics, which turned toward the examination of the mutual relationships between a concrete historical tradition and the human self-consciousness, liberated theology from being a metaphysical, supernatural enterprise which was rapidly being discredited by the natural scientific perspective.

The obverse side of this retreat from metaphysics and the threat of science was Ritschl's statement to his age that the "natural" processes in which they participated were more than they themselves would often admit, since they were actually the correlates of the divine reality. Furthermore, he challenged his times to acknowledge that the leveling of human self-consciousness and man's psychic life to a place of subjection within a natural nexus of cause and effect would in the end be a destruction of the very human spirit which they exalted. Wrzecionko sees this as a pointed apologetic which demonstrates how seriously (and in Wrzecionko's view, wrongly) Ritschl took the spirit of his times, a spirit which proudly and even arrogantly sang the praises and glories of the human spirit and its achievements.

Before we interpret Ritschl's antimetaphysical bias and his strategy of concentrating solely on Christian community and revelation as a retreat from the ferment and challenges of his age, we must be clear in what ways he was accurately interpreting the thrust of his era. This was an era marked by the demise of the older metaphysical God and the metaphysical method of talking about God. Ritschl was concerned to carry on both an attempt to overcome his age and to offer an apologetic to it. It goes without saying that his was a *relatively* conservative approach among many liberal alternatives. His rejection of metaphysics went along with an unquestioning acceptance of God and the traditional picture of God as heavenly father (he fully expected to be reunited with his wife after death, in heaven), and he was convinced that his innovations were a return to Jesus and the authentic reformation. But he was only relatively conservative; he made no attempt to rescue metaphysics or supernaturalism or to gloss over their passing.

Ritschl's Norm

We can conclude our survey of Ritschl's method by describing in more detail the factors that were normative for his historical method, most of which have already been discussed implicitly in our survey. Many interpreters of Ritschl, including myself, have argued for a single norm in his work—Jesus Christ as set forth in the New Testament, Luther, the historical tradition as such, and his constructive category of the dual relationship between God and man which received expression in his concept of the kingdom of God.[37] Effective arguments have recently been made for each of these. As a result of these several arguments and their mutual criticisms, we are probably wisest to conclude that there are several normative elements in Ritschl's thought, each of which can appear paramount when his system is viewed from a certain perspective. Three of these suggested norms belong together as historically received factors—Jesus, Luther, the tradition—while the concept of a duality of religion and ethics is a constructive category built of dogmatic and philosophical elements. Ritschl was convinced that his dual concept of the God-man relationship, expressed powerfully as the kingdom of God, was at the heart of Christian faith and that it was a word his generation needed to hear. He was also convinced that this was a faithful representation of what Jesus preached as the revelation of God and of what the authentic Christian tradition, including Luther, witnessed to. Ritschl could not have effectively interpreted his tradition from Christ to his own nineteenth century, nor participated in that tradition, if he had not possessed such a category of meaning and interpretation. At the same time, he could not, in good conscience, have affirmed this concept of Christian life if he had not been convinced that the authoritative persons and moments in the tradition witnessed to its substance and its importance. His attention to history gave breadth and persuasiveness to his dogmatic concepts, but we cannot avoid the judgment that those concepts (and their philosophical undergirding) rendered his reading of the historical sources partial and, in some respects, seriously defective. History and dogmatic creativity were so closely wedded in his method and in his person that it seems impossible to argue that one or the other was normative over the other, even though his own intention was to let historical revelation rule his dogmatics.

III. RITSCHL'S SIGNIFICANCE FOR HIS OWN TIME

We have argued, partly in reliance upon new studies of Ritschl, that he worked under the consciousness that he had a message for his own day and that this consciousness helped to shape his total theological work. We have examined that message and its methodological principles in some detail; now we must ask about its significance. *Positively*, we may say that Ritschl's significance lies in his effectiveness in bringing together more creatively than any of his contemporaries the theological concerns of his age and its recent past, and in his ability to synthesize those concerns with his own categories in the formulation of a message persuasive to a great variety of his contemporaries. *Negatively*, we must say that Ritschl also made a great number of his contemporaries feel that the wind had been taken out of their sails by his system. The one judgment explains his popularity and influence, the other the bitter criticism he drew from his opponents. Because he drew together so many elements in his work, very few of his colleagues in the church or in the theological and philosophical faculty were left untouched by him. We can test this thesis by briefly observing Ritschl's impact on a number of his contemporaries.

To the Hegelians and the Tübingen school of F. C. Baur, Ritschl seemed to be a conservative traditionalist. He stung them by insisting that a concentration upon the revelation in the New Testament demanded a revision of their overarching theoretical schemes for interpreting Christianity, viz., their concept of the Spirit manifesting itself in history and fulfilling itself through the movement of conflict from thesis to antithesis and synthesis. Since they considered this scheme to be essential for objective scientific thought, Ritschl's demurrer appeared to be a lack of nerve, a retreat from the critical implications of historical truth. To many pastors and theological students, however, Ritschl's insistence that speculation must be subordinate to biblical revelation was more consonant with what they conceived to be the imperatives of their faith. Alongside this explicit polemic and appeal, however, lies the implicit strategy of Ritschl's antimetaphysical stance which wagered its future on a surmise that the metaphysics of Hegel and Baur was passing away, in which event theology was better advised to concentrate on the obvious historical sources available and their significance for life. Ritschl's advocacy of revelation over speculation was also a decision that in the future Kant's critique of metaphysics would prove correct. But while he was rejecting the superstructure of Hegel and Baur, he took over their critical apparatus and brought it to even greater refinement and inspired his disciples to surpass himself in this regard. In the process, he retained the Hegelian-Baurian concern for the whole of history and for the interpretation of Christianity in terms of its total development.

In his decision against Hegelian metaphysical speculation, Ritschl relied upon the Kantian critique of metaphysics and the Kantian emphasis on will and the moral law, in concert with Schleiermacher's ethics and religious emphasis. Ritschl was sharply critical of Schleiermacher's romanticism and individualism, which he thought were pietistic in their consequences. But in his decision for Kant and his subsequent concentration on the ethical and religious self-consciousness of man, he found Schleiermacher's detailed and methodical discussion of that self-consciousness invaluable. In the long run, Ritschl linked his work to Schleiermacher's in both historical studies and in probing the dynamics of the religious consciousness, albeit modifying the latter with a Kantian concern for the will.

Ritschl's relations to orthodox, confessional Lutherans and pietists were especially significant, since they formed a hostile environment for him and his father before him. He very nearly defeated the confessionalists on their own ground, since he championed Luther and the confessions every bit as strongly as they, devoting years and many treatises to demonstrating that he was in fact the true Lutheran. And, as Lotz has shown, even though Ritschl was greatly mistaken in some of his Luther-interpretation, his work—especially as it was an impulse for the work of Karl Holl—may have been more significant in the long run than that of the more orthodox Lutherans, even that of Theodosius Harnack.[38] Far from leaving his adherents without a strong sense of Lutheran identity, he intensified it in men like Wilhelm Herrmann and Adolf von Harnack. It might be said as much as anything else, that Ritschl's work was a vigorous description of what it meant to be a reformation Christian in his day—at least he thought it was.

As for the pietists, they consumed as much of Ritschl's time and effort as the confessionalists. He said that his ten years of work on the history of pietism was necessary in order to hold up to his pietist contemporaries their own history and demonstrate openly how wrong they were.[39] This seems an almost compulsive dedication of a decade's work, but it also indicates what Ritschl thought was at stake. In one sense, focusing as he did on the Christian style of life or *Lebensführung*, he was in direct competition with the pietists and therefore had to beat them at their own game. He had claimed that unless the reformation of Luther, Calvin, and Zwingli could foster a strong piety or life-style, it could not claim to be a true interpretation of Christianity.[40] He did not, in other words, believe that a preoccupation with piety and a living religion were in error; rather, he disagreed with the specific option which pietists set forth. He considered the pietists to be the manifestation, within churchly protestantism, of the same perversions that were rooted in medieval catholicism and its left-wing protestant (i.e., for Ritschl, nonchurchly protestantism) offshoot, the anabaptists. Several observers have rooted Ritschl's success in the healthy version of piety which he fostered. He rested it in the New Testament and in Luther, thus stealing the thunder of the pietists with one hand and attempting to eradicate them with the other.

A number of Ritschl's theological peers had committed themselves to mediating between the modern world view and critical scholarship on the one side and traditional faith on the other. This group, practically speaking, simply had to accede to Ritschl, since he fulfilled their program with more skill and force than they could themselves.[41] The case of Martin Kähler is an instructive example, since we now know from recent studies that far from being an alternative to Ritschl, he stood with Ritschl on many of his most important emphases and even borrowed from him for some of his most characteristic ideas.[42]

One of the reasons that Ritschl's opponents failed in their attempts to have Ritschl censured is that his popularity was simply too great. Another, perhaps less important reason but nevertheless worthy of mention, is the high regard he enjoyed in governmental, university, and some ecclesiastical circles. It is ironic that the "new thing" that Ritschl did theologically and philosophically did not possess within it a thrust for new things culturally, politically, and socially. His was not the image of a typical conservative or "establishment" figure although his social and political impact led to such a characterization. When in 1886 protests were at a high pitch in confessional circles— leading to an attack at the 1887 provincial synod—Ritschl was receiving forty-seven out of a possible fifty-eight votes in his election as pro-rector of the university. Colleagues and provincial officials took over much of his defense at the synods. He had earlier declined four calls to the Berlin faculty where the confessionalist leader Hengstenberg was strong. Yet as revolutionary as many of his ideas were, his social impact was conservative, probably due to his call for vocational obedience, his thorough authoritarianism, which marred his emphasis on divine providence, and his success at linking his theological opponents, the confessionalists, to an anti-Prussian political position. Ritschl had been in the Prussian elite since birth and he knew how to conduct himself discreetly. Although he was controversial, he never permitted his person or his name to be attached to a specific party or to partisan newspapers or periodicals. As thickly involved in controversy as he was, his political shrewdness deserves some admiration.

Finally, Ritschl's thought attempted to help the protestant church of his day bolster itself against the onslaughts of both a rising secularistic culture which despised the church (and for protestants, these critics were joined by catholic opponents) and a modern scientific world view which threatened the faith of the church. David Lotz has argued suggestively how Ritschl's interpretation of protestantism can be viewed as an almost point-for-point refutation of the antiprotestant polemic of two prominent contemporaries—Jakob Burckhardt of Basel, with whom Ritschl may not have been familiar, and Paul de Lagarde, who was a colleague and sharp foe at Göttingen.[43]

Lotz focuses particularly on the formal address which the university faculty senate (with Lagarde dissenting!) delegated Ritschl to deliver in 1883 on the occasion of the four hundredth anniversary of Luther's birth. But in a sense all of Ritschl's work comes into play here, especially the work on justification and reconciliation. The substance of the several critiques of protestantism was that protestantism undercut human freedom and the need for a moral reordering of society by its insistence that God alone ordained man's salvation through a justification to which man could contribute nothing and by its tendency to retreat from involvement in the practical affairs of society into a world of objective, partially obscure dogmatic propositions. Lagarde's school of historical studies insisted that since the doctrine of justification was polemical in Paul's writing, it is of only occasional importance and therefore cannot be considered to be the essential theme of Christian faith. The anti-protestant critics also charged that the reformation was responsible for the cultural disintegration of the great ancient and medieval traditions of western society and that its true colors were evident in the libertinism and anarchism ascribed to the anabaptists. Ritschl's work bears within it a clear, if implicit, answer to these charges. He insists that the essence of the Lutheran understanding of justification was that God liberated man to live freely *in* the world, through his vocation, without reliance upon artificial props whether in the form of an ecclesiastically controlled state or a repressive sacralized social order. The freedom of the Christian man which the reformers proclaimed was the very antithesis of the anabaptist theology, since it committed the Christian to working for the righteousness and justice of society at every level and valued every worldly occupation and institution in its own right, without demanding that it be "Christian." True reformation faith was thus eminently practical and only secondarily dogmatic in its expression. It may be that Ritschl's sensitivity to this kind of attack on protestantism contributed to his insistence that Christian faith supports vocational obedience to the established order.

We have already clarified Ritschl's assessment of the modern scientific world view and its threat to faith by reducing man's significance in a vast chain of cause and effect which subordinated him to nature. Ritschl challenged this view by insisting that the failure properly to distinguish between physical and psychic (and spiritual) realities meant a failure to understand man. With this challenge he offered the kingdom of God as a holistic system that incorporated both man and nature with God in a way that preserved the authentic being of both.[44]

If it is true that in Ritschl's age traditional supernatural and metaphysical religion, as well as traditional views of man and traditional protestantism were on the defensive, it seems that the aggressive forces were those that threatened the death of metaphysics, which would later be the death of "God," and substituted an age of "one-dimensionality," which would be the death of man. Ritschl felt the strength of these forces and plotted a strategy to meet them. The death of metaphysics he did not mourn, and he devised a strategy for living without it. The death of man through one-dimensionality was more fearful for him, so he challenged it with a theology that insisted that every action and reaction within man's dimension was correlative to another dimension which was God.

Although Ritschl's foes and competitors were at many points correct in their criticisms of his thought and even though their own work was at points more satisfactory than his, and, furthermore, even though it cannot be said that he won every battle (the ecclesiastical scene in Germany, for example, was hardly relinquished by the confessionalists and pietists), it must be said that no other single theological work of his generation gathered in itself so many strands of intellectual, religious, and cultural meaning and synthesized them in a creative manner—both intellectually stimulating and practically edifying (even "preachable")—as Ritschl's did. This is his significance for his own day: that he spoke his particular message to an epoch that was shaped religiously by confessionalists, pietists, and Prussian unionists; philosophically and theologically by Kantians, Hegelians, and Schleiermacher; culturally by free-thinking liberal and anti-protestant secularists; as well as by classical German protestantism and Vatican I catholicism, by great social unrest, and in politics by the Prussian state and its radical opponents. The passion that marked both his friends and his foes is explained by the fact that he entered the fray on so many fronts and deeply touched so many raw nerves. As a consequence, his work dominated many university theological faculties. The succeeding generation of Ritschlians includes outstanding men in every field of theology. His influence was felt in Sweden, England, and in America (where the social gospel and many liberal religious thinkers were impressed by his thought). In Europe, the generation that was to overthrow Ritschlianism was largely trained by Ritschlians.

IV. RITSCHL'S SIGNIFICANCE TODAY

We have portrayed Ritschl in terms of his times and his own thought, suggesting the significance of the word that he spoke to his contemporaries. Now we ask: What is the assessment of our own day? What is his significance for us?

After the bitter controversies that centered on Ritschl himself had died down, the number of articles and book-length studies subsided to a trickle after 1910. Even though the Ritschlian school taught and trained most of the next generation of dialectical theologians, these pupils in the main chose to gloss over their own ties to the Ritschlians and focused instead on what may be termed a vigorous and even malicious attempt to discredit Ritschl himself and, to a lesser extent, his school. The silence concerning origins and the ensuing denunciation had their effect. Emil Brunner tarred Schleiermacher and Ritschl with the same brush of criticism, whereas Karl Barth restored Schleiermacher, only to blister Ritschl with disdain in what must go down as one of the most influential ten-page essays in the history of theological interpretation.[45] Barth's point was that Ritschl was not all that important anyway, when compared to Schleiermacher, and that he represented the effort to repristinate enlightenment theology, to give religious and theological support to bourgeois nineteenth century German society.

Since 1960, however, there has been a resurgence of interest in Ritschl which can be explained by the fact that the passing of the anti-Ritschlian dialectical theology has liberated us to look more honestly at the nineteenth century. The present attitude toward Ritschl is that his theology represents a significant input to the present theological situation and that it is therefore necessary to carry on dialogue with him, whether his work is evaluated positively or negatively. We can understand how Ritschl is a man to be reckoned with. On the one hand he so energetically brought together in his work the elements of his generation that all theology now stands on his shoulders, even that which goes beyond him and/or rejects him.

On the other hand, since the generation of theologians which dominated the first half of the twentieth century suppressed an adequate critical evaluation, it is only now that theologians are free to engage in an open self-conscious dialogue with Ritschl's work.

One of the tests by which the validity of any work of the mind and spirit is determined is its usefulness in stimulating further thought—sometimes even a work that is marred by serious errors is rendered valid by history in the sense that it is provocative of significant subsequent developments. With this in mind, we ask: What seems to have become of Ritschl's powerful statement to his own generation and what seem to be its prospects now?

In his recent study, Rolf Schäfer demonstrates how Ritschl appears to us as a curious blend of conservative and liberal, even though he is invariably (and rightly so) viewed as a figure in the history of German liberal theology. Our survey has shown some of the grounds for this ambivalence. He saw the need, philosophically and theologically, for a "new thing," and to a large extent he carried out his vision. But his vision did not include a rejection of much tradition, and it did not call for a change socially and politically. We have described how Ritschl was a child of the Prussian system in which he grew up and in which he and his father served with distinction, and how his call for obedience within society's vocations had a conservative thrust. Obedience and work in those vocations was the force for realizing God's kingdom. Ritschl is not conservative because he did not envision creative and reforming actions within those vocations (for example, educational reforms, which he supported as a member of the provincial examining committee), but rather because he gives no hint that those vocations might be shattered by changes in society and thus rendered more fluid or radically reshaped both in their own form and in their relation to other vocations.[46] Ritschl was not uncritical of his society, and there is no evidence that he divinized it, but he simply had no inkling that there was any other societal form in which God's kingdom might be served. Thus, in an ironic way, his impressive concern for the world, his intimate wedding of religion and ethics, and his vision that the kingdom of God pertains to this world—all of these were undercut by his commitment to the vocational structure of his own society. Formally, there is no reason why his thought cannot be a force for change and liberation; but materially his own investments of meaning gave an unfortunate conservative thrust to his work. For example, in his day there was great ferment for the democratization of society and greater social justice. Despite Bismarck's fairly advanced welfare policies, conditions among the working class population in Germany were miserable. In this setting, Ritschl's emphasis on the high possibilities of vocational obedience must have seemed ironic to persons outside the middle and upper classes—unless he meant that the worker and the political revolutionary had a vocation to change society, which he did not! Ritschl must not be pictured as a man who was content with his times and their achievements, nor as one who did not challenge the establishment of church and state, university and culture. We must conclude, however, that he was almost totally captive to his own elitist social class, and that his feeling for the transience of the metaphysics of his day was not matched by a sense of the impermanency of its societal forms. And this aspect of the man and his work has proven to be singularly unproductive, up to this day, because to a post-World War I generation this aspect made Ritschl seem culture- and time-bound to the "other side" of the dividing line between modern and postmodern epochs.

Theologically, Ritschl's ambiguous conservative/liberal stance has contributed to his being a bridge figure spanning the modern and postmodern periods. His work has been rejected or simply left unregarded at those points where his cultural conditionedness tied him indissolubly to the modern age, that is to the enduring validity and adequacy of the nineteenth century system of society, religion, and values. It was this that the dialectical theologians of the first half of the twentieth century rejected, and it is this conditionedness that perhaps angered Karl Barth the most—a man who took social and political differences almost more seriously than theological disagreements! They were the theologians who witnessed the collapse of the pre-World War I European dream, and they naturally spoke in terms of man's precariousness, the evil and weakness of institutions, and the fragility of human existence in a way that qualitatively marks them off from Ritschl and his achievement—even though, as we shall discuss later, they had close affinities with Ritschl theologically. A good deal of Ritschl's ethicism, drawn from Kant and

Schleiermacher has appeared to be a dead end, since it breathed an air of authoritarianism and exhorted obedience to the cultural and religious system—an obedience which our century's experience must conclude is more than a system has a right to demand. Furthermore, the philosophical and historical supports for the ethicism in Ritschl's system are also now being called into question. The mysticism, anabaptism, and pietism that he rejected in a single-mindedly neo-Kantian manner we now see were elements of creative ferment within the modern system.

It is clear, however, that as a bridge figure Ritschl was able to make a massive contribution to later generations. We can summarize under four categories the elements of his achievement that have proven productive of fruitful development, even up to the present time.

IMPETUS FOR HISTORICAL-CRITICAL STUDIES

We have already called attention to this aspect of Ritschl's work. His own historical work is impressive, including comprehensive treatments of early church history, reformation developments, the history of pietism, and the history of the doctrine of justification and reconciliation. The output of the so-called Ritschlian School is staggering: Adolf von Harnack's studies of the history of dogma, Ernst Troeltsch's historical work in ethics, not to mention hosts of others in every field of church history, including the often overlooked Ritschlian influence on Karl Holl and other early workers in the "Luther Renaissance." It is not that these men were wholly under Ritschl's influence (which they were not) nor that without him they would not have been excellent historians (they surely would have been). Rather, the point is that Ritschl personally encouraged them and inspired them and his influence upon them is unmistakable. Even more important for our assessment of Ritschl's meaning and significance is that his decision, based on what he learned from Baur, to commit his own resources to a critical-historical investigation of Christianity and to insist that such an investigation be a foundation for the constructive dogmatic expression of the Christian faith has not only been vindicated, but has become so productive of fruitful advance that it is reckoned a basic assumption for theological work.[47]

RESOURCES FOR DIALECTICAL THEOLOGY

That the dialectical theology of Karl Barth, Emil Brunner, Rudolf Bultmann, and Friedrich Gogarten lived in a different world from Ritschl and branded him its arch-heretic cannot obscure the fact, as Paul Jersild has brought out, that the main contours of Ritschl's theology furnished a framework which dialectical theologians could incorporate for their own ideas.[48]

Here we must distinguish between the Barthian and the existentialist wings of dialectical theology. Three of Ritschl's most important and most strenuously argued assertions provide formal resources for his twentieth century Barthian antagonists: his insistence that theology must base itself on the revelation of God in Jesus Christ as portrayed in the New Testament (what developed into Barth's so-called Christo-monism); his adamant rejection of any "natural" theology or philosophical statement of the Christian faith; and correlative argument that the theologian must irrevocably take his stand within the community of believers, the church, and do his theologizing from that standpoint. Other assertions that Barthian theologians share, at least formally, with Ritschl are a concern to reappropriate Luther and the other mainline reformers for dogmatics, a rejection of Schleiermacher's emphasis upon feeling as the main resource for theology, a rejection of historical positivism, and a rejection of romanticism, mysticism, and aestheticism in theology. In these areas of commonality, it is not a question of isolated points of agreement; rather, we are dealing with issues which Ritschl and the Barthians alike made central to their programmatic efforts to renew dogmatics in their respective generations. For some of these members of the dialectical theology, these elements were mediated through Wilhelm Herrmann, a close friend and disciple of Ritschl, who was a respected teacher of both Barth and Bultmann. Paul Jersild has shown that despite Barth's rhetoric of rejecting Ritschl, there remains a surprising bond of continuity between the two theologies, specifically in their doctrine of God. Perhaps the fundamental bond, however, is their common effort to build a theology exclusively upon the distinctive Christian revelation in the New Testament message of Jesus and their common effort to maintain this position polemically against other options in their times.

Some of these very Ritschlian elements which the dialectical theologians found useful are now proving less fruitful, both in their Ritschlian and in their dialectical forms. The restriction to the New Testament revelation, with its corollaries of restriction to the community of believers and rejection of philosophical resources for stating the Christian message, as these found expression especially in Barth, have proven confining to many in the present generation, since they seem to offer little resource for taking seriously the secularization and unbelief which press upon us today in a form that neither Ritschl nor Barth felt. Nevertheless, we must not forget that these so-called restrictions may also be interpreted as a *response* to secularization in both Barth and Ritschl and not simply as *retreat* (see pp. 26–29, above).

For the existentialist wing of dialectical theology, represented in the work of Bultmann and Gogarten, Ritschl's preoccupation with the self-consciousness of man was of great significance. This dimension of his thought was particularly mediated to them through Herrmann, and it provided an antecedent thrust toward their existentialist orientation. Their reliance upon the philosophies of Heidegger and Buber, for example, can be construed, as Wrzecionko has done, as a direct elaboration of Ritschl's methodological decision to avoid metaphysics by turning to the self-consciousness of man (see the essay "Theology and Metaphysics") as the arena within which theology was to probe the encounter with historical revelation.

HISTORICAL AND HERMENEUTICAL METHOD

Ritschl is a remarkably contemporary partner in dialogue for theologians and historians who are today concerned over the question of historical method and its function in the art of interpreting the past, and his suggestions for his own time have proven to be of continuing usefulness. We refer here not simply to Ritschl's insistence upon critical-historical tools and techniques for historical and theological study, but also to the way in which he stated theology's relationship to historical methodology. We note three aspects of this relationship: (a) the insistence that Christianity must be understood in terms of its *whole* development; (b) the acknowledgment that every theologian and every generation stands in a relative position within the historical process, from which is carried on a dialogue with the past and the present; (c) the necessity, for the adequate carrying out of this method, of perceiving the dynamics of the historical consciousness of man, that is, the need for a phenomenological description of man's historical consciousness.

(a) The concern for interpreting Christianity and its individual manifestations in light of the whole development of the Christian religion through its successive periods is now so deeply rooted in the consciousness of German and most western theology, that it hardly needs mention. It is one of the most important methodologies for biblical studies, where it functions as "tradition criticism" and "redaction criticism," but it is also prominent in studies of the history of later periods and in theology itself. Ritschl insisted in employing this totalistic approach in interpreting the doctrines of justification and reconciliation, and in his studies of Luther, orthodox confessional Lutheranism, and pietism. He placed his own theological proposal as the contemporary climax of the interpretation of Christianity's development.[49] In systematic theology, the work of Wolfhart Pannenberg, in dialogue with the philosophy of Hegel and Hans-Georg Gadamer, as well as the work of Gerhard Ebeling, building on both Barth and Heidegger, are two of the most important examples of how Ritschl correctly assessed the significance and ongoing fruitfulness of this methodology, which he did not originate, but which he did plant irrevocably in the discipline of dogmatics.[50] Ritschl himself, although his perspectives were impressively broad and inclusive, is superseded in the even more inclusive work of these men, who reckon not only in terms of the Christian tradition, but also place that tradition more effectively in its cultural setting than did Ritschl.

(b) When we take the historical approach, interpreting Christianity in terms of its total development, critically investigated, we are ultimately forced to recognize the relativity of each phenomenon and epoch—including our own—within the whole process. Consequently, we are engaged in a dialogue with past and present, on the basis of which we speak our own word in our own epoch, with a view toward the future possibilities of that word. Gerhard Ebeling has put this in classical contemporary form for theology in his book, *The Problem of Historicity*; Ebeling's argument shows how close Ritschl was to the contemporary discussions in his explicit awareness of the dialogical character of the historical approach. This is borne out especially in Ryan's analysis of Ritschl's kinship with Schleiermacher, Dilthey, and Ranke in respect to historical methodology. Ritschl devoted considerable effort to interpreting his own "present age" so that he could carry on dialogue with it and through it with past and future. In other words, Ritschl's method made its investments in a line that has proven fruitful, even among those who feel uncomfortable with the specific results that he obtained in his own time. Studies by Schäfer, Wrzecionko, Lotz, and myself all point to a basic defect which mars Ritschl's intentions to carry out this dialogical principle.[51] Although each of these writers expresses the defect in slightly different terms, they stand agreed that the presuppositions which Ritschl brought with him to the dialogue with past and present served not only as a key to unlock the meaning of Christianity's historical development, but also as serious blinders that vitiated the impressive skills and breadth of intention with which he approached the dialogue.

(c) The past two centuries of western experience with the historical mode of thinking have taught us that man does not merely *use* the historical method, but rather he *is* a historical being. This insight has gone hand in hand with a close phenomenological analysis of man's psychic and intellectual processes as he is caught up in the historical process of assessment and dialogue. To mention only a few who have made great contributions to this analysis: Schleiermacher, Dilthey, Heidegger, and the contemporary phenomenological school, including Gadamer, Ebeling, and Paul Ricoeur. This phenomenological analysis has attained a high level of sophisticated description. Ritschl stands in this tradition. In fact, his entire polemic against the use of metaphysics in theology was predicated on the argument that metaphysics could not distinguish between physical and spiritual entities, and therefore it could not do justice to the distinctiveness of man and to that dimension of human existence where the encounter with God and the theological enterprise take place. In connection with this argument, he produced a rudimentary phenomenology of man's psychic processes, mainly in his effort to show that classical metaphysics distorts our understanding of these processes. His argument requires a more profound depth of analysis, however, and here, we must conclude, is the place where Ritschl contributed least to the future of the historical method. He stands well below the others in this tradition in his grasp of how man functions within the dialógical process of history. This must be said, even though his concentration on the psychic life of man, as the arena within which the encounter with revelation was to be charted, gave a formal impetus for full-scale phenomenological work and encouraged his followers to do what he did not do.

Ritschl himself seems to have been content to understand the dynamics of human life in generalizations drawn from his own style of life. He found it almost impossible to understand from within and thus with fairness those religious and cultural movements (uncongenial to him) which were deeply concerned with the inner dynamics of man's psyche and mind—pietism, mysticism, romanticism, and the concentration upon human consciousness which was part of Schleiermacher's theological legacy. Since these movements were all active at the same level as he was—committed to discerning the encounter with revelation within man's own self-consciousness—he seems to have looked upon them more as foes to be vanquished than as comrades in the same battle. Schäfer's critique is here much to the point, that although Ritschl formulated a clear and healthy image of Christian life-style, he slighted—with regrettable consequences—the interior life of individual persons, submerging this dimension in his concern for the corporate practice of religion and in his formal ethicism.[52] Lotz joins Schäfer and Jersild in calling attention to the way in which this seriously flawed Ritschl's understanding of Luther and his doctrine of justification, since he could not deal adequately with human despair over one's sinfulness and the inner torments which accompany the religious and ethical life.[53] Thus, in his *Instruction in the Christian Religion,* Ritschl could devote more attention to the ambiguities concerning the pursuit of recreation than any other specific ethical problem!

To summarize: The tradition of historical interpretation in which Ritschl stands has given great attention, at least since Schleiermacher, to two factors: man's stance in a process of relative moments in history with which he carries on dialogue, culminating with a word spoken to his own generation; and the description of the inner dynamics of man's life as a historical being. Ritschl attended carefully to the first of these and contributed to our understanding of it. And although he acknowledged the importance of the second factor and framed his argumentation so as to be dependent upon it, he contributed much less to it. The result of this was that his dialogue with past and present was in some respects extraordinarily stunted, primarily in the direction of an ethicism which achieved a dominance which Ritschl himself did not intend and also in the direction of an insensitivity to the dark side of despair, ambiguity, and inner torment in human existence.

Theology Centered on the Kingdom of God

Ritschl stood in a tradition, from Kant through Schleiermacher and Rothe, that understood the importance of the kingdom of God for Christian faith and which interpreted the kingdom in both eschatological terms as a religious reality given by God and as an ethical mandate governing man's life. He made a decisive contribution to this tradition by demonstrating that the kingdom of God was central to the New Testament picture of Jesus and his preaching, and that the Jesus of the Gospels simply cannot be understood apart from this message. Whereas an earlier study by Christian Walther negatively assessed Ritschl at this point, newer works by Schäfer and Metzler have reacted more positively to his achievement.[54] Ritschl was the first to make the kingdom of God "the crucial, all-embracing term of systematic theology," so forcefully implanting the concept in the doctrinal system that eschatology could never again simply be left for the end of the catechism.[55]

In 1892 Ritschl's own son-in-law, Johannes Weiss, followed by Albert Schweitzer (who built on Weiss's studies, even though he received more notoriety for the view), leveled a fundamental criticism at the Ritschlian view, only three years after the latter's death. He charged that even though Ritschl is correct in emphasizing the centrality of the message of the kingdom of God for the New Testament picture of Jesus, his conception of the kingdom actually owes more to the enlightenment ethical interpretation that dates from Kant and Schleiermacher than it does to New Testament sources. Weiss himself claimed (and Schweitzer supported him) that it was impossible to hold a concept of the kingdom that was both eschatological and ethical, both God's gift and his ethical demand for men, and further that the New Testament clearly pictures Jesus as emphasizing the eschatological rather than the ethical. Weiss concluded that the New Testament concept was unusable for dogmatics and that Ritschl's ethicized view was to be preferred to the biblical concept. Ritschl's disciples, notably Herrmann, Troeltsch, and Walter Rauschenbusch in America, followed suit. In the years that followed, this critique gained ground and was seen as the decisive negation of Ritschl's views, albeit generally accompanied by the opinion, contrary to Weiss, that Ritschl was *not* to be preferred to the New Testament, although the interiorizing of eschatology by the existentialist theologians is not far from Ritschl's ethicizing of it. Walther continues this recent trend of pitting Weiss against Ritschl, to the discrediting of the latter. Schäfer reopened the question by challenging Weiss's interpretation of the New Testament and suggesting that Ritschl's views are more viable as biblical exegesis than the critics have allowed. Thus, he continued to pit Ritschl and Weiss against each other. Norman Metzler, with support from Wolfhart Pannenberg, speaks in contrast of the "Ritschl-Weiss historical-theological nexus,"[56] whose value is enduring and whose real implications are just now being fully unfolded by the current "eschatological" school of theology, which includes Pannenberg, Carl Braaten, and Jürgen Moltmann. The suggestion is that Ritschl and his tradition were correct, that the kingdom of God in the New Testament and in Christian dogmatics *is* both eschatological and ethical, but not in the precise way Ritschl set forth. That is, the kingdom is not to be conceived, as Ritschl did, as a reality which is to be realized in and through man's concrete ethical actions, actions which thus fulfill both God's highest good and man's, offering self-fulfillment for both God and man. Rather, the kingdom is a future reality realized only by God, but which proleptically gives shape to man's ethical action. That is, it gives shape to present action, even though it is a future reality to be consummated. This is so because man lives under the impact of that coming kingdom which was also present in Jesus through his resurrection. I have previously suggested that Ritschl's success in concretely relating the kingdom to the dynamics of human action is notable and still stands as a challenge to the eschatological school.[57] However one evaluates the discussion, it appears that Ritschl's insights on the kingdom as a central, if not all-embracing, issue for Christian faith is another example of the fruitfulness which his theology has had for succeeding generations. Metzler goes so far as to say that "the Ritschlian concept of the kingdom must be considered the norm and touchstone of any modern discussion of the kingdom of God."[58]

V. CONCLUSION

We have interpreted Albrecht Ritschl by applying his own historical method to the phenomena of his own life and work. He spoke a word to his own age that was so appropriate and so in resonance with his contemporaries in Germany that despite its weaknesses it became the dominant theology of his generation. It has proven fruitful up to this day in several major areas of theological concern, even though parts of it have been rejected or permitted to lie dormant. Such an analysis of Ritschl—in light of his significance for his own day and his fruitfulness for subsequent generations—is only possible because of the numerous new studies of the particular facets of his thought. A full picture of Ritschl and his significance is not yet possible, since there is still much in his work that lies unexamined, but we can now assess him appreciatively and critically in a way more responsible than at any previous time since the 1870s. We are in a position to discern that even though many of his specific interpretations now appear faulty and even though he himself did not always match his intentions with performance, he nevertheless still stands as a significant guide for the *manner* in which Christian theology is to be done, that is, for theological methodology.

NOTES

1. The primary source for Ritschl's life is the biography in two volumes written by his son, Otto, shortly after his father's death. Unless otherwise noted, it is the source for all of the biographical details in this essay. See Otto Ritschl, *Albrecht Ritschls Leben*, 2 vols. (Freiburg, i. B.: J.C.B. Mohr, 1892 and 1896).
2. Ibid., I:3.
3. Ibid., I:45–50. Also Peter C. Hodgson, *The Formation of Historical Theology: A Study of Ferdinand Christian Baur*, in Makers of Modern Theology, ed. Jaroslav Pelikan (New York: Harper and Row, 1966), chapter 2. Also Karl Löwith, *From Hegel to Nietzsche* (Garden City: Doubleday Anchor Books, 1967), Section V.
4. See Darrell Jodock, "F. C. Baur and Albrecht Ritschl on Historical Theology" (Ph.D. diss., Yale University, 1969).

5. Ibid., pp. 175–85.

6. Otto Ritschl, II:315, 317.

7. *Die Entstehung der altkatholischen Kirche.* Eine kirchen- und dogmenge-schichtliche Monographie (Bonn: Adolph Marcus, 1850: Zweite, durchgängig neu ausgearbeitete Auflage, 1857). Jodock's work is a thorough study of the significance of the differences between these two editions. The following discussion is based on his study.

8. Jodock, "F. C. Baur and Albrecht Ritschl on Historical Theology," chapter 4. See also Rolf Schäfer, *Ritschl.* Grundlinien eines fast verschollenen dogmatischen Systems (Tübingen: J. C. B. Mohr, 1968), pp. 161, 176.

9. Adolf von Harnack, *History of Dogma,* trans. Neil Buchanan from 3rd German edition (1893), 7 vols. (New York: Dover Publications, 1961).

10. David Lotz, "Albrecht Ritschl's Interpretation of Luther's Theology: An Exposition, Analysis, and Critique" (Th.D. diss., Union Theological Seminary, New York, 1971).

11. See Philip Hefner, "Albrecht Ritschl and His Current Critics," *The Lutheran Quarterly* 13 (May, 1961): 103–12.

12. Unfortunately, this fact (which Ritschl explicitly noted) was not taken into account by the first English translator of the work, and so it has gone down in English as *Instruction in the Christian Religion.*

13. Otto Ritschl, I:101.

14. Ibid., II:391.

15. The following works are useful for this discussion:
Norman Metzler, "The Ethics of the Kingdom" (Doctoral diss., Evangelical-Theological Faculty of the University of Munich, 1971).
Michael Ryan, "The Role of the Discipline of History in the Theological Interpretation of Albrecht Ritschl" (Ph.D. diss., Drew University, 1967).
Rolf Schäfer, *Ritschl* (see note 8, above).
Christoph Senft, *Wahrhaftigkeit und Wahrheit.* Die Theologie des 19. Jahrhunderts zwischen Orthodoxie und Aufklärung (Tübingen: J. C. B. Mohr, 1956).
Christian Walther, *Typen des Reich-Gottes Verständnisses.* Studien zu Eschatologie und Ethik im 19. Jahrhundert (Munich: Chr. Kaiser, 1961).
Paul Wrzecionko, *Die philosophischen Wurzeln der Theologie Albrecht Ritschls* (Berlin: Töpelmann, 1964).

16. Lotz, "Albrecht Ritschl's Interpretation of Luther's Theology," pp. 91–98. Philip Hefner, *Faith and the Vitalities of History: A Theological Study Based on the Work of Albrecht Ritschl,* in Makers of Modern Theology, ed. Jaroslav Pelikan (New York: Harper and Row, 1966), chapter 2.

17. Lotz, "Albrecht Ritschl's Interpretation of Luther's Theology," pp. 117–28.

18. Ibid., p. 19.

19. Ibid., pp. 117–28.

20. Walther, *Typen des Reich-Gottes Verständnisses,* chap. 6. Also Metzler, "The Ethics of the Kingdom," pp. 105–10.

21. Metzler, "The Ethics of the Kingdom," pp. 2–3, passim. See also, Philip

Hefner, "The Concreteness of God's Kingdom: A Problem for the Christian Life," *The Journal of Religion* 51 (July, 1971): 189–93.

22. Metzler, "The Ethics of the Kingdom," pp. 201–4. See also, Rolf Schäfer, "Das Reich Gottes bei Albrecht Ritschl und Johannes Weiss," *Zeitschrift für Theologie und Kirche* 61 (1964): 66–88.

23. Metzler, "The Ethics of the Kingdom," p. 204.

24. Ryan, "The Role of the Discipline of History," pp. 336–58.

25. Hefner, *Faith and the Vitalities of History*, chapter 3, especially pp. 99–100.

26. Ibid., p. 100. Wrzecionko, *Die philosophischen Wurzeln*, pp. 141–42, 218–19.

27. Hefner, *Faith and the Vitalities of History*, pp. 70–90.

28. "Prolegomena," *History of Pietism*, see pp. 51–147 below.

29. Ryan, "The Role of the Discipline of History," especially chapters 4 and 7.

30. Ibid., pp. 329 f.

31. Ibid., pp. 335–59. Metzler, "The Ethics of the Kingdom," pp. 207 ff. Schäfer, *Ritschl*, pp. 121–213.

32. Horst Stephan, "Albrecht Ritschl und die Gegenwart," *Zeitschrift für Theologie und Kirche*, N.F. 6 (1935): 21. See David Mueller, *An Introduction to the Theology of Albrecht Ritschl* (Philadelphia: Westminster, 1969), pp. 149–50.

33. This is the opinion of Ernst Haenchen, "Albrecht Ritschl als Systematiker," in his *Gott und Mensch* (Tübingen: J. C. B. Mohr, 1965), pp. 409–75. Also Senft, see note 15, above, and Karl Barth, see note 45 below.

34. Hodgson, *The Formation of Historical Theology*, pp. 70–73.

35. Wrzecionko, *Die philosophischen Wurzeln*, pp. 22–33.

36. Ibid., pp. 52–140.

37. Jodock, Ryan, Schäfer argue for Jesus in his New Testament witness. Lotz emphasizes Luther, although not as an exclusive norm. Hefner has argued for the tradition as such. Wrzecionko argues for the philosophical norm, as does Gösta Hök, *Die elliptische Theologie Albrecht Ritschls*: Nach Ursprung und innerem Zusammenhang (Uppsala Universitets Årsskrift, 1942), p. 3.

38. Lotz, "Albrecht Ritschl's Interpretation of Luther's Theology," p. 202 f.

39. Otto Ritschl, II: 320 ff.

40. "Prolegomena," *History of Pietism*, see pp. 51–147 below.

41. James Hastings Nichols, *History of Christianity, 1650–1950* (New York: Ronald Press, 1956), p. 285.

42. Schäfer, *Ritschl*, pp. 113–14. Ryan, "The Role of the Discipline of History," pp. 22–23.

43. Lotz, "Albrecht Ritschl's Interpretation of Luther's Theology," pp. 209–18.

44. Hefner, works mentioned in notes 11 and 21 above.

45. Karl Barth, "Ritschl," in *Protestant Thought from Rousseau to Ritschl* (New York: Harper and Row, 1959).

46. Schäfer, *Ritschl,* pp. 123–28. In 1887, on the occasion of the 150th anniversary of the university, Ritschl as pro-rector gave the keynote address. He used the opportunity to analyze the three main political forces at play in the life of the university—clericalists, free-thinkers, and social-democrats. He leveled sharp criticism at the first two, which drew their fire in return in newspaper editorials aimed at Ritschl. The speech argued that university professors should be freed from political pressures and distractions. For an extended discussion of Ritschl and his relationship to his cultural milieu, see Fritz Fischer, "Der deutsche Protestantismus und die Politik im 19. Jahrhundert," *Historische Zeitschrift* 171 (1951): 473–518, esp. pp. 499–501.

47. Ryan, "The Role of the Discipline of History," and Schäfer, *Ritschl,* both give full accounts of Ritschl's wedding of history and dogmatics. Hefner, *Faith and the Vitalities of History,* summarizes his historical studies and their conclusions.

48. Paul Jersild, "The Holiness, Righteousness and Wrath of God in the Theologies of Albrecht Ritschl and Karl Barth" (Doctoral diss., Evangelical-Theological Faculty, University of Münster, 1962). Excerpts in *The Lutheran Quarterly* 14 (1962): 239–57, and 328–46.

49. See Ryan, "The Role of the Discipline of History," passim, and Hefner, *Faith and the Vitalities of History,* passim.

50. Wolfhart Pannenberg, ed., *Revelation as History* (New York: Macmillan, 1968). See also his "Redemptive Event and History," "Hermeneutic and Universal History," and "On Historical and Theological Hermeneutic," in *Basic Questions in Theology: Collected Essays,* Volume 1 (Philadelphia: Fortress Press, 1970). Gerhard Ebeling, *Word and Faith* (Philadelphia: Fortress Press, 1963), especially "The Significance of the Critical Historical Method for Church and Theology in Protestantism," pp. 17–61. Also his *The Problem of Historicity* (Philadelphia: Fortress Press, 1967) and "Sola Scriptura und das Problem der Tradition," in *Schrift und Tradition,* ed. K. E. Skydsgaard and Lukas Vischer (Zurich: EVZ Verlag, 1963).

51. Schäfer terms this restriction "biblicism"; Wrzecionko describes it as a philosophical bias; Lotz calls it a tendency toward ethicism; Hefner argues for a restricted view of life-style. Both Ryan and Jodock seek to rescue Ritschl from this charge.

52. Schäfer, *Ritschl,* pp. 178–81.

53. Lotz, "Albrecht Ritschl's Interpretation of Luther's Theology," pp. 129 f., 151–61.

54. Metzler, "The Ethics of the Kingdom," pp. 438 ff.

55. Ibid., p. 204.

56. Ibid., p. 438.

57. See note 21, above.

58. Metzler, "The Ethics of the Kingdom," p. 1.

"PROLEGOMENA"

TO *THE HISTORY OF PIETISM*

"PROLEGOMENA" TO *THE HISTORY OF PIETISM*

The History of Pietism was the product of Ritschl's last active period, consuming the decade 1876–1886, after his major works in dogmatics were complete. He undertook a thorough study of the original sources, a task that made great demands on the libraries he used, since he had to call for books that had long been out of use. He dealt with every available treatise, devotional booklet, or other literary vestige of Dutch, German, and Swiss pietism. The reading had a great effect on him and his moods, at times exciting him and at others depressing him, since he was always aware that he was dealing with a phenomenon that was alien to himself. The great and intriguing question is why a man would devote ten years of his life to the study of a movement to which he was opposed. The answer may lie in the fact that pietism was so concerned with the Christian life, which was also Ritschl's major concern in his academic thought. At any rate, the work grew to three volumes of what is Ritschl's clearest, most easily comprehended writing. The "Prolegomena" lays out more lucidly than anything else he wrote how he employed the categories of "way of living" as a key for interpreting the Christian religion and its various groupings.

This "Prolegomena" first appeared, in a slightly different form, in the *Zeitschrift für Kirchengeschichte* in 1877. Apparently Ritschl wanted to float the idea before putting it in more permanent form. The first volume of the work appeared from Adolph Marcus in Bonn in 1880, followed by the other two volumes in 1884 and 1886. This is the first English translation of this work.

"Prolegomena"
to *The History of Pietism*

I. THE SCOPE OF THE TASK

There have been contradictory assessments of the nature and significance of that phenomenon in the history of the protestant churches which we call pietism, just as there have been totally different judgments about its extent. This twofold disparity in comprehending pietism strikes one when he compares the two monographical studies by Max Goebel and Heinrich Schmid which have been undertaken in the last generation. Schmid[1] recognizes under the rubric of pietism only that series of manifestations within the Lutheran church of Germany which were occasioned by Philipp Spener[2] and which reached their term in the course of the controversy between Joachim Lange in Halle[3] and Valentin Ernst Loescher in Dresden.[4] He rightly denies the allegation that Spener was conforming directly and intentionally to his older contemporary, the reformed separatist Jean de Labadie,[5] when he reluctantly established the conventicle. Accordingly, however, he separates the manifestations of pietism in the Lutheran church from similar events in Calvinism with the result that he pays no attention at all to the latter and does not even raise the question of whether the two phenomena are to be derived from the same source. In addition, he is so convinced that Spener's movement is central to pietism that he makes the false estimate that pietism originated in the Lutheran church and subsequently spread from there into the reformed provinces as well (p. 468). Moreover, it is surprising that he excludes from his *Die Geschichte des Pietismus* [*The History of Pietism*] not only the founding of the *Brüdergemeinde* [Moravian brotherhood] by Zinzendorf and its historical development, but also the phenomenon of Württemberg pietism and the theology of Johann Albrecht Bengel and his followers. This branching of pietism, in itself, contradicts the estimate by which Schmid makes the transition from his historical portrayal to a judgment concerning the nature of the pietist movement: "Pietism continued to stimulate and win individual souls, but from an ecclesiastical perspective it also proceeded to work in a disintegrating and destructive manner" (Ibid.). Is it further the case, for this historian, that the series of manifestations in which pietism clearly showed itself as representative of ecclesiastical interests and revealed its efforts to subject under its own domination those souls which would not permit themselves to be won over to it, does not even exist? Or does he deny that, in terms of church law, pietism attempted to hold these persons on a leash like a child and even to silence them? It might even seem an insignificant thing to try to understand this incorrect delimitation of the material which the Erlangen church historian has set before us, but a comparison of this work with Johann Georg Walch's *Historische und theologische Einleitung in die Religions-streitigkeiten der evangelisch-lutherischen Kirche* [*Historical and Theological Introduction to the Religious Controversies of the Evangelical Lutheran Church*][6] pushes us irresistibly to attempt such an understanding. Schmid's book is neither more nor less than an elegant extract from the fifth chapter of Walch's work, which deals with the pietist controversies and extends from the middle of the first volume through the middle of the third. Using this method, Schmid thus elicits the impression that the history of pietism consists solely in controversies, whereas the documents of pietism are actually for the most part ascetical books and hymns. A particular verification of my suspicion about this book is offered by the fact that Schmid enlarges upon Gottfried Arnold[7] and Christian Thomasius[8] in a postscript (p. 472), as Walch does, presenting both men at the conclusion of his portrayal of the controversies, separated only by a series of mystical enthusiasts to whom Schmid correctly gives attention. If my conjecture is correct, that the material of Schmid's *History of Pietism* is only an extract from the work of Johann Georg Walch, then it is fully understandable that we look in vain for Zinzendorf and Bengel in his book, because Walch dealt with them only in the sequel to the above-named work, which first appeared in 1739. One is tempted, as a proof of that piety with which dogmatics, alone among the sciences, is favored, to recommend the Erlangen church historian's enterprise for everyone to read and marvel at—that is, that in 1863 he has restricted his presentation of pietism to the perspective of 1730! The only mitigating circumstance would be the fact that even in Schmid's own book (p. 454) there is a reference to Loescher's comment that piety also possesses desires, drives, and demands which have been ordered and established in a perverse manner. By the very fact that Schmid has appropriated Loescher's expression as an evaluation of pietism's worth, he will be all the more vulnerable to the criticism of his historical perspective which follows from this very reasonable observation. He finds that the error of this sort of piety is rooted in a doctrinal error of Spener. In his judgment, Spener was in agreement with Lutheran doctrine as a whole, but differed on the question of what was the correct estimate of the organization of the Lutheran church. The establishment of the conventicle supposedly called into question only the "third order" of the church, namely, the congregation, whereas it justified its churchly activity solely on the assumption that this "third order" worked in cooperation with the other two orders (pp. 436, 445).[9] In addition, Schmid also takes exception to pietism on the grounds that Spener's manner of emphasizing the necessity for *active* faith (i.e., good works as the test of justification) created a confusion of this faith with sanctification (p. 448).

The phenomenon of pietism is not at all exhausted by this interpretation and derivation. One receives this impression immediately when he surveys Goebel's description of these same manifestations in the reformed and the Lutheran churches.[10] His research of the entire material has led this author to suggest the interpretation that pietism, in all its types, is the diminished or attenuated form of the same movement which appeared as anabaptism in the sixteenth century. Goebel's interpretation opens a wide horizon for church-historical research, and the value of his observation is totally independent of the use which he himself makes of it. Since he comes to his work with a personal commitment to pietism, which he considers to be a powerful force for renewal in the face of the stagnation and corruption of the protestant church, he also makes a very favorable judgment on anabaptism. Alongside the violence of the anabaptist movement, he recognizes their efforts to reform the ethical and political order as a *more thorough, more decisive,* and *more perfect* continuation of the reformation of Luther and Zwingli (I, 137–39). This evaluation of pietism and anabaptism requires all the more justification since Goebel himself could not withhold certain qualifications of his positive interpretation, for he termed the reform of the anabaptists at the same time a degeneration of Luther's reformation and he considered the renewal which pietism opened up for the protestant church to be one-sided. This uncertainty in Goebel's judgment also indicates that his observations on the phenomena he studies are neither complete nor exhaustive. Both the pietistic phenomena and anabaptism demand more precise investigation if their relationship to each other is to be confirmed and their common form perceived with certainty. For every conscientious study of pietism will have to concern itself with the scope of the vista which Goebel has opened up for us. In this sense I have imitated his work. It is also my personal desire, however, to testify how provocative Goebel's diligent and many-sided research has been in guiding my own work. Even where I have had to contradict his judgment and where his presentation has not satisfied my own demands, I have nevertheless been reminded of his eager diligence and his characteristic accuracy. Just as he has won for himself a lasting place in the writing of church history through the aforementioned work, so also I, and indeed all who have known him and had associations with him, will never be able to forget his friendliness, helpfulness, impartiality and unpretentiousness.

II. THE REFORMATION IN THE
WESTERN CHURCH OF THE MIDDLE AGES

Wherever it exists, pietism claims to have reformation significance for the protestant churches. No less have the anabaptists felt that they themselves brought the work of restoring the church—which was begun by Luther and Zwingli—to its proper end. Therefore, both phenomena stand in strong analogy to each other and, accordingly, it is not improbable that pietism might stand in the close relationship to anabaptism which Goebel suggested. But even if a protestant theologian did recognize in pietism the diminished form of that tendency by which anabaptism wished to reform the church, we would still require more than the simple assertion that anabaptism is the logical fulfillment of Luther's reformation, especially since Luther and Zwingli and their own contemporary followers were of a totally different opinion. They saw a renewal of monasticism in anabaptism, which was something quite different from their own ends and means, and a protestant theologian cannot rightly disregard this judgment of the reformers nor deviate from it. Rather, one must ask himself very precisely whether anabaptism merely displays a *quantitative* difference from the reformation of Luther and Zwingli (as the consistent extension and carrying out of a task common with theirs) or whether there is a *qualitative* difference, a difference in kind, between the two attempts to restore the church. We have not yet fully realized the task which arises from this dilemma, and this defect is closely related to the fact that protestant church historians have had an excessively narrow interpretation of the concept of "the reformation," a concept they have subsequently used to throw light on a whole range of phenomena.

It is well known that certain tendencies in the second half of the Middle Ages have been designated by protestant church historians as "reforming," as the prehistory of the reformation of the sixteenth century, as the forerunners of "our" reformation which is seen as the only distinctive one. As criteria for their judgments, these historians have divided their sources, making use partly of the rejection of the veneration of saints and the like and partly of the actual or apparent acknowledgment of the doctrine of justification by faith and the acknowledgment of the exclusive authority of holy scripture for Christian doctrine. In addition, however, they have also counted opposition to the constitutional representatives of catholic ecclesiasticism as a chief mark of the reformation character. They have even gone so far that, for a long time, they considered the dualistic thought and ascetic life of the Albigensians to be a "forerunner of the reformation," simply because they set themselves in opposition to the Roman hierarchy. With similar justification, one could with certainty also convince himself that there is the closest relationship between the anabaptists and our reformers, merely because the former stand in an even sharper opposition to the Roman church than the latter. If this criterion is essential and decisive for the concept of the reformation of the church, then in the name of Luther and Zwingli we would have to abdicate in favor of the anabaptist or Manichean reformation. It is a pity that both are choked in blood! This interpretation of history, which culminates in Karl Ullmann's *Reformatoren vor der Reformation* [*Reformers before the Reformation*],[11] merely serves to confuse everything. This interpretation originally grew out of the esteem which these historians held exclusively for Luther's reformation, but by means of the categories to which they have restricted themselves in comparing historical phenomena, they have only succeeded in effacing the distinctiveness of the reformation. In particular, this method of historical comparison is guilty of the greatest injustice against the Middle Ages of the western church. The Middle Ages is always regarded only as the footstool for the Lutheran reformation and is almost never examined on the basis of the tendencies which were intrinsic to it and which are thus justified relatively in the light of the existing circumstances. The basis for this inadequacy lies in the too-narrow and illiberal concept of reformation which is employed. By "reformation," these historians always mean first of all opposition to the legitimate or traditional form of the church, and they seldom are receptive to the question of whether or not it might be possible to have reformations in the church which were accomplished directly by ecclesiastical authority or in cooperation with it. Consequently, they do not understand even Luther's reformation in a full and correct manner.

Gotthard Viktor Lechler,[12] to be sure, recently betrayed some misgivings about this failure of church historians to secure a broader concept of the reformation for themselves. As he undertook to portray the *Vorgeschichte der Reformation* [*Prehistory of the Reformation*] (i.e., the reformation of the sixteenth century) in order to put his hero John Wycliffe[13] in proper perspective, who should he discover in his path but Pope Gregory VII[14] as the leader of a reform party which strove after the *moral purification* and the *liberating of the church* from its dependence upon the world, i.e., upon the power of the state (p. 37). Similarly, he recognized the impulse for an *inner renewal and reform of Christendom* in the two great mendicant orders of the thirteenth century (p. 80). Now these are truly the two epoch-making realities which give shape to the history of the western church and which transmit to us, at the same time, the material by which we are able to amplify any concept of the reformation of the church. And it will become clear that this amplification does not hamper our understanding of Luther's reformation nor lessen our esteem for it. But Lechler has not made use of these observations; he quickly blurs their significance for the history of the church in the Middle Ages by comments which grow out of his bias in favor of the particular forms of the Lutheran reformation, on the one hand, and which make success or failure the criterion for judging historical intentions, on the other. Lechler decides that he should not dwell on the reforming significance of Gregory but, instead, quickly turns to the varied manifestations of opposition to the church whose reforming intentions he validates in familiar fashion as forerunners of Luther's work. Why? Because one can hardly sense "the warm pulse of the pious Christian heart" in the great pope, because the priestly celibacy which he established for the moral purification of the church accomplished precisely the opposite of what he intended, and because the elimination of lay investiture[15] did not accomplish the desecularizing of the church. But is this a justifiable assessment of Gregory? How would we judge Luther's reformation if we used this criterion? Does the "pulse of the pious Christian heart" beat in the controversy over the doctrine of the Lord's Supper, or is it not much more the concern to guarantee objective ecclesiasticism? Furthermore, is there really a correspondence between the result of Luther's reformation, namely a separate church which stands under the constraint of scholastic doctrine, and his reforming intention to guide all Christians in the direction of their religious freedom over the world and their moral obligations toward human society? He who weighs Luther's reformation against concerns of the "pious Christian heart" and the intention of the reformer himself against his success could well miss the significance of the reformation of the sixteenth century—and many have done this. But if we do not permit ourselves to be confused in our assessment of Luther by the experiences of the mystics and converts to catholicism in the epoch subsequent to syncretism and romanticism, then we ought not let Lechler's comments falsify Gregory's reform either! Lechler also deals very superficially with the reform of St. Francis.[16] He does not

even describe its goals and means; but merely says that the well-
known divisions in the Franciscan order dampened the very hopes
which the order itself aroused. If this is supposed to mean that there
was no success at all in efforts at reforming the church in this manner,
then, as we shall see, Lechler is quite wrong.

Now then, if we are to survey adequately the scope of phenomena
within the history of the medieval church that are pertinent to the
concept of the reformation, we must take the following into account.
The two reformations which Lechler allows—that of Gregory VII
and Francis of Assisi—have their common point of origin in the
monastic reforms which permeate the history of the medieval western
church in all possible forms and degrees. In particular, the liberation
of the church from the power of the state, which the great pope
undertook, has its roots in the reform of the Benedictine order which
culminated in the congregation at Cluny. And Francis based the
reform of the church which he sought on the establishing of the
Franciscan order which, like all newly established orders, carried
within itself the intention to reform monasticism. Now in the catholic
interpretation of Christianity, that monasticism which turns away
from the world stands as the true, perfect Christian life. In comparison with it, the worldly Christianity of the laity is wholly subordinate, even as they are admonished to a merely passive discipline
through the sacraments. By "reformation," the Middle Ages understood quite explicitly only the renunciation of the world, which
continually had to be intensified from time to time. Romans 12:2,
in the Vulgate,[17] is determinative for this point of view: *Nolite con-
formari huic seculo, sed reformamini in novitate sensus vestri* ["Do
not model yourselves on the behavior of the world around you, but
let your behavior change, modelled by your new mind"]. Reformation of monasticism, or the defense against the always-spreading
secularization of monasticism, therefore, qualified in the Middle
Ages as reformation of Christianity generally. When judged in this
light, the history of the western church in the Middle Ages is an
almost unbroken chain of attempts at ecclesiastical reformation.
Against this general background, the Cluniac reform of the Benedictine order and the establishment of the Franciscan order stand out
as the epoch-making events. This assessment is borne out concretely
by the fact that the Benedictine rule at Cluny was intensified by the

vow of silence and that through Francis the renunciation of personal property, even by the monastic community, was introduced into the general monastic obligations. Both had identical aims— to preserve the freedom from the world to which men felt themselves called and for which they strove, within the forms of monasticism, against backsliding into worldliness. If it is true that all reforms of the monastic orders and all the foundations of new orders proceed on the basis of this common goal, then it is also true that the reform of the relationship between church and civil power which Gregory VII conceived was only the application to the legal ordering of the whole Christian church of that principle which governed the authentic Christian life. If it were so that the Christian life, in the form of monasticism, should be freed from the worldly factors which had stunted its growth, then it did not seem fitting that the power of the secular state should interfere in the legal ordering of the church of Christ. Now it is not accidental that a Cluniac monk should set for himself this task of liberating the church, since the reformed congregation at Cluny was brought into touch with the concerns of the whole church by virtue of the fact that it was directly under the supervision of the pope. Also, since Cluny was well aware of the significance of this position during the time of its flowering, it followed that the Cluniac monks attempted to lay down the rule that secular spirituality [the spirituality of Christians outside the monastic orders] should accept the canonical pattern of life, i.e., a pattern in the closest possible analogy to monasticism. Within this same line of development, we also find the view that marriage of priests should be eliminated. It was through this prohibition that Gregory VII thought that he could most effectively undergird his liberation of the church from the state. The Cluniac reform of monasticism, therefore, brought along with it the monastic reform of the clergy; and a church which was represented by such a clergy could not tolerate dependence upon the secular state: this is the context in which Gregory's epoch-making significance as reformer is to be understood.

We can form an adequate assessment of the significance of the Cluniac and Gregorian reform, however, simply by tracing the course which this movement took within the Middle Ages itself. In the first place, the goal of reforming monasticism does an injustice to the great masses of church members. Furthermore, the ever-recurring necessity for reforming monasticism is a clear proof of the purposelessness of undertaking to shape Christian perfection in the statutory forms of simplistic renunciation of the world. Finally, the fact that a church, richly endowed with property and legally structured, is independent from the state is no assurance that that church is liberated from what we would call "the world" in a moral sense, for in this latter sense property and law are thoroughly secular conditions and structures. The church which wishes to be structured substantially by the marks of material property and legal functioning is plainly a part of the world. We must also add that the same church had to exalt itself to dominion over the world since it could not exist in the same place (or should we say persons) in indifference to the state once it had freed itself from imperial investiture. And since the church presented itself as the original possessor of the secular sword it therefore betrayed the fact that it was first led down the road of secularization by Gregory. But this result had received its *de facto* rectification already in the Middle Ages. Not, to be sure, in the reform councils of the fifteenth century, but in the system of national churches. It is a direct abrogation of the Gregorian reform that in England, Spain, and France—indeed, through a formal concession by the pope in the two last-named lands—the *appointment* of the bishops came to be in the hands of the kings. Even in Germany a system of state churches was created to the extent that the Holy Roman Empire transformed itself into a confederation of secular and spiritual princes, and the possession of the bishoprics in Germany was made useful to the social and political demands of the upper and middle aristocracy.

Nevertheless, the reformation of St. Francis of Assisi designates a new epoch in the western church during the same period in which the Gregorian system unfolded its farthest-reaching consequences. To be sure, as the founder of a new order, Francis thought that he was simply attaching himself to the line of his predecessors; and he thought that his efforts to insure that the Franciscan brothers remained far removed from the world through the severe means of total poverty differed only in degree from previous founders of monastic orders. In spite of this he had the unmistakable intention to renew authentic Christianity, that is to say, the religion of Jesus, through his order, and his contemporaries understood the success of his life in precisely this sense. The older, more detailed Rule of St. Francis, comprising twenty-three chapters, lays down the rule in the introduction: *Vivere in obedientia et in castitate et sine proprio, et domini nostri Jesu Christi doctrinam et vestigia sequi, qui dicit . . .* ["To live in obedience and in chastity and without property, and to follow the teaching and example of our Lord Jesus Christ, who said . . ."]—and it cites Matt. 19:21, 16:24, Luke 14:26, and Matt. 19:29.[18] The approved rule of Honorius III, which came later and which encompassed twelve chapters, determined that the *vita fratrum minorum* [life of the Franciscans] would "observe the gospel of our Lord Jesus Christ by living in obedience, without property, and in chastity."[19] It is a matter, therefore, of the monastic vows of continence being intensified, but with the intention that they should correspond to the general commands of Jesus upon his disciples and to Jesus' own example. Accordingly, the precepts of the individual orders also made constant reference to the principles of universal service and forgiveness which the gospel sets forth, and in particular the monastics of St. Francis were literally charged with the precepts which Jesus gave to his disciples that they should travel through the world without purse, money, or staff, and that they should always greet those whom they met with peace and seek hospitality. Added to this was the obligation to preach to the masses with the intention that, so far as possible, the Christian principles of universal self-abnegation might also be recognized as valid and actually practiced among the laity which the church had neglected up to that time. Peter Waldus had previously attempted to do the same thing, but the ecclesiastical authority had not permitted him.[20] In spite of this, Francis and Dominic simultaneously with each other took up the same task again a generation later and they received ecclesiastical approval both of their motives and of the means by which they set out to accomplish their goal. Such preaching for repentance or commendation of the ascetical life to the laity meant that an attempt was being made within the catholic church itself to resolve the alienation that existed between the Christian perfection of the monastics and the utterly passive Christianity of the laity. It was explicitly recognized by both contemporary and later witnesses that these undertakings, particularly that of St. Francis, amounted to a reformation of the church, i.e., the restoration of primitive Christianity.[21] Neither the warm pulse of the pious heart nor the earnest concern for the judgment of the gospel is missing from the reformer of Assisi; rather, the entire life-style of this extraordinary man indicates a level and inner profundity of Christian sensibility, as well as a breadth of human love, which none of those other men have attained to, whom we otherwise distinguish with the title "reformer of the church." The reforming intention of St. Francis has been anything but a failure—but we need not insist that the consequences of his work must be identical with those of Luther and Zwingli in order for them even to qualify as manifestations of a reformed Christianity. For Francis's goal, which was to transport the ascetical life out from behind the walls of the cloister into the society as a whole, is totally unlike the intentions of the reformers of the sixteenth century, just as the specific means which Francis employed would be quite foreign to those men.

It is said that St. Francis's preaching for repentance was a powerful impetus for the masses to enter the cloistered life. That is quite understandable since the principles which Francis proclaimed as the substance of catholic Christianity had only been exercised up to that time in the particular form known as monasticism. Therefore, it was up to the reformer to introduce the ascetical form of life into the civil society as well. To this end, in addition to the men's order of the *fratres minores* and the women's Order of Poor Clares, he established the *ordo tertius de poenitentia* [third order of penitence] which was composed of lay congregations of men, and women as well, for whom he provided a comprehensive rule of twenty articles.[22] Thus we see the direct consequence of his restoration of primitive Christianity in this half-monastic association of laity who remained in their secular situations. Entrance into these tertiary communities—which was possible only after a certain period of testing—was meant to obligate the entrant so fully that he could leave only if he were transferring to a full-fledged monastic order. Married women required the permission of their husbands before they were accepted. Members were required to draw up their wills soon after their entrance into the order, so that they could relinquish all concern for their property. They were prohibited from participation in revelling and dancing, specifically from dramatic presentations, and even from indirect support of such entertainments. The vow was granted to the tertiaries only in specifically designated cases since taking an oath was forbidden in the circumstances of daily life. Bearing arms was permitted only for the defense of the Roman church and the fatherland, for in general they were held to complete pacifism. A cheap cloak was prescribed for clothing, neither black nor white—hence, grey. In addition, the tertiaries were held to diligent attendance at worship services, observance of the canonical hours, frequent confession, regular communion, four weekly fast days, visiting the sick within the order, participation in the burial of members of the order, and, finally, subjection to the regular visits of their superior (*ministri*). Similar associations grew out of the groups that followed the Dominican order and the later orders of the Augustinians, the Minims, the Servites, and the Trappists. The Jesuits also formed such congregations of laity. Thus, in this respect, the impulse of St. Francis has been efficacious in the Catholic church throughout the epoch that followed his own life. As far as the Middle Ages is concerned, however, the Franciscan and Dominican preaching proved its reforming intentions in the spreading of an asceticism which accommodated itself to the conditions of living among those who were married and active in civil pursuits and thus it narrowed, at least, the gulf between monastic and laity. In general, this undertaking corresponded more fully to the Christian imperatives of equality and corporate unity than the reform in the first half of the Middle Ages which restricted itself to monasticism alone. When we look at the means which were employed for its purposes, however, it is particularly clear that the significance of the Franciscan reformation is only relative—namely, that it amounted simply to the foundation of a new type of monastic order.

In just this manner, the Franciscan reformation stood intentionally in service to the medieval system of the western church, in that it concentrated on the catholic perspective on the Christian life. The principle of absolute poverty and renunciation of property which St. Francis set forth for his order was, in itself, an occasion for conflict between the ascetical reform of the church and the papal dominion of the world. The representatives of the papacy were well aware that the spiritual sword could neither gain nor maintain dominion over the secular sword unless the preponderance of worldly property was in alliance with spiritual authority. Arnold of Brescia[23] had had to do penance with his life for entertaining the opposing view, namely, that the clergy and monks who possessed property could not be blessed. Therefore it is understandable that the popes would not tolerate the principle of complete renunciation of property, even in the limited domain of the Franciscan order, for they must have recognized in that order a quiet rebuke of their system, and they must also have feared that a general rebellion against the property rights of the church which laid claim to worldly goods would come out of it. The "spirituals" in the Franciscan order actually did raise this opposition to the highest imaginable degree. Thus we see here the phenomenon of a reformation, as fully catholic in its conception as the Franciscan, turning about, at least partially, to oppose the ecclesiastical system. And, as a logical conclusion from the reforming principle of their master, the "spirituals" judged that the papacy and the church actually followed the Antichrist, since they did not revert to the example of apostolic Christianity but, rather, sought to repress the Christianity of the "spirituals," which corresponded to the gospel of Christ himself. They concentrated their efforts, however, on actions which would leave to the future the reformation which would be equal to the level of degradation which the church had reached—a future in which the eternal gospel of the Spirit would be efficacious. Such an outlook is perhaps a silent admission that even the intensifying of the Franciscan ascetical means for reform was not sufficient to lead the church directly toward perfection. I will grant that the hope for the future reformation through the eternal gospel was directly determined by the conviction that there would also be a final judgment of damnation upon the antichristian degradation of the church along the lines depicted in John's Apocalypse. The medieval church thus became the master of this movement. After the storms and conflicts which the "spirituals" aroused in the thirteenth and fourteenth centuries, for which many of them had to do penance on the funeral pyre, they permitted themselves to be pacified by virtue of their recognition as the *fratres regularis observantiae* [Brothers of the Strict Observance] by the Council of Constance. From then on, for the remainder of the Middle Ages, none of their repugnance for the Roman church appeared on the surface. Nevertheless, it is difficult to believe that this voice could be fully confined to the circle of the order. The silent obedience of the monks disguised many impulses from the distant observer which could become the common property of many within the smaller circle simply through partial hints. Even if the fifteenth century did not offer us a single document indicating that the Franciscan-Observants had propagated their fundamental objection to the secularization of the Roman papacy among themselves and their tertiaries, it would not follow, from this absence of documents, that their objection had died out completely in that period.

The phenomena of the Middle Ages that I have set forth in this short survey fall under a concept of "reformation" which has a much broader scope than the one which dominates the protestant view of history. "Reformation" in this sense is the restoration of the proper relationship between Christianity and the world which is based on the assumption that that relationship has passed over into a confusion of Christianity with the world. This general concept refers both to the individual Christian life and to the position of the church in the world. The two reformation epochs which I have described are particularly conditioned by the fact that they are governed by the catholic interpretation of the Christian life as being monastic in nature, as well as on the catholic view of the church as a legal entity. For this reason, these examples of reformation had as their goal, on the one hand, carrying out the ever-recurring and ever-intensified task of detaching monastic perfection from life in the world and, on the other hand, the spreading as widely as possible monastic perfection to the laity who were to remain in their families and in their civil occupations. Thus, the reformation of the church which Gregory VII undertook was concerned with detaching the divine legal structure from the influences of the secular state which was spoken of as the organism of sin. But the reformation strategy, which the "spirituals" had in mind, meant the liberation of the church from secularization in general—certainly, the degree and extent to which this was attempted remain in the dark since the enterprise was left to a supernatural intervention of God in the future and was not taken directly in hand by any man.

It is especially noteworthy that the Franciscan reformation of the catholic church was based on the principle of the primitive church, which was still free of confusion with the world (see p. 63). This

view was certainly not restricted to the circle of the Franciscan enterprise, nor is it to be considered an exclusive characteristic of theirs.
On the contrary, the example of the societal situation of the earliest
church in Jerusalem was the standard for nearly all of the reformation movements in the second half of the Middle Ages. It first
appeared in the writings of Joachim of Fiore (died 1212).[24] Simultaneously (about 1170) Peter Waldus, the forerunner of St. Francis,
was engaged in restoring the apostolic life through the actual
observance of the commands of Christ, in voluntary poverty, and,
above all, through evangelical (i.e., ascetical) perfection. Against
the popular tradition which asserts the close relationship between
this phenomenon and the reformation of the sixteenth century, it is
always necessary to refer to the testimony of Herzog that this
"reform stands on catholic soil and was rooted in it."[25] Even though
Peter Waldus did not represent this demand to restore the primitive
church from the very beginning, the Waldensians have been accustomed to legitimizing themselves through that claim.[26] Furthermore,
the Bohemian Matthias von Janow (died 1394)[27] entertained the
idea of a similar reformation. After 1457 the community of the
Bohemian Brethren undertook a form of life in his example, similar
to that of the Waldensians, in the territory which was set in tumult
by the Hussite wars. Through their founder, Brother Gregory the
Barefoot, they seem to have been derived from the Franciscans.[28]
This imitation of the church in Jerusalem maintained its specific
catholic character even as late as the sixteenth century. This same
ideal also governed that double form of the "modern devotion"
which occurred in the Netherlands—the Windesheim Congregation
of regular Augustinians and the Brothers and Sisters of the Common
Life—associations whose specific catholic character cannot be denied.[29] Just how fully this norm corresponds to the catholic way of
reforming can be seen, finally, in the fact that the Jesuits have
extolled the Indian congregations which they founded and supervised in Paraguay as being replicas of the earliest Christian congregations.[30]

I will demonstrate later how the reformation of the sixteenth
century relates to the concept of reformation which has emerged as
the decisive one for the western medieval phenomena that I have
just assessed. But the historical outline of the western church which

I have suggested here does entail a measurable reduction of the category of "forerunners of Luther's reformation" which has been current since the time of Flacius. The manifestations that I have discussed above in reference to the Franciscan reformation would have to be stricken from Flacius's category. It would be still another task to define the catholic counterreformation of the sixteenth century according to that category. Meanwhile, as we come to the conclusion of this discussion, it should be recalled that the eastern church exhibits nothing similar to the reforming efforts which have kept the western church perpetually in turmoil. That church has been at peace since the sixth century as far as its liturgy and ecclesiastical customs have been concerned. In its territories church and state have been closely intertwined, because the ecclesiastical customs are also folk customs and because the church can either identify with the patriarchal despotism of the state or remain so neutral in respect to that despotism that there is no conflict. Since it is concerned only with the stability of the liturgical structure and custom, the church can maintain this stance. In the territory of the eastern church it is much more possible for the Russian Czars to rule the church in their realms indirectly, as the Byzantine rulers did at an earlier time, and—conversely—for the Patriarch of Constantinople to be provided with judicial powers and rights of taxation within the Turkish empire, as the political head of his comrades in the church or of his nation. The problem of the relationship between church and state does not even exist for the eastern church while in the west it has exercised the church and occupied the attention of the state continually for centuries.[31] The eastern church has had equally as little occasion to reform monasticism or to found new orders, nor has the stance of monasticism in relation to the laity come into question, nor the relationship of the secular clergy to the monks. Neither do we find any particularly ascetical congregations among the laity, nor has the marriage of priests been challenged. On the other hand, the married priests have never set themselves against the privilege of the cloisters, from which the bishops are chosen. No reformations in the western sense have appeared there, either because all of these things have always remained in their stable order in the eastern church or because men have not felt deeply the disorder which might exist.

Apparently the western church stood in the same relation to the empire of Charlemagne which the eastern church enjoyed with respect to the Byzantine emperors. The church appeared to be incorporated within the Frankish state; the organs of the church stood at the disposal of the chief of state, to be employed for moral discipline and schooling; even the church councils were under the guidance and confirmation of the emperor, who was designated the regent of the holy church. Only the fall of the Carolingian monarchy made it possible for the papacy to achieve independence and ecclesiastical dominion over the state. But the rise of the papacy was not accidental, nor did it come about simply because of the fall of the Carolingian empire; it would be incorrect, moreover, to assume that the western church would have continued in a relationship of dependence upon the state, like the Byzantine church, if that empire could have maintained itself. For the western church possessed a spiritual legacy in Augustine's teaching concerning the superordination of the city of God over the earthly city, and this legacy pressed to disrupt the Byzantine combination of church and state. Byzantine Christianity lacked this sort of fundamental ethical-political vision. Therefore, that church was indifferent towards those changes in the equilibrium between Christianity and the world which have caused the western church to open itself to repeated reformations, the effects and countereffects of which have both filled out and distinguished its history.

III. THE DISTINCTIVENESS AND ORIGIN OF THE ANABAPTISTS

According to Goebel, anabaptism is the more basic, more decisive, and more perfect reformation, which is to be recognized as "the child of the reformation" which Luther and Zwingli undertook, even though they abandoned it in 1522 and 1524 respectively. If we follow through with this assertion, we can trace the lineage of anabaptism back to Luther and Zwingli in two senses: first, the earliest manifestations of the movement appeared several years after the reforming work of Luther and Zwingli had begun; secondly, many of its leaders were first adherents of the two reformers, prior to their own obvious deviations from those reformers. But these circumstances do not adequately prove that the one phenomenon is the descendant from the other. That which comes later is not, by virtue of the fact that it is something different, necessarily caused by its predecessor, and the adherence of later anabaptists to Luther and Zwingli could be coincidental; it all depends on whether these two reformations *specifically* held to the same purpose and course. But such is simply not the case. Luther defined the Christian life thus: that through the religious virtues of humility, confidence in God, and patience, the Christian is free lord over all things, subject to no man, and that through the moral exercise of his civil occupation, he is obligated to every man. The same holds true for Zwingli, even if it is not so precisely formulated. Both men interpret the moral law as free and independent recognition of the demands which duty imposes; they place the Christian life in the realm of civil society, and they recognize the legal structure of the state as the chief guardian of the exercise of the Christian life, of the ordering of public worship, and of the work of religious instruction. In comparison, one can ascribe a superiority of perfection to the anabaptist pattern of life, only if he believes that detailed statutory rules for the external conditions of life are a necessary and valuable supplement to the freedom that goes along with the moral law. Moreover, one might judge that the anabaptists were more thorough in their reform of life if he holds that it is more useful and more successful to practice Christianity by renouncing as far as possible the ordinary conditions of human life, rather than transfiguring and purifying the given structures of human society through the motives of universal love for neighbor. Finally, one might extol the anabaptists for their greater decisiveness, in that they blazed the trail for a statutory sanctity or, to put it more bluntly, for a statutory sinlessness. But just how little these means succeeded in attaining autonomy and purity in formation of the character is demonstrated by the ease with which these marvelous holy people fell into antinomian aberrations. Thus anabaptism pursued the task of reforming the Christian life in a direction that is diametrically opposed to the intentions of Luther and Zwingli. As reforms, both phenomena are comparable and, in a few situations, similar; but when they are compared in terms of the distinctive characteristics of their respective movements, they appear as complete opposites, rather than as related to each other.

For protestant theologians it is clear that the reformation of Luther and Zwingli, at least in principle, moved beyond the stage of Christianity which unfolded from the second century on and which is described in particular as the catholic stage of Christianity. In contrast to this, it is evident that the motives and goals, the means and the specific regulations on which the anabaptists stand are, as a whole, of medieval lineage, and that that age provides the closest analogies to their movement. For proof of this assertion I reach back to the accounts of Heinrich Bullinger.[32] In that the anabaptists defined themselves as the one, righteous, God-pleasing church of Christ, they put the weight on the active life and on the "visible improvement" of that life in their circles—something which was sought after as little in the protestant as in the papal church. On this basis they censured the protestant doctrine of the satisfaction worked by Christ and justification by faith, since this doctrine seemed to assert that men became righteous before God through faith and not through works. They further censured the teaching that the law cannot be fulfilled, since scripture prescribes keeping the law. In these two principles of life the anabaptists stood on the side of catholicism. From the Christian imperative of love, they deduced furthermore that the Christian should not be permitted to hold property or goods, since love would much rather prefer to hold all things in common with the brethren. This principle is only the generalization of a rule which, up to that time, was held as a condition of Christian perfection by monasticism.[33] Moreover, the anabaptists held themselves partly indifferent and partly averse to the state and its arrangements. They denied that religion belongs to the competence of the state and that the Christian has any need to live by civil laws. According to their view, Christians do not resist force, and they have prepared themselves for suffering—therefore they do not seek legal protection from the state. This means that they cannot occupy any office of authority, nor are they permitted to bear arms or use them, nor may they take an oath. These principles grow out of a differentiation between the Christian religious community and the secular state, a differentiation which has its closest analogy in the principles of Gregory VII, and it ultimately refers back to Augustine's polarity between the city of God and the city of man. The logical conclusion of all of these principles is that the community of the righteous and guiltless should separate itself from members of the protestant and papal churches. Since they could never tolerate a passive adherence to the community of the sanctified, as these latter churches acknowledge in their practice of infant baptism, but rather only the active, ascetical qualities of their group, the anabaptists were led to practice adult baptism as the only correct form of reception into the true community of Christ—or else the rebaptism of those who were baptized as infants. Among all the principles of this group this one innovation is to be understood as a necessary consequence of their way of structuring life, and its individual features can be shown to be more or less developed in medieval catholicism.

Bullinger designated these marks of the anabaptists as those which were in part common to all their sects (except for individual modifications) and in part (excluding deviations) served as characteristics of the masses for which he recommended the term "general or common baptists." Generally, they fall into two groups: the one depends on individual inspiration, and the other on the letter of the Bible. The first group originally appeared in the Zwickau prophets, the other in the Zurich prophets. It is customary to say that in each respective group we find a heightening of the reformation principles of Luther and Zwingli. The intensification of the authority of holy scripture is said to be evident in Conrad Grebel's[34] deviation from Zwingli, and the revelations of the Holy Spirit among the baptists are said to be simply the natural development from the immediate certainty of salvation to which the individual is led by the doctrine of justification by faith. But this series of phenomena presents yet another side. When we compare the biblicism of Grebel and Zwingli, we see that it is but a means of defending totally different claims concerning the Christian religion. Biblicism was the easiest and, for that time, the most self-evident means available for such a defense. For his part, Zwingli stood with Bible in hand to represent the gospel of divine grace and the moral law, whereas Grebel represented a social and ethical organization of the Christian church as binding, even though it was derived from a historical epoch that lay far in the past. The educated people of the time tended to restrict themselves to the general principles which Grebel set forth, but we must enlarge our picture of these phenomena by comparing the response of these educated men with the actual application which was made of that principle among the uneducated adherents of the movement. The "apostolic baptists" looked only at the letter of scripture, according to Bullinger. Since they relied on the example of the apostles, they traveled around as preachers without staff, shoes, purse, or money; because the Lord had said that the apostles should preach from the rooftops what was whispered in their ears, they climbed up on rooftops and preached from there; since it is written in scripture that one should become a child among children, they behaved as children; because discipleship to Christ supposedly entailed that one should abandon wife and child, house and trade, they became tramps and let themselves be supported by the brethren. A related group, the "separated spiritual baptists," wanted to have nothing more to do with the world, and therefore they regulated both the material and style of dress, eating, drinking, sleeping, standing, and walking; whenever they saw someone laughing, they called down woes upon him in the name of the gospel; for the same reason, they shunned all weddings, festive meals, singing, and stringed music; in addition, they rejected the fraternal and guild associations in which they might have to mingle with different types of people, and also the bearing of arms. Would one really wish to interpret these oddities—whose only analogy in church history is the monomania of the Russian Old Believers[35]—as being the logical continuation of the movement which Zwingli began? One might be forced to this assumption by the legend that the "formal principle"[36] predominated in Zwingli's reformation. But on the basis of the anabaptist consequences that followed from this so-called principle, one could also be convinced that actual life never follows such wretched schemes. Zwingli's view of Christianity differs from that of his anabaptist opponents in its profoundest depths, namely, his view is far from the catholic form of life, whereas theirs links itself closely to the ceremonial-legal tendency of catholicism. The fact that both base their directly contradictory claims on the binding character of the word of God and the holy scripture indicates that this norm is not a distinctive characteristic of the reformation of Luther and Zwingli, but that, on the contrary, it has played a role in other movements as well. The ceremonial-legal substance of this norm gives us cause to suspect that its roots lie in the Middle Ages.

The appearance of ecstasy and inspiration which the other groups of anabaptists gave has likewise nothing in common with the personal assurance of salvation which comes from faith based on justification through Christ. It is rather the case that those pathological manifestations which portray the most arbitrary, most worthless, or most wanton impulses as if they were divine commands stand completely removed from the humility and patience, as well as from the faithfulness to the pursuit of one's vocation, in which the evangelical assurance of salvation sets itself forth. The nearness of the return of Christ and his judgment, which the anabaptists proclaimed in their ecstatic excitations as the means by which his kingdom will be established, are indeed similar to the presupposition of the coming end of the world which went along with the work of Luther and his comrades. But while it is true that these presuppositions of the two parties are identical in content, the Lutherans never made them a particularly important part of their gospel, whereas the anabaptists made them the chief substance and leading motif of their preaching for repentance. Ecstasy and inspiration are the kinds of phenomena which are much more at home in monasticism, since they are possible effects of the ascetical life, and thus they received a certain esteem in the Middle Ages. Therefore, this mark of anabaptism is also oriented in the same direction as the ones we assessed before. The ecstatic proclamation of the nearness of Christ's return likewise finds its analogies in the Middle Ages; but its particular location will be designated in the later course of this investigation.

Everywhere, anabaptism sprang from the bosom of the urban artisan population. This reforming movement was basically untheological, in spite of the fact that it won for itself many clerics and monks whose level of education enabled them to lead the movement and defend its principles through speaking and writing. For example, the mystical theology represented by Andreas Carlstadt[37] and Hans Denck[38] and the general thrust toward restoring the so-called apostolic stage of Christian society were, in themselves, totally indifferent to one another. Now I will grant that mysticism is reputed to stand in a particularly close relationship to the Lutheran reformation. But it is really only a much more pronounced phase of catholic piety, as I will show in the following section. And even though Luther shared this theological tendency for a time, it nevertheless did not lead him to those ideas through which he became a reformer; rather, the traces of mysticism in his writings disappear as his reformation viewpoint clarified itself. The vision of the Christian life that is distinctive to Luther, as it is presented in *de libertate christiana* ["Concerning the Liberty of the Christian Man"],[39] is directly opposed to mysticism. Mysticism teaches escape from the world and renunciation of the world, and it places the significance of the ethically good action and the formation of virtues far beneath ecstatic union with God. Luther taught that the Christian religion leads to spiritual dominion over the world, and he placed the same value on the service of ethical action toward other men as on those activities which comprise man's reconciliation with God. Mysticism in the Christian church is actually a growth of neoplatonism, for the leading idea, which is common both to this philosophy and to mysticism as well, is that God is not the world but that he is the denial of the world. This idea is the expression of a paganism that has despaired of its own foundations and is in itself subchristian for that very reason. Furthermore, the piety which corresponds to this idea of God, which seeks ecstatic reunion with God so that the world in general and creatureliness in the form of one's own person can be denied—this piety is possible only if the ascetical renunciation of the corporeal and social conditions of human existence has preceded it. For this reason, and since it declared the monastic asceticism invalid in general, Luther's reformation cannot be related to mysticism. Indeed, the two exclude each other: the teaching of Luther is that human existence is to be understood in terms of the opposition between sin, for which we are responsible, and the divine grace in Christ; whereas mysticism sets man's self-assessment within the opposition between creatureliness on the one hand and its dissolution on the other hand into universal, divine being. Furthermore, mysticism does not set forth a higher religious view than that which Luther opened up for us; nor does Luther's theology find its natural fulfillment in the mysticism of Carlstadt and Denck. Rather, Luther's structure for understanding salvation is of incomparably greater significance than the mystical method, which is high-flying but unfruitful. Therefore, since mystical theology is at home in the circle of the anabaptists, this demonstrates that the anabaptist reformation received its *Leitmotiv* from the catholic-ascetical Christianity of the

Middle Ages, to which mysticism, at the very least, is quite congenial.

But now what is the particular area within medieval Christianity from which anabaptism sprang? In order to answer this question,[40] we must first of all keep in mind that this reformation, which is alleged to be more thorough, was without a doubt first set in motion essentially through the example of Luther and Zwingli. With very few exceptions, the adherents of this reformation were first attracted through the reformation of Luther and Zwingli prior to the time they hit upon those differences which distinguished their tendencies from those of these men. The Lutherans could make good use of the saying (1 John 2:19), "they went out from us, but they were not of us." But how is it to be explained that men who were oriented toward legalistic and ceremonial sanctity and toward the restoration of a per-fectionist social system for the church could even temporarily put their trust in Luther and Zwingli? We can imagine that the later anabaptists were won over by the fact that these reformers exalted the authority of the preaching of the divine word, because this had always stood as well in their own circles as the highest standard for the reform of the Christian life. If we may accept this presupposi-tion, then it is understandable how the preaching of Luther and Zwingli won the urban masses for them so quickly, and also how they lost these same masses, as it became evident that their preaching of the gospel did not lend itself to the purposes of a particular ascetical sanctity in whose terms these masses were accustomed to judge the significance of Christianity. Now the "preaching of the gospel" is also the proper rubric for understanding the reformation of St. Francis, although the tendencies of this reformation were totally different from Luther's efforts. Accordingly, the question of the origins of the anabaptists and of the basis for the changing atti-tudes which they assumed both as adherents and foes of Luther and Zwingli, leads one to the assumption that a resuscitation of St. Francis's reformation made its appearance in them and that it was aroused by their efforts to emulate Luther and Zwingli. When I first set forth this research in the *Zeitschrift für Kirchengeschichte* (vol. II, no. 1),[41] I sharpened this hunch into the hypothesis that the anabaptists emerged directly from the circle of the Franciscan tertiaries, in particular, from the Observants.[42] Since I could not support this hypothesis through any documentary evidence at that time, I wanted to give an interim sketch of how the study of the documents which I was suggesting should be carried on. Should it turn out that nothing concrete could be ascertained on this point, I would not persist in this particular hypothesis since that which is pertinent to anabaptism can be clarified even without it.

Therefore the anabaptists, whose piety itself bore the mark of the monastic and the ceremonial-legal, gave notice that they originally understood something different by the term "reform of Christianity" than what they had learned from the reformers; and this was expressed through the opposition to Luther and Zwingli, which followed after their original adherence to those reformers. With few exceptions, the anabaptists were men of literary education who belonged to the lower artisan class. However, for three hundred years this class had been the sphere of activity for the mendicant orders that had settled in the cities, of which the Franciscan orders were the more popular. To be sure, the mendicant orders showed various signs of secularization in the fifteenth century, and in many places in Germany they gave the civil authorities occasion to interpose themselves with reforming action. But this did not diminish their impact upon the masses. They applied themselves to preaching, and therefore also to the task of interpreting holy scripture, and thus they gained the upper hand over the parish clergy, who were uneducated and lived gluttonous lives. While they were adept in bringing these clergy into contempt on the one hand, on the other they impressed the masses, according to Erasmus's testimony, with their appearance of sanctity.[43] If we try to picture to ourselves the kind of Christianity that had spread among the lower classes in the cities at the end of the Middle Ages, we can only think of the pattern of the Franciscans, even if we omit for the moment the existence of the congregations of tertiaries. And if one spoke of the reformation of the church in these circles, it would only be understood in a Franciscan sense, namely, as the direct reform of mores. George Witzel[44] came to Luther with this expectation, *omnia fore purius christiana* ["that all of Christendom would become more pure"], only to find later that he did not know what to make of Luther, since the latter undertook no direct measures to this end. All the prophecies of a general reformation of the church which were mentioned at the end of the fifteenth century and which were later referred to

Luther were, without a doubt, meant in the sense of this expectation. The customs and intentions of the anabaptists coincide so precisely, in part with the rule of the Franciscan tertiaries and in part with the first rule of St. Francis, that one cannot deny that herein there is a genetic relationship. It is thus all the more striking, precisely at this point, that this similarity has not been noted by any church historian up to this time. The "apostolic baptists" to which Bullinger refers, who set out to preach under the conditions which Jesus laid down for his disciples (Mark 6:7–9), correspond literally to the heading in the first rule of St. Francis, article 14, *quomodo fratres debeant ire per mundum* ["In what manner the brothers ought to go forth through the world"].[45] Bullinger does admit, but in an offhand manner, that among the apostolic baptists who had relinquished private property there were "several new Barefoot Ones, that is, men who were like the Franciscan monks," who held that it was a sin to travel at all with money, whereas others were not opposed to the money as their share of the common property. The anabaptists based their rejection of the idea that the state had any competence within the church on the premise that Christians were called to suffering and therefore did not need civil protection against injustices. This fully corresponds with St. Francis's admonition, in the same source, that his brothers in the world should govern themselves directly according to Matt. 5:39–42. Accordingly, one can also understand that the anabaptists exceeded the restrictions concerning taking oaths and bearing arms which were placed upon the tertiaries by making them into absolute commands. They were well enough acquainted with the Sermon on the Mount that they could subject themselves to this gospel of Christ under all circumstances. Modest clothing, gray in color and cut specifically in the style of the monk's cowl, was prescribed for the tertiaries, and participation in worldly pleasures was forbidden. Concerning the "separated spiritual baptists," Bullinger reports that in order not to appear like the world they issued regulations for clothing and they censured all manifestations of joy and cheerfulness "exactly like a new monastic order." In all these points of reference, the identity of the anabaptist reformation with that of St. Francis springs to mind. But there is yet another very instructive point in this connection. When the movement put its very existence within the civil order at stake through its abrupt renunciation of taking oaths and bearing arms, Melchior Hofmann,[46] who was so influential everywhere, acknowledged once again his obligations to the state in respect to the oath and bearing arms. In this instance, he actually returned to the stipulations which corresponded to the rule of the Franciscan tertiaries.

From all these marks of agreement, we are quite well justified in concluding that the anabaptists were the kind of people who were filled with the Franciscan ideal of Christianity, even when they thought that they could discern the instruments of a corresponding reform of the church in Luther and Zwingli. They felt themselves obligated to take up the reformation of St. Francis after they found their expectations disappointed, since Luther and Zwingli had apparently turned away from the work of raising the level of asceticism among Christian people. The fact that the anabaptists almost universally preached the return of Christ and the establishment of his earthly thousand-year kingdom is another point of agreement with my hypothesis. The despair that is expressed in this regard, over improvement within Christianity by means of the ordinary forms of ethical training, exhibits a distinctive strand within that thinking which renounces the world. The dominant motif within that strand of thought is the view that the task of Christianity is not to formulate the moral rules of life in the world and order them supernaturally; rather, the ordinary regulation of moral life in the world and the rule of Christianity are mutually exclusive. This is also the fundamental view of all monastic asceticism, be it inside or outside the walls of the cloister. This urgent expectation of a forcible rupture of all human ordinances through the return of Christ clarifies once again the monastic substratum of the anabaptist movement. But the fact that the heavenly kingdom of Christ is to appear on earth, that is, under the continuation of the conditions of the world, seems to stand in contradiction with the point of view to which I have just referred. This aspect of anabaptist thought springs from the other motif within medieval Christianity, the Augustinian-Gregorian assumption that the kingdom of God must accommodate itself on earth through ethical-political ordinances. There may be a contradiction between the monastic principle of escape from the world and the hierarchical principle of the political dominion of

world and state, but since it embraced both elements of this contradiction, the system of western catholicism was not rendered
impracticable. The anabaptists, however, merely effected a modification of this catholic synthesis, in their monastic tendencies despair-
ing at the secularization of the hierarchical system of the vicar of
Christ on the one hand, while considering the earthly kingdom of
Christ itself as a practicable form of the Christian life, on the other.
If it is thereby established that medieval images are at work precisely
in this expectation, then this particular expression of that expectation points us again to the soil which has been seeded with the well-
known set of dualisms which the spiritual Franciscans posited. I will
grant that things are more ambiguous after the Observants were
legalized through the Council of Constance. As a matter of fact, we
see a thoroughgoing, harmonious reciprocity between the papacy and
the Franciscan orders in the fifteenth century. Indeed, Erasmus
observed that the mendicant orders took pains with their relations to
the pope when it might bring them an advantage, but otherwise the
holy father was no more a reality for them than a dream.[47] One has
to assume that this inner independence from the papacy was stronger
and more widespread among the Franciscans than among the
Dominicans, for the latter were charged with the Inquisition and
therefore were more closely bound to the papacy. This is also verified by the fact that Luther's opposition to the pope received wide
approval among the Franciscans. That this approval was due to the
gospel of God's free grace and justification by faith more than to a
basic censure of the secularization of the church and the papacy is
doubtful. In any case, the artisans who had been affected by the
diverse activities of the Franciscans recalled again, when they heard
Luther, how the church had been secularized under the papacy;
nevertheless, they also experienced the inability to break through
this secularizing of the church in Luther's reformation. With this in
mind, it is quite understandable that in their ascetical impulse for
reform, their recollection of the eternal gospel also became more
vivid—a gospel whose fulfillment seemed to stand all the nearer to
them as the hopeless, antichristian character of the church became
clearer. But now, in the sixteenth century, the slogan of the movement was "the visible return of Christ himself," rather than "the
eternal gospel, based on the Holy Spirit." This expression was also

set forth in the Joachite Books,[48] and without a doubt this vision from the apocalypse was more popular than the vision of the eternal gospel based on the Holy Spirit. With this modification, therefore, the anabaptists' expectation is nothing but the renewal of the storm caused by the spiritual Franciscans.

Finally, the fact that the anabaptists shared the perspective of mystical theology can be fully explained by recalling that the preaching of the members of the mendicant orders transported mystical piety from its usage within the cloisters out into the parishes. When the anabaptists followed leaders such as these, who extolled resignation to God as the highest calling, and when they not only experienced ecstasies and visions but even believed that in them they received impulses from God, they indicated thereby that they had stood for some time under the influence of the mystical traditions which had come down from the mendicant orders to their particular congregations. Therefore, there is nothing that is included in the dominant views of the anabaptists that is not explicable in terms of the impact that the mendicant orders, specifically the Franciscans, made upon the urban lower class masses. For this reason, when viewed from the outside, the reformation which the anabaptists undertook appears more decisive and complete than that of Luther and Zwingli. Luther did not even intend a reform of Christian life, but, rather, a reform of doctrine and worship as well as of the teaching office, and he had only an indirect effect on the practical amendment of life, to the extent that he established the proper foundation for moral training. Zwingli, to be sure, aimed directly at improving mores, in that he brought the restricting legal power of the state into relationship with the power to arouse which preaching on matters of faith and obedience possessed. But who can continue to give a favorable assessment of anabaptism, in light of the fact that it bases amendment of the Christian life on renunciation of the world and contempt for the civil order, in view of the fact that it prescribes communal ownership and the cut of the clothes, forbids cheerfulness and joyfulness, and in view of the fact that it points the way for a fundamental freedom of the flesh through its imagined sinlessness? Such principles as these aim at goals which are diametrically opposed to the intentions of Luther and Zwingli, and the antinomian side of this movement is not an accidental appendage.

If the norm of the Christian life is to be arrived at, in any sense, through ascetical rules in statutory form, then one might let himself be impressed by the facade of the anabaptist impetus for reform. But if the Christian life has to do with the totality of character formation on the basis of the law of freedom, then the error of the monastic and statutory position of the anabaptists is clear beyond any doubt. This is what demonstrates that this reform is not the more thorough and complete, but rather that it is simply another kind of reformation, diametrically opposed to that of Luther and Zwingli. This conclusion is fully clarified by the probability that anabaptism took its origin from the sphere of the Franciscan reform, since the opposition between this reform and Luther's is established. It is true that a number of Luther's and Zwingli's adherents afterwards appeared as anabaptists, but even this phenomenon does not destroy the hypothesis I have set forth. The attachment of those ascetically inclined artisans to Luther and Zwingli was possible because the authority of the divine word and the holy scriptures was just as decisive for the adherents of the Franciscan reformation as it was for Luther and Zwingli. It is true that that authority was understood in totally different ways in the two types of reformation and that opposing styles of life are derived from it. Although the masses of ascetically inclined urban artisans first permitted themselves to be drawn to the side of Luther and Zwingli through the slogan of "reform based on God's word," they turned away from those two reformers just as quickly and struck out on the path of anabaptism when they failed to find their ascetical ideal confirmed in those reformers. Under these circumstances, it is also understandable why the authority of the holy scriptures could not settle the differences between these two movements, since it was a purely formal authority which was utilized differently by each side. As a consequence, the decision against the anabaptists was actually occasioned by the force of the civil authorities, rather than by the force of a theological norm.

IV. CATHOLICISM AND PROTESTANTISM

The fact that the authority of holy scripture is invoked both by our reformers and by the anabaptists at the same time, but with opposing meanings, indicates that we can neither explain nor adequately describe the distinctiveness of our reformation through

the commonly used formula of the "two principles of the reformation."[49] Actually, the so-called formal principle, which asserts the
exclusive authority of holy scripture for faith, life, and theological
knowledge, was already acknowledged by the Franciscan monastic
theologian, Duns Scotus.[50] The fact that the theology of the
Franciscans nevertheless incorporated a great deal of the ecclesiastical tradition did not diminish the significance of the scripture
principle for them; neither did the fact that protestant theology
transmitted a mass of ecclesiastical traditions from the very beginning compromise the significance of holy scripture for protestants
nor their fundamental esteem for it. Such a position makes Duns a
representative of the reformation tendencies of the founder of his
order rather than an isolated "forerunner" of Luther. Neither did
this same scripture principle take on specific meaning for Luther and
his comrades until they found themselves in opposition to the
Dominicans and Thomists and to that action at Trent[51] which made
the equation of tradition with scripture the fundamental principle
of the catholic church. It would be much sounder to claim that the
original meaning of the reformation of the sixteenth century is based
on the so-called material principle, the doctrine of justification
through faith. Even though this concept was already expressed
before Luther—for example, by St. Bernard[52]—it was only in an
accidental manner, with no real tie to the opposition against the
catholic system which gave Luther's doctrine its significance. But a
principle of doctrine cannot be established on the basis of Luther's
assertion of justification by faith. On the contrary, it is only a
characteristic conclusion to be drawn from the principle of divine
grace, which, *when it is related to* other knowledge, serves for
ordering and evaluating the Christian life in a relevant way. The
formula of the two principles of the reformation, and the manner in
which it is customarily employed to interpret the reformation, expresses an inadequate assessment of this epoch-making phenomenon.
Such an assessment would only lead one to believe that the reformation of Luther and the others called a new form of theological school
into being, and not that it had set in motion a new phase of the Christian style of life [*Lebensführung*]. In addition to this shortcoming,
the formula of the two principles was put together in a very fortuitous
manner, with no comprehensive reflection upon the facts.[53] Schleier-

macher has explained how the formula may be rightly interpreted and what its usefulness is, namely, that within the diversity of protestant theologians, the acknowledgment of these two principles is the least that must be attributed to a theologian if he is to qualify as a protestant [*evangelischer*] theologian.[54]

In light of the common characteristics of western Christianity which were presupposed at the time, the distinctiveness of ecclesiastical protestantism—that is, that which is common to the reforms which Luther, Zwingli, and Calvin carried out—over against Latin catholicism, can be set forth under as few as three headings. These are: the substance of the image which serves as the norm for the Christian life [*Lebensideal*], the estimate of what is most important in the Christian community, and, finally, the judgment of the relation of the state to the Christian religious and moral community.

If the reformation of the sixteenth century had exhibited no ideal for the Christian life [*Ideal des christlichen Lebens*], we would be hard put indeed to demonstrate with certainty that it possesses epoch-making significance and lasting validity alongside the catholic form and phase of Christianity. And, in the light of the three-hundred-year history of the progressive splintering of its community, our faith that God will sustain protestantism until the end would be shattered. Catholic Christianity finds this governing image for its style of life [*Lebensideal*] in monasticism, in the bond created by the obligations of poverty, chastity, and obedience (to the superior in the order). These are understood as touching upon the universal law of God. In these particular virtues, it is said that one attains the supernatural destiny which Christianity holds out for man, a destiny which was not provided for in man's original creation. Since man enters into the life of the angels in this way, the monastic condition, thus conceived, is really Christian perfection. That protestants are filled with a sense of the quantitative imperfection of all their accomplishments is by no means a conclusive antithesis to this catholic position. This qualification does not deny the catholic position in any fundamental way; rather, it only clouds the issue. The works-righteousness or self-righteousness which popular opinion teaches us to ascribe to the catholics is no more frequent among them than it is among orthodox and pious Lutherans. If protestantism is to prevail against the practical weight which catholicism carries in its cultivation of monasticism and in the spreading of monastic piety, even among the laity, then it must be able to produce a standard of qualitative perfection. And it has been able to do just this.[55] Just as a chief characteristic of the condition of sinfulness is the lack of fear and trust in God, so also—according to the Augsburg Confession[56]—perfection consists of fear and trust in God through all the conditions of life; this is more fully expressed as fear, trust in God's merciful providence, prayer, and the conscientious carrying out of one's vocation.[57] Such a description of perfection is expressly intended as the antithesis to the catholic view of monasticism. It is true that this idea is not prevalent in Luther's private writings,[58] and Melanchthon gives it no place in his doctrinal writings. Thus, it is all the more significant that the Apology of the Augsburg Confession[59] not only frequently echoes this idea, but even gives it classical expression at one place.[60] There the meaning of the assertion of justification by faith is demonstrated—namely, that such justification clarifies how the sinner comes to possess trust in God's providence in all the situations of life in which he finds himself and whence he actually derives that trust.[61] This is the distinctive test of reconciliation with God, that one is also reconciled with the course of the world which God directs, no matter how hard it may strike him. In contrast, the doctrine of justification by faith has no *direct* intention of explaining the good works of the believer or engendering them. If that were the intention, we would have to prefer the catholic doctrine of justification. And it is in this context that the practical significance of the Lutheran doctrine comes to light, the practical significance which gives it its place as the *primus et principalis articulus* [first and principle article]. That is to say, the importance of this doctrine becomes clear only as Christians have to strive after their perfection precisely in the midst of their regular intercourse with the world and in their vocations within the domain of the secular society. How can their worldly anxieties and temptations to cowardice give the monastics cause for such faith in God's help, defense, and redemption from tribulations—these monastics who are free from these weaknesses, according to the testimony of St. Bernard?[62] Therefore, in our reformation's governing image of life-style, faith in God's providence stands next to prayer and regard for secular vocation as the place where love for man is practiced in mutual reciprocity. This interpretation of the secular vocation is similarly a specific principle of protestantism; it is the practical expression of the fact that protestantism is conceived as filling and penetrating the world, rather than renouncing it. This significance and effect are inherent in the principle, even though they are not systematically grounded and derived from it by the reformers.[63]

But, I can hear someone say, the concept of perfection is a subordinate matter for the reformers, since it only occurs in their polemic against the catholic concept of perfection.[64] If I were to understand this remark as an assertion that the concept of Christian perfection is a matter of indifference for the total reformation view of life as such, then I would have to concede that it is supported by the fact that the concept is seldom enough discussed. Apart from this, however, it seems to me that even if this concept of perfection does flow from the pens of the reformers only when they polemicize against the catholic regard for monasticism, that in itself is an indication that it holds a primary significance for them. Or am I mistaken in asserting that the distinctiveness of the reformation of the sixteenth century is to be understood at one single point, over and above its specific agreement or disagreement with catholicism? And is it not true that monasticism stands as the authentic form of Christianity in catholicism? A person who has spent his life in the nineteenth century, untouched by catholic patterns of life, might form the opinion that a concept which is antithetical to monasticism would be in itself of subordinate significance for the reformers. But this would not be true for the sixteenth century, despite appearances to the contrary. And even though the Augsburg Confession seldom speaks of the term "perfection," nevertheless the substance and significance of the concept is attested by the interpretation of Adam's perfection before the fall, which Luther and Calvin both set forth, in agreement with each other,[65] inasmuch as the redemption spoken of in Christianity is supposed to reinstate the perfection which Adam possessed in relation to God. But the description of Adam lacked one thing which was necessary for the reformers' own situation, namely, the imperative which confronts the Christian to prove his Christianness within his secular vocation through good or publicly useful action; however, they emphasized this one mark of perfection so consistently that it tended to make up for all the other marks.

This principle fundamentally transformed the entire society and gave the catholic opponents, for example, Georg Witzel,[66] occasion to assert that the reformation led to epicureanism and paganism. If the reformers never doubted the importance of worldliness, but rather always lifted it up, regardless of the fact that there was also a pejorative form of worldliness (which was also relevant to the practice of their principle), should we then assume that they wanted to be known as the patrons of a distinctive imperfection in the moral life? Should we not, rather, understand them in this respect as representatives and guardians of a distinctive perfection of Christian life? Let me posit the converse: The reformers took no constructive interest in the matter and spoke only from a polemical perspective when they reflected upon the ideals of Christian perfection that were current in their own time; therefore, they did not possess any internal impulse to set forth an image which in its wholeness would govern the Christian style of life [Lebensideal]; all they could do, or wished to do, therefore, was to give fragmentary rules for Christian living. Here I would admit that protestantism stood at an immense disadvantage vis-à-vis catholicism, and I recognize that I must take pains to justify my concurrence with the former. Perhaps I should assume that the weakness I have described is counterbalanced by the amplification which pietism sought to make effective within a Lutheranism that was in itself imperfect; then, however, the question would arise whether the last state were not worse than the first. To put the matter briefly, if the independent significance of the reformation concept of Christian perfection is denied, then I cannot help but regard that the soul-saving significance of pietism really begs the question. Indeed, the image of life-style [Lebensideal] or evangelical perfection which the reformers asserted describes the distinctiveness of their undertaking, particularly in that the discriminations between perfect and imperfect Christians, monastics and laity, or pietists and nonpietists, are made with a norm which is the same for all. To a certain extent, St. Francis pursued the same intention; but through just the opposite means, so as to extend monastic piety as far as possible throughout the laity. The basis for this effort in the Middle Ages was found in a reformation patterned after the example of the church in Jerusalem. This authority was also brought up against the reformers in Wittenberg by Georg Witzel, in criticism of their undertaking as it pertained to the ethical imperative.[67] But Melanchthon, with his sure sensitivity, recognized the monastic style of this example. If it should be confirmed that pietism is similarly sustained by the authority of the example of the primitive church, then Melanchthon's critical judgment against Witzel is especially noteworthy, since it presupposes the familiar idea of Christian perfection.

The second major point of comparison between catholicism and protestantism is the determination of the relation between the religious and legal communities that are included under the rubric of the church. The catholic principle at this point reads as follows: that these two functions coincide throughout, that there is no religious function of a Christian type which does not fall within the framework of the legal structure of the western church, and that this legal structure serves as the direct warrant for the correct exercise, maintenance, and propagation of all religious functions within the community. Accordingly, either of these functions could be legitimated as the end and the other would stand as the means, in reciprocal fashion. In protestantism, on the contrary, the common legal structure of the church stands unconditionally only as the means for the corporate religious activity, or, in other words, the latter is always held to transcend the framework of the legal structure, and it would never be said that it coincides with the former.

Third, catholicism understands the state either as a form of the sinful world or as God's means for ordering the world, with the stipulation that it is of less value than the ecclesiastical legal structure and must unconditionally accommodate itself to the claims of that structure. In the protestant interpretation, the state is a good thing, as the legal structuring of human activity which is as such legitimated by God; to be sure, of less value than the religious community within Christianity, but in itself nevertheless a support of that community, since the care of the law is the corresponding means for the freedom of religious and ethical activity.

If one asks, on the basis of the aforementioned marks of protestantism, how this relates itself to the concept of reformation spoken of in the twelfth chapter of Romans, it certainly appears as if protestantism is far removed from this standard. "Do not model yourselves on the behavior of the world around you!" [Rom. 12:2].

Is esteem for one's vocation in society together with rejection of
monasticism not in direct contradiction to this admonition? Is
esteem for the state as a special support of the combined religious
and ethical activity within Christianity not a significant concession
to the world, especially when one recalls that from this relationship
the transfer of the church's legal structure to the state first came
about? To the contrary, I would observe that with respect to one's
vocation in society the important thing is that the vocation be carried
out in a spiritual rather than in a worldly fashion; and with respect
to the state's legal supervision of the legal functions of the church,
the important thing is that the religious activities of the community
—which in fact make it the church—be bothered as little as possible
by legal, that is, worldly, concerns. The thrust in both cases is therefore governed throughout by the other clause, "but let your behavior
change, modelled by your new mind" [Rom. 12:2]. But at the same
time, it is precisely the fundamental differentiation between the legal
and religious functions within the church and the fundamental regard
for the disparity in their respective worth that stands in direct
harmony with the first admonition. The catholic view of the church,
however, runs directly counter to it. Law is primarily the concrete,
secular ordering of man's common life; all ecclesiastical law is therefore also secular. The catholic view concerning the law of the catholic
church, that this law is directly and unconditionally divine and
supramundane, involves a specific conforming of Christianity to the
world. Accordingly, protestantism has not renounced the principle
of reformation, but is sustained, contrariwise, by the intention to
conform to it to a greater extent than is the case in catholic Christianity. Which of these two forms of Christianity nevertheless gives
the greater impetus for secularization is a question that ought not be
discussed here.

Thus far in my comparison between the two forms of western
Christianity, the catholic concept of Christian perfection has been
determined by the traditional formulas of monasticism. Officially,
catholic perfection is exhaustively described by the three monastic
virtues; nevertheless, the full scope of this perfection is actually
arrived at only through the contemplative form of piety to which the
monks are held. We cannot afford to overlook this phenomenon at
this point, because it is only through it that the opposition between

the protestant and catholic concepts of perfection is fully understandable. For faithfulness to one's secular vocation is opposed to the three monastic virtues. Furthermore, what is the importance of the fact that faith in God's providence and the prayer which that faith supports are counted as part of protestant perfection? These functions find their corresponding opposite in the contemplation which is imposed upon the monastics and which, on the surface, seems to aspire to much higher things. It must be noted, however, that in the second half of the Middle Ages, this devotion was, in part, expressly counted as a mark of the monastic and, in part, had also extended itself among the masses, as was the case with the tertiary orders and related forms, like the Friends of God,[68] and the Brothers and Sisters of the Common Life.[69] However, the prototypical statement of this devotion, and the one that was normative throughout the entire Middle Ages, was set forth by St. Bernard in his eighty-six sermons on the Song of Songs.[70] Without a knowledge of this typical outline of devotion, one can have no full understanding of catholicism. Bernard made such a highly influential application of the allegorical exegesis and ecclesiastical use of the Song of Songs that he explained the bride of Christ no longer as the church, but rather as the individual believing soul. To be sure, the familiar interpretations of the church fathers also occur in his work, and once (56, 1) he also gives expression to Athanasius's exposition that the visit of the bridegroom to the bride refers to the incarnation of the divine word. In advance then, one can imagine that, when compared to these expositions, Bernard's interpretation was especially important for determining the direction piety took. I will note here that in his lectures Luther expressly rejected Bernard's explanation, since he interpreted Song of Songs as applying to Solomon's political rule.

The background for the range of Bernard's ideas, which we want to consider at this point, was a most comprehensive acknowledgment of divine grace. It is well known that this stands generally in his sermons as the highest and dominant theme; consequently, his concern for human freedom, which is shown in his theoretical theology, drops totally out of sight. From this perspective, Bernard serves to establish for us the fact that a thrust identical to that of our reformers had its roots in medieval Christianity. Nevertheless, it is pertinent to try to find the boundaries of this consensus in the

practical consequences of St. Bernard's reform movement. To do
this, it is appropriate to undertake a precise analysis of the piety
which is inherent in the sermons on the Song of Songs. Thus, for
St. Bernard, it was firmly established that believers had to lead their
lives in trust in the fullness of God's mercy, and not trust in their
own merit or in the feeling of their own powers (14, 4; 21, 11);
and on occasion he was able to give as precise an expression of
justification by faith as a protestant could desire (22, 7, 8, 11).
In another connection, to be sure, the compassion of God through
the forgiveness of sins is acknowledged as the effective ground of
merits (61, 5; 68, 2). One ought not view this as though catholic
piety were disposed predominantly or overwhelmingly toward works-
righteousness. This tradition of interpreting catholicism among
protestants is shaped by judgments that grew out of Luther's special
and very one-sided experiences, and it is in need of considerable
correction. Still, the fact that Bernard does not give up on merit
completely, in spite of his energetic stress on God's grace, but rather
maintains it intact, causes one to doubt from the outset that the basic
presupposition in his work which is common to us both will lead
to wide-ranging consequences which we can both accept. In this
connection we must above all pay attention to the fact that Bernard's
sermons are directed only to monastics. Their situation, however, is
such that they enjoy in the cloister "peace from the cares of the
world and the vicissitudes and afflictions of life, in that they are
directed to lead a life that is exceptional in its holiness and virtue"
(46, 2). Consideration of the first verse of the Song of Songs, "O
that he would kiss me with the kisses of his mouth," leads to the
conclusion that we "extend ourselves in trust (*fiducia*) to the same
degree that we grow in grace" (3, 4). But in this context this verse
finds an application totally different from what it would have to find
to retain a protestant sense. For the sphere to which the protestant
Christian is directed for testing his trust in God is simply nonexistent
for the listeners of St. Bernard who are protected from the manifold
cares of life in the world (see pp. 86–87 above). Rather, the trust
in God which he means points to the sphere of individual contemplation and to the benefits which are sought therein; and at the same
time this trust to which he refers is motivated by something other
than the simple acknowledgment of reconciliation with God through

Christ. In the third sermon, Bernard proclaims that one does not get to kiss the bridegroom's mouth before he has succeeded in kissing his hands and feet. The first kiss is the act of penance for sin; it directs itself toward the feet of the stern Lord, which symbolize his compassion and his righteousness; in the reciprocal relationship of these factors, however, the Christian does not long continue in either despair or in false security (6, 6–8; 11, 2). Since the penance would nevertheless be pointless if its results were not firmly established through abstaining from sin and through works of piety, the second kiss signifies the whole spectrum of active sanctification, in which one is supported by the hand of the Lord. Thus growth in grace is signified, and it consists in extending oneself in trust in God. Only he who has experienced divine grace in the first two kisses, that is, in the consummated penance and in the active sanctification which consummates itself, is permitted to claim with more ardent love and increased trust the wonderfully sweet and gracious kiss from the mouth of the bridegroom, the kiss in which he becomes *one spirit with the Lord Jesus*. Therefore, one experiences this kiss only on a level of perfection which seldom exists (4, 1). "My beloved is mine and I am his" (Song 2:16)—no one dare strive for this height of reciprocal love, to which the soul is entitled through wondrous grace, who has not merited the experience through special purity of disposition and holiness of body (67, 8). Or whoever longs for peace in contemplation has to take the lead through exercise of the virtues of that sacred peace, since the enjoyment of contemplation is due only to him who is obedient to the commandments (46, 5). One has only to read how Bernard at one point counts up his good works and afterwards proceeds to say that all of these come from habit, not from inner sweetness; therefore, he who has only produced what he owes is termed a useless servant in the gospel. "Perhaps I do fulfill the commandments in one way or another; but in so doing my soul is like land without water; therefore, let him kiss me with the kisses of his mouth, so that thereby my sacrifices might be rich" (9, 2).

The protestant Christian, who also considers himself a useless servant since he is only doing his duty, at the same time entrusts his salvation to the reconciliation with God which he has experienced in Christ. St. Bernard's stance is somewhat different however, even though he, too, experiences no salvation in his fulfilling of the

commandments. For him, this experience is a trial both of God's
grace and his own merit—it is a trial through which he gives himself
to be aroused to that trust in God or thirsting for God which will
bring him satisfaction in his bridal love for the Lord Jesus. In the
interpretation of this image, the marks of the *humiliated* and suffering Son of God emerge at times very significantly, whereas the marks
of his divinity and dominion are, according to the circumstances,
intentionally repressed through the description of the love which is
directed toward him. On the other hand, the satisfaction which is
sought in the bridegroom is affected by the fact that he is also the
word of God and that he stands in place of God. Accordingly, in
the portrayal of the contemplative processes, God can be interpolated
for Christ without any difficulty. It is all the more striking then, that
the description of love which Bernard intends here expressly pushes
aside the barrier between God (Christ) and the person of the
believer which is set by God's sublime nature.

The soul loves ardently, it is so intoxicated with its own love that it
does not heed the majesty. Oh what power of love, what trust in the
spirit of freedom! Perfect love casts out fear (also awe?) (7, 2). I am
driven by ardent desire, not by reason; raise no complaint against the
presumption toward which passion drives. Caution warns us, certainly,
but love outweighs it. I know very well that the king's honor desires
judgment, but love, rushing precipitately, disregards judgment; love will
neither be moderated by counsel nor bridled by modesty, nor governed
by reason (9, 2). The beloved is present, the master is away, the king
disappears, propriety has left, and awe is laid aside. Between God's
word and the soul a very private dialogue is carried on, as between two
neighbors. Mutual love and tenderness flow into each from the one
source of love. Accordingly, words sweeter than honey soar from both
sides, and there hover about the glances that are filled completely with
ecstasy. Finally, he calls her 'beloved' and names her 'the beautiful
one'; he repeats himself, and he receives the same endearments in turn
from her. Truly, this is sublime vision, in which the soul is lifted to the
level of trust and then again to the level of acceptance where it comes
to know Jesus, the Lord of all things, no longer as Lord, but rather
only as beloved (45, 1, 6). The soul that loves is driven by desires,
drawn on by yearning, it conceals its merits; the soul closes its eyes to
majesty, opens wide its longing in the sense that it directs it toward
salvation and bestirs itself with full confidence toward that salvation.
Finally, without trembling and without reserve (*inverecunda*) it calls

God's word back to itself and confidently begins the game (*deliciae*) again, in which, with her accustomed freedom, she calls him not Lord, but Beloved (74, 4; see also the even stronger expressions in 79, 1).

Bernard even concedes that this love for the God-man is in a certain sense sensuous.

> Notice that the heart's love is to a certain extent fleshly (*carnalis*), because it is directed more to the flesh of Christ and because what Christ does and commands in the flesh grasps the human heart. And when that heart is filled with this love, it is easily incited to that sort of talk.

But the love which is supposedly passionate in this connection is said, at the same time, to be prudent and powerful—prudent in that the sensuous movement of that love itself renders the attractions of the flesh ineffective; powerful in that it hews to the line of the church's rule of faith (20, 4–9). Besides this, however, we notice that the sensuously formed excitements which the text of the Song of Songs sets before us are transformed allegorically into spiritual functions. The soul, which is called happy in Song 2:6 because it lies on Christ's breast and in his arms, is reminded that it has to prove itself through fear and hope (51, 5). Generally, however, the goal of contemplative ecstasy is that one should attain the purity of the angels, that in the knowledge of God one would not remain entangled in sensuous images, but rather would transcend the illusions of corporeal likenesses. One cannot hope for the peace that he strives for until this prior goal has been achieved (52, 4, 5).

We must ascertain precisely the characteristics of this love for Christ which I have described, this love which is attributed to the perfect believers; for from the very beginning it is alien to protestant piety. Above all, however, we must observe that this sketch of passionate love for Christ contradicts the common protestant assumption that the catholic approach is to posit the God-man only as a strict judge set at the greatest possible distance from the believer. Just as, in accord with Luther's experience, we frequently judge that catholic Christianity consists in striving after works-righteousness in the timid fear that accompanies servile work, so too, the assumption has taken root among us that, for all practical purposes, Christ stands for catholics only as a strict, inaccessible judge, whose grace is surreptitiously obtained through the intercession of the saints. We have every reason for wanting to set this opinion straight. It is true that in catholic piety Christ holds this position I have just described in penance (see above, p. 93), that is, at the beginning of the religious life, but not in an exclusive sense. St. Bernard's thinking is not just different in form from the stereotyped picture of Christ as stern judge—it contradicts that picture. As I have suggested, the reason why most comparative studies of Lutheranism and Roman Catholicism do not introduce this dimension into their discussions goes back to the accidental fact that Luther had no experience of it in his monastic life. But in reality, Bernard's method, which leads the believer through the context of divine grace to passionate love for Christ, serves us as a direct introduction to the flowering of monastic piety. Luther, on the contrary, became acquainted as a monk only with the withered shell of monastic devotion which was already emptied of its fruit. According to the introduction which St. Bernard provides for the monk who is firm in his sanctification, love for Christ should disregard the divine sublimity; the soul on whom God has bestowed grace should experience and enjoy the benefits through which the God-man satisfies his yearning as if he and Christ were on a level of equality. The soul may be just as quick to rejoice in the fact that it has been lifted above its original position as it is to take God's humbling of himself as the occasion for its sensuous passion to be aroused toward him. Since the opposition of these two points of view has never been clearly delineated, the latter has prevailed to the extent that this passion for Christ has served to neutralize the drive for this world's goods and the pleasures that go with them. Only under this supposition does the other view come into force, namely, the view that the sensuous intuition of the God who humbles himself turns into the formless spiritual immersion in God which characterizes the ecstatic goal of blessedness in which the benefits of eternal life are even now experienced in advance. The balancing of these opposing methods of the spiritual life proceeds according to the laws of feeling itself [Gefühl]—the one method pulling Christ down in the interests of drawing close to him in a passionate and sensuous manner, at the cost of his sublime nature; whereas the other method seeks a union with him in one spirit through an elimination of sensuous elements and by participating in his sublimity. Since the sensuously colored passion for the God-man also includes in itself a spiritual intention, the apparently purely spiritual elevation of feeling to the state of ecstasy can be understood as resting on the expectation that the tension of the overexcited sensuous drives will be lessened. This is why I say that the balancing of these contrasting methods proceeds according to the laws of feeling.

Although such a devotional method rests upon clear images of Christ, since, indeed, it points us to excitations of feeling which have to be linked to Christ, those images are nevertheless by no means uniform. For Bernard, the image of God who humbles himself is twofold in nature; in the first place, it is framed with no reference to his sublimeness, only afterwards to become entirely commensurate with that sublime nature which guarantees that the soul is elevated over its own creaturely limitations. In contrast, the protestant Christian is under the imperative to find personal religious meaning in the fact that the God-man who humiliates himself is identical with the sublime divinity, and also in the converse. For this reason, we must be careful not to overestimate Bernard's apparent agreement with the protestant point of view in the following explanations. Bernard recognizes the love of the bridegroom in his works of redemption and says that every redeemed man must to some degree hold them vividly in mind. In connection with this theme he raises two points, namely, the form and the consequence. The form is the humiliation of God, the consequence, our being filled with God (11, 3). To be sure, it is particularly important for Bernard that these conditions be effective as the basis of the distinctive devotion which his sermons aim at eliciting. The work of redemption, therefore, should not be understood here as if it could explain for every believer how he has been restored in the image of God and to dominion over the world (21, 6, 7), rather, it is to be understood as that which "allures in a coaxing manner, justifiably compels, closely binds, and sharply arouses" love, the passionate excitement for Christ. In addition, however, it is emphasized that one must make real for himself individually the whole spectrum of efforts through which the God who humbles himself has authenticated his love. For

the same God who without effort created the world through his
simple command endured in his earthly preaching those who would
oppose him; in his actions, the hostile onlookers; in his torments, the
scoffers; and in his death, those who would malign him. See how he
loved! Learn, therefore, from Christ how you should love him (20,
2, 4).

The basis for the protestant faith which subordinates itself to Christ
is simply the regard which the believer has for the love of God
which is efficacious unto redemption in the obedience of Christ,
whereas the passionate love of equal for equal which Bernard represents, demands that the total achievement of Christ's love be divided
up into its individual strands. Consequently, Bernard explains in
connection with Song 1:13 ("My beloved is to be a bag of myrrh,
that lies between my breasts"):

> Since the beginning of my conversion (i.e., my entry into monasticism)
> I have undertaken to bind this bag to myself and to lay it on my
> breast—a bag which is made up of all the anguish and bitterness of
> my Lord, especially that which has to do with the distress of the child-
> like life, that is, the toil of preaching, the weariness in travel, vigils in
> prayer, the temptations in fasting, weeping in sympathy, and finally
> dangers from false brothers, the invectives, blows, mockery, abuse,
> nailing, and the like. Among the many types of this scented myrrh, I
> have not omitted that which he drank on the cross and with which he
> was anointed at his burial. I wish to express my remembrance of the
> fullness of the sweetness of these things as long as I live; in eternity
> I wish to remember these mercies in which I have found life (43, 3).[71]

He applies this interest differently in the exposition of Song 2:14
("O my dove, in the clefts of the rock, in the shelter of the cliff").
Here Bernard presents an explanation which he borrows from
another, but which he represents with his own conviction, namely
that

> the clefts of the rock refer to Christ's wounds, for the rock is Christ.
> The sparrow makes its house in these clefts and the turtledove its nest;
> in them the dove finds safety from the hawk. And truly, where may
> the weak find safety and peace except in the wounds of the savior?
> Men pierced his hands and feet and stabbed his side with the lance,
> and through these openings, it is permitted to me to drink honey out
> of the rock and oil out of the hard stone; that means that I may taste

and see that the Lord is sweet. The secret of the heart is revealed through the rents in the body, the secret of piety and the depths of God's compassion. Are these depths not laid open through the wounds? Where would it be clearer than in your wounds, Lord, that you are sweet and mild and richly compassionate? (61, 3, 4).

We can see that the most important elements are preserved also in these words, and in accordance with the principle that it is only by contemplating the humiliated God that one attains the vision of his majesty. "For the direct exploration of his majesty is full of terror, whereas the exploration of his merciful will is as comforting as it is devout" (62, 5). In spite of this, St. Bernard starts down a very steep path when he emphasizes the reciprocal relationship between the suffering form of Christ, which he has to explicate in its individual aspects, on the one hand, and the passionate love, on the other hand, which goes beyond Christ's majesty and embraces him as an equal, as a neighbor, and as a friend.

It is clear that Bernard wishes to lay hold of the mercy of God in the suffering form of Christ or, in other words, he wishes to contemplate the suffering God in individual manifestations of Christ's passion, a passion that testifies to his concern for men. From such a perspective, he is concerned throughout with the divine significance of Christ. He expresses this when he says that in his feeling for individual acts of suffering he finds the "fullness of sweetness" and that in the wounds of Jesus he receives the impression that the Lord "is sweet and mild and full of compassion." This estimate of Christ's suffering is to be made in the context of the believer's relations of equality with the bridegroom. Since, in Jesus' undeserved and voluntary suffering, one gets to know the fullness of his love for the individual who practices contemplation, one should permit himself to be moved to a correspondingly high level of reciprocal love and sacrifice for Jesus. This particular thrust of the total view which Bernard sets forth comes from the statement that the bitter experiences of Jesus should be appropriated in a sweet taste of his love, and they should bear the shape of the same. It is clear from this that Bernard does not wish to conclude that one should lose himself in the inexhaustible pity and dejection which arise from comparing his own guilt with the guiltlessness of Jesus. He really intends a religious impression of an entirely different sort. But the question arises, nevertheless, whether the method which he prescribes really does necessarily lead the believer through the bitterness of suffering with Christ to obtain a taste of sweetness from his suffering, and further, whether in striving for this impression one really does justice to the full significance of redemption. As a theologian, Bernard knows very well that the power of faith to overcome the world arises from one's inner realization of the majesty, divinity, and dominion of Christ over the world (21, 6, 7). Moreover, at one point, Bernard is able to articulate in exemplary fashion the significance of Christ's person as the God who humbles himself.[72] Still the taste of sweetness to which he was able to penetrate in contemplation upon Jesus' love in the bitterness of his sufferings—this taste of sweetness does not necessarily follow from nor is it the clear test of the divinity of Christ's love. When we observe the phenomena of medieval piety, which nourished itself directly on the contemplation of Christ's suffering, we see that endless numbers of people never went beyond the point of aimless pity and dejection. In the devotion of the monks and the nuns, we get a much deeper impression that this devotional method led to gloomy abasement than we do that it served to elevate and liberate.

Furthermore, the fact that Bernard could transform the impression of bitterness into sweetness through contemplating that the meaning of Christ's suffering was really that of love, or that he could harmonize the desirable and the repugnant or joy and pain—this is by no means a trustworthy proof that he impressed both the divine sublimeness of Christ and the experience of his human humiliation upon his memory at the same time. To be sure, there is a certain analogy between Bernard's remembered impressions, which constitute a problem of cognition, and the experiences of Christ, which are questions of a complex sense-impression. In the divinity of the man Jesus, seemingly contradictory opposites do have to be thought together. And when the manifestations of Christ's suffering are tasted at the same time as bitter and sweet, we are presented with a paradox. In itself, this paradox contains no contradiction; for the bitterness follows from the impression of suffering, whereas the sweet taste adheres to the thrust of the love which permits Christ to suffer voluntarily. Outside of this, however, this love which is perceived as sweet points to no fundamental mark of divinity which would necessarily exceed the measure of human being. On the contrary, it is simply the ideal man, who lives for me, who lets me have his perfection [*Schönheit*], whose suffering causes the experience of bitterness to find an echo in the pleasure of sweetness; and Bernard is able to experience the feeling of sweetness only because he relates to the Lord Jesus on the basis of equality in this situation. The amalgam of bitterness and sweetness that we have to interpret before we can understand and assess Bernard's position possesses a character customarily associated with spiritual epicureanism, and therein it reveals rather a close relation to certain sensuous excitations of feeling than an analogy to the problem of how one comes to know the phenomenon of God-manhood. Even if it were true that this cognition impresses itself upon a person through the intuition of the suffering of Christ and from that gives the impression of redemption, still it is not advisable to venture into the specificities which Bernard recounts and to arouse the pain and ecstasy of sympathy from them; rather, one must assure himself of the total significance of redemption in the fact of the power of Christ's obedience to overcome the world. For the perception of Christ's divinity lies in the fact that his love wins victory over the world in his suffering; and we test this perception in feeling when we experience the elevating impulse for our own dominion over suffering and the world on the basis of reconciliation with God through Christ. This is the protestant understanding of the matter, which does do justice to the divinity of Christ. On the contrary, Bernard's contemplation can elicit a passionate love for neighbor and a willingness to serve which also transforms the most bitter into sweetness; but that is merely the cult of the ideal man which modern sentimentality has learned to apply to others besides the Lord Jesus. Thus at this point, we come to a perfectly clear opposition between protestant and catholic piety which we dare not overlook.

Since Bernard attended to the reciprocal relations between the soul and its bridegroom as if they were real, the question arises as to how this reality is to be put to the test. How can we disregard the objection that what we are dealing with here is the activity of the imagination? To this we hear the answer:

When I feel that the sensitivity for understanding holy scripture is being opened up for me, or a wise saying wells up, as it were, from my inmost depths, or mysteries are unveiled by a higher light, or, as it were, the inner depths of heaven are spread out before me and from above a rich fullness of contemplation in the spirit is poured out, then I do not doubt that the bridegroom is present (69, 6). . . . The soul should not consider itself to be perfectly united with God until it has the strong *feeling* that God abides in it and it abides in God. I am one spirit with God when I am once convinced that I cling to God as those who are in love (71, 6). . . . Sometimes when the word has come to me, I have not been able to feel just when it happened. I have *felt* its presence and afterwards remembered it; sometimes I could sense its coming in advance, but I could not directly sense its coming again or its leaving. By what means would I have recognized its coming? It is lively and powerful; as soon as it enters into me, it awakens my sleeping soul, sets it in motion, it soothes and wounds my hard heart. I have recognized the presence of the bridegroom only by the movement of my heart, and I have experienced his power when my sins ran away and the desires of the flesh were restricted (74, 5, 6).

Although sense experience generally does not distinguish between the feeling subject and the object which arouses that experience, the reason which always coexists with sense experience does posit this distinction. As a consequence, it is possible to become one spirit with God through the intentional elevation of religious desire (which is also supported by sufficient corporeal means) and still make this normal rational distinction between oneself and God. For this reason, Bernard holds the expectation that the goal of the mutual relationship of love is the vision of God, though not without some limitations. For he reserves the vision of God as he really is to life in the beyond, and he grants only that God appears in the present to those whom he will, as he will (31, 2). Occasionally he even circumscribes this vision of God according to the experience of Moses, so he says that man cannot see God's face, but rather only his back (61, 6). Nevertheless, the most important assertion in this regard is that

> this experience of the soul and its commingling with God's word which lies beyond any bodily feeling and beyond the power of the imagination, is produced only through God's condescension, when the ardor of holy desire and the incessant groanings of prayer draw the bridegroom close (31, 4–6).

One could be tempted to assess this assertion as magic, except that the mystical union is ascribed throughout to the will of God or of the bridegroom and is seen as conforming to an expanding experience. For

> when a person seeks the bridegroom through vigils and *entreaties*, through many exertions and a rain of tears, and when the bridegroom does make himself present, then he slips away suddenly just when one thinks that he holds him fast, and when he again confronts the weeping soul that pursues him, he does, to be sure, permit himself to be grasped, but not to be held fast, since suddenly, as it were, he vanishes away once again (32, 2). . . . When the soul feels grace, it recognizes the presence of the word, when not, it protests his absence and strives after his presence. Thus, the word is called back through the yearning of the soul which has once had his sweet presence bestowed upon it. But the word comes and goes according to his own will, as when he pays a visit at twilight and shows himself unexpectedly (74, 2, 3).

Therefore, it is always only in a momentary way that it is possible to substantiate the presence of the bridegroom through the passionate excitations of feeling. The price of these pleasures, however, is the barrenness and slackness into which the soul falls, ever deeper and for even longer periods of time, in proportion to the unnatural character of these exertions which precede the pleasure (9, 3; 14, 6; 32, 4; 74, 7). And it is hardly appropriate to give the admonition that the enjoyment of grace is not to be counted as a securely held possession, inviolate through inheritance, as if this advice would keep one from losing courage and becoming unnecessarily disconsolate when the bridegroom withdraws himself (21, 5). For a constant certainty of grace is not achieved in the isolation which Bernard describes thus: "The soul that beholds God beholds him as if it were itself beheld only by God. In such confidence, the soul enters into this mutual relationship between God and itself as if nothing existed at all outside itself and God" (69, 8). At this point, I would only add the observation that this postulate of mysticism does not find a counterpart in that piety which is properly protestant. Churchly protestantism gives no sanction for such egoism. Yet Bernard is in a position to rebuke the monastics for claiming this privilege of mystical vision only for themselves, because on another occasion he reminds them that in truth the church is the bride and that the prerogatives of the one catholic community which comprises the purpose toward which the world tends cannot be claimed by any individual soul who belongs to the church, no matter how great its sanctity might be (68, 7).

> For which of us is able to possess any of the gifts of grace perfectly, in such a way that he is not at some time unfaithful in his speech and half-hearted in his works? But it is the church which in her totality never has a defect from which it is intoxicated or odorous. For what is lacking to the church in one person, it possesses in another. The church is odorous in those who make friends for themselves among unrighteous mammon, and it is intoxicated with those servants of the word who sprinkle the earth with the wine of spiritual joys, make the earth itself intoxicated, and harvest its fruits in joy. This church can call itself the bride with boldness and certainty. Therefore, although none of us takes it upon himself to call his soul the bride of the Lord, nevertheless, since we belong to the church, we justifiably claim our share of this honor. Without contradiction, we can say that each one of us shares in that which we all possess together (12, 11).

This is actually a confession which cuts across all of the previously portrayed claims of the soul to be the bride, by referring back to the older exegesis of the Song of Songs. All of those statements about the special distinction of the individual soul, whereby it seems to be made autonomous from all the other members of the church, in immediate relationship to God and Christ—all of these are rendered invalid in the light of Bernard's assertion concerning the church! But I will not draw this conclusion, since it appears that each alternative is valid for the speaker in the place where it appears—or each is imagined.

But this much is clear indeed, that the mystical vision which comprises the particular immediate relation of the individual soul to God under such equivocal conditions did not at all intend that this relation should develop beyond its catholic forms into protestantism, and there turn into the kind of evangelical Christian who is filled with awe and trust in God in the midst of life's distresses and who is exceedingly diligent in the service of God within his secular vocation. The two forms of piety are different or, to be more specific, they are opposed in their fundamental characteristics. And no little weight should be placed upon the fact that the sentimental piety with

its mystical thrust is expected only of monks who have no opportunity to test their faith in the temptations which arise from the
cares of human life. This consideration serves perfectly to determine
the character of the opposition between catholic and protestant
Christianity. Grace is the dominant factor for protestant piety, but
not, on that account, exclusively the possession of protestants, since
it is also central to catholic piety as well. But the consequences and
the applications of this highest principle are different for the
monastics who live a life free from cares and for the protestant
Christians who remain within the midst of their secular conditions
of life and who must stand the test of their faith within the inescapable cares of those conditions. The latter must so conduct themselves through trust in God and the prayer which proceeds from
that trust that, on the basis of their reconciliation with God or their
redemption from guilt and evil they overcome the forces which hold
man's life in check. In contrast, the monastics and their devotees in
the catholic church may prove their redemption through Christ in
the exercise of equality with him in sentimental pathos and sentimental desire which reaches to the height of the unity of their spirit
with Christ and God—at least as long as this enjoyment lasts and
does not deteriorate into the barrenness of experience. From this
we may conclude that the certainty of reconciliation as it is expressed
in trust in God is the necessary presupposition of sanctification for
the protestant Christian, whereas for the catholics the enjoyment of
redemption in tender intercourse with the redeemer is a possible
appendage to their sanctification.

V. LUTHERANISM AND CALVINISM

If we may suppose now that pietism, in principle, restored the
thrust of the anabaptists within the sphere of the Lutheran and
Reformed churches, we still have the further question of which of
the two protestant churches was more receptive to pietism's seed.
And from this general investigation, our first task is to isolate the
prior question of how far one may carry the analogy between
Zwingli's reforming intention and that of the anabaptists. Although
it is well known that the theocratic form in which Zwingli developed
his plan for reformation did not become or remain normative for
the formation of the Reformed church in Switzerland, nevertheless

that tendency of his is pertinent to at least a portion of the anabaptists. Zwingli clearly did not impute to the state merely the direct
task of protecting Christianity and reforming the church; he also
considered it advisable that the state should extend this reformation
through political force. In a similar manner, the anabaptist group
which was led by Hans Hut,[73] considering itself to be the true Israel,
proposed to exterminate all godless Canaanites by the sword, and
the anabaptists in Münster acted on this same impulse. This violent
attitude, to be sure, is an exception to the basic peaceableness and
subservience with which the anabaptists generally responded to the
force applied against them. Nevertheless, this deviation is quite
understandable as anticipatory of the coming power of Christ to
judge and rule, which the anabaptists expected. Thus the theocratic
perspective engendered on both sides a sanctioning of force for the
purpose of carrying through the Christian reform. Of course, there is
a great disparity between the two—Zwingli applied the means of
the existing state to the ends of a truly moral ordering of life; the
anabaptists, on the contrary, sought with their morally questionable
and reprehensible ends to overthrow the civil order. Accordingly, the
Münster theocracy of the anabaptists can hardly be viewed as the
consequence of Zwingli's Zurich theocracy. Indeed, there is neither
a logical nor moral connection between the moral and antimoral
ends, respectively, of these two tendencies, between Zwingli's legal
attachment to the existing civil order and the radical overturning
of the civil order in Münster. The constitution of state and church
in Zurich, directly under Zwingli's leadership, is therefore least of
all disposed to grant the anabaptists' claims concerning the validity
of their perfect Christianity. On the contrary, in fact, the opposition
to them in Zurich was so forceful precisely because the people there
were confident of the Christian justification for the existing civil and
moral order.

Even in his own lifetime, none of the Swiss social classes accepted
Zwingli's theocratic perspective, and in Zurich itself this highly
significant proposal was abandoned when the catastrophe occurred
in which Zwingli met his death. From then on, within the entire
sphere of the sixteenth century reformation movement, the principle
came to be accepted that the service which the state could render
to the Christian religion could be justified only by individual terri-

tories and that it could only be a protective service. In other words, Christian unity was sought only in unity of confession, not in unity of legally constituted organization, and hardly even in unity of liturgical forms. We need not discuss here how the commonality of confession split apart in the Lutheran and Reformed groups. By contrast, one other function of the church does come to mind, besides the ones already described, which brings with it a different manner of classifying the territorial churches. I am referring to the church's function of discipline. The polemical theologians of the sixteenth century were not clear in their own minds that there are divergences of considerable significance between the Lutheran and Reformed churches in their regard for church discipline. Even in our own century adequate attention has not been given to this matter.[74] It is very easy to demonstrate, in this respect, however, that Calvinism stands opposed not only to the whole of Lutheranism, but also to the ecclesiastical order of German Switzerland, or to the actual sphere of Zwingli's activity. Calvinism was able to occupy this area with its doctrine and its official confession (with the exception only of Basel), but not with its discipline; and even in the matter of doctrine, a Zwinglian undercurrent has always remained active. In addition, Calvinism has not been able to make its form of discipline stand in the German territories which acknowledge its authority in doctrine, as in the Palatinate, Bremen, Hesse, Anhalt, etc. In this regard, it has been able to establish its validity only in the areas outside Germany, and in Germany it was able to take hold in eastern Friesland, as well as in Julich, Cleves, and Berg only by reaching out from the Netherlands. Therefore, if church discipline is considered a worthy basis for classifying the reformation churches, Calvinism outside Germany must be set in opposition to the German sphere, which embraces Lutheranism and Zwinglianism. Indeed, Calvin could not carry out his work of establishing the church in Geneva except on the basis upon which the shaping of the reformation churches took place in the spheres of Luther and Zwingli, namely, through the authority of the state. Under such circumstances, church discipline came to be in the hands of the civil authorities throughout the German and Swiss territories. But there were various principles at work in bringing this to pass. In part, the medieval practice of church discipline assumed the form of secular penalties which the state simply took over in the wake of the reformation. In part, the one distinctive penalty of the church, exclusion from the Lord's Supper, could not be left to the individual pastors but had to be taken over by the provincial consistories. Or where a particular authority was established to exercise the ban, as with Bucer (1531) in Ulm (four men from the town council, two pastors, and two members of the congregation), it was prescribed that this authority could excommunicate only at the command of the town council.[75] Nevertheless, this course of things within the German sphere (particularly the Lutheran) of the church's development did not take place simply because of external, accidental considerations; rather, from the very beginning this development was governed by a certain theory concerning the respective competencies of church and state.

The two branches of the reformation between which we are differentiating here agree on this point: that church discipline is not necessitated simply by general considerations for social order, but, rather, by consideration for the honor of Christ or for the particular character of the Christian community.[76] As we know, Calvin concluded from this that the church must be in possession of specific legal organs for excluding public sinners. These organs could not be developed without support and even cooperation from the state, but yet they were to be independent of the state in their activity. In any case, the power of the state was to stand as a ready servant of the disciplinary decrees of the consistory and not as a higher authority over them. For the power to discipline is in God's behalf and, according to the prescriptions of holy scripture, it is an inviolable attribute of the church. But the Lutherans deviated completely from this norm. Franz Aepinus, in the Church Order for Stralsund (1525), and Johann Brenz, in the Church Order for Schwäbisch-Hall (1526),[77] agree that the church bears only the organs of grace, and that, accordingly, the maintenance of the Christian life through means of law or discipline is ultimately an attribute of the secular authority or of the state.[78] Accordingly, Brenz asserted that discipline was exercised in the ancient church in conformity with Paul's precept only because no Christian governmental authority was then in existence. Since general legal authority has come into the hands of Christians in the meantime, the necessity for church discipline has largely disappeared. In those specific cases where Brenz does prescribe church discipline, however, it is only in the sense of a substitute action because and for so long as the state does not hold sex offenses to be punishable, even though they transgress both divine and *imperial* laws.

The idea is clearly expressed in this discussion that in principle the church can have no punitive authority over its members since it is the community of divine grace and the bearer of the proclamation of grace. And therefore, when it does occur that this authority is attributed to the church, this can be explained only as an accidental defect in the relation between church and state in a certain epoch. However, when the state is conscious of the moral character of its penal authority, within a Christian frame of reference, the church must dispense with its disciplinary authority, in order to mold in a more definitive manner its own character as a religious community. This conclusion that the necessity of discipline is only conditional for the church stems from a contemporary of Luther, who actually only attained a second-rate significance. Although none of the later church orders include similar ideas, this man's discussion must be regarded as normative for the direction this issue took in the sphere of the Lutheran reformation, because his thinking conformed the most precisely to the dominant concept of the church at the time. When a person judges that it is a mark of the weakness of the German reformation that, in part, it left the church's power of discipline directly to the state and, in part, subordinated it to the judgment of the state-church administrative authorities, he unconsciously has the Calvinist ideal in mind. What is considered a "weakness" is justified in principle by the Lutheran thought which Aepinus and Brenz represent, that as the organ of divine grace, the church cannot be a fundamental organ of punitive authority at the same time. And this standpoint is confirmed indirectly by still other witnesses.

In the second generation of the development of Lutheran churches, the man to whom I am referring, Erasmus Sarcerius, superintendent of the worthy earldom of Mansfeld, wrote a volume entitled, *Von einer Disciplin, dadurch Zucht, Tugend und Ehrbarkeit mogen gepflanzt und erhalten werden* [*Concerning a Discipline whereby Culture, Virtue and Honorableness Might Be Planted and Maintained*] (1556), wherein he discussed the urgent need for this discipline and the means for restoring it.[79] It strikes us in reading this work that he has the German people rather than the ecclesiastical community in mind as the subject of his discipline. The conscience of the people is to be developed on account of the decline of morals, and, as proof of this need, he compares the present with the description of the Germans given by Tacitus. Accordingly, he makes the claim for the secular authority that it is the vicar of God for the purpose of restoring discipline; and when he adds that the clergy are also called to the same task, his exact words are that they are obligated by their office *to assist* in establishing a discipline. One has further reason for doubting that this book is concerned with an imperative of church life when, on the basis of examples taken from both Christian and pagan periods, the legislative and judicial functions of the state are recommended as means for establishing such a discipline, specifically the imperial parliament, the provincial parliaments, municipal ordinances, and all types of courts. This undertaking will further alienate many contemporary theologians since the author brings these proposals to bear upon complaints about the immorality of the royal courts and of the jurists—matters which have no bearing on the church's interest. Such a structure of demands and proposals in which the secular legal basis for discipline is combined with the ecclesiastical basis, would be entirely unintelligible if one thought that the term "a discipline" referred to the catholic and Calvinist practice of separating public sinners from the cultic community. But this meaning of the word seldom comes into force in Sarcerius's usage. By "discipline" he normally means the much more comprehensive imperative of *good morals,* which are the fruit of true penance and whose restoration is effected chiefly by the preaching of the gospel, that is, next to the law of the civil order. The customary meaning of discipline, as the punishment of the church upon those who publicly transgress God's will, "for their own improvement and as a horrible example for other persons"— this meaning is only appended by Sarcerius to the means and ways by which the divine law is brought to realization among the people.

We would make a more beautiful and more worthy beginning toward a discipline if every citizen would reform one man; then in time, everyone would be reformed. Thus, the head of every house would first lay the foundation for a common discipline in his own house, for himself and his kin, in that every man would bring his wife, children, and servants up to their best. Then it would be that much easier for the authorities and the clergy to set up a common, public discipline (namely, through punitive force).

Since Sarcerius also prescribes for the clergy by what means they have to restore a discipline, ten chapters of the work in question deal with their personal attitude, the proper management of their houses, their faithfulness in preaching on penance, grace, duties, and virtues, and with the holding of synods and visitations; and only after this are they advised to exercise ecclesiastical penalties and to impose public penance. The final two chapters are very characteristic of the whole book, in that the establishment of good *schools* and, again, common fraternal admonition are suggested as particularly effective means for setting up and maintaining a discipline.

When we recall in what sense the reformers of the sixteenth century took over the imperative of ecclesiastical discipline from the catholic tradition, and in what sense it formed the imperative for Calvin's life at the same time, then we recognize that Sarcerius has shifted the meaning of this imperative considerably. The dicipline which he wishes to carry out is the *moral training of the entire nation*. To this end he could bring civil legislation and government together with the principles on which the Christian religion structures the common life, and even in such an order of priority that the latter takes precedence as means for the secular authority. However, since he bore in mind the original meaning of ecclesiastical punitive discipline he could rightly maintain that it is feasible and effective as a means for restoring public morality only when it can rely on the substructure of the moral training of the nation. Nevertheless, the conviction does emerge rather clearly that the ecclesiastical process of punishment will seem superfluous to the extent that the task of training the nation is successfully carried out.

> For where there is discipline, there everything goes well and right in an orderly manner; there every citizen does in his vocation what it is his obligation and duty to do; there is obedience and everything good; there is peace and unity; there men render to God what is God's and to the civil authority what belongs to it.

If one wishes to know the Lutheran position with respect to church discipline, he dare not restrict himself to the perception that this discipline has somehow been curtailed because it was transferred to civil organs. Currently, this point of view usually also includes the judgment that thereby an essential function was lost to the Lutheran church, and that Calvinism surpasses Lutheranism because it retained this function. When one is in such a mood he generally disregards the fact that discipline has been no less impracticable in Calvinism than in the Lutheran church. However, in order to understand the position of Lutheranism authentically and fully, one should recognize what a much more comprehensive and sound enterprise Sarcerius has set forth as a replacement for traditional church discipline. And this enterprise, in spite of all the difficulties, has not remained unheeded in protestant Germany. When one reads in Sarcerius's book the profoundly bleak descriptions of the moral conditions of his time, as well as the complaints lodged against the conduct of the upper classes in his society—persons whom he nevertheless expected to accept his admonitions—then one must marvel at the power of his practical idealism and the patience which accompanied his belief that the task could be carried out. From this line of thinking, it is also plain that the Lutheran acceptance of church discipline is only a conditional one. It is expressed in the following formulation: "If church discipline is to take place, then it is only possible under the assumption that there has been a prior civil and religious training of the nation in morality." Meanwhile, it will be objected that Sarcerius is not a sufficiently legitimated representative of Lutheranism. As though it were to be reckoned to Luther's adherents—Sarcerius among them—that they had disposal over their own ideas! The essence of his point of view can be authenticated directly in Luther himself.

In the exposition of the prophet Joel which Veit Dietrich published from Luther's lectures of 1547,[80] Luther concerns himself with the widely held view that the ban, as exclusion from the Lord's Supper, had fallen into disuse partly through the carelessness of the clergy and partly through the disfavor of the civil authorities. Against this, he asserted that the guilt for this lay with the entire Christian society. Everyone failed in this task, namely, to warn and admonish his neighbor against injustice and lack of discipline, so as to reform him. Thereby, out of the fear of men and due to their own anxiety, people assured themselves that they would be treated in similar fashion by others. The actual cause of the decline of the ban, then, was the circumstance that true Christians were so small in number. This view of Luther led to the conclusion that if the ban were to come into usage, it would be necessary, above all else, to train the nation in true Christian morality. But at the same time Luther calls attention from another point of view to the fact that the ban has only a relative worth for the church, for it directs itself only against public scandals. Nevertheless, as Luther explains, the private sinners who share in the sacraments of the Christian church are also banned, *de facto,* by God. Thus they fall under God's judgment even though they deceive men by their appearances. From this it follows that the exercise of ecclesiastical punishment against public sinners does not achieve its purpose of purifying the church of sinners; rather, the fear is aroused through this activity that the hypocrites are the ones who will present themselves in the church as worthy. Even if Luther did not use these precise words, he nevertheless suggests these considerations, since they serve to verify his argument for the purely relative significance of the ban for the church. As much as he argues *in thesi* for the usefulness of the ban and the clergy's duty to exercise it—even in this context—he still is hardly of the opinion that the church has had one of its essential functions curtailed simply because the ban has fallen into disuse.

Calvin's opposing point of view finds its clearest manifestation in the manner in which he brings the authority of the New Testament to bear in this case. As a man of the second generation of the reformation, he stood less free vis-à-vis the authority of holy scripture than did Luther; as a matter of fact, he distinguishes himself at this point from Lutherans in general. This disparity occurred because Calvin regarded not only the religious train of thought of the New Testament, but also certain social structures of the first Christian communities as permanently binding, whereas Luther and the true Lutherans abandoned the latter. In Calvin's opinion, the installing of pastors and doctors of theology as leaders of the church after the apostles, without permitting a distinction in rank among them, was a holy, inviolable, and eternal law—a structure which God had established, and not a human invention (*Institutes,* IV, 4, 6, 7). Similarly, discipline as punitive power was seen as an attribute of the church which the Lord had foreseen as necessary (IV, 12, 4).

The threat of punishment which Paul raised in the name of the church against the members of the Corinthian congregation stands for Calvin as the divine sanction for the entire range of discipline which is granted to the church. Brenz, on the contrary, could discern only a momentary need of the church in this passage, since there was not yet any Christian civil order at that time. In this divergence, the difference between the Lutheran and Calvinist views is clearly not merely one of discipline but rather one of the use of the Bible in the church as well. With regard to what pertains to the social ordinances of the first Christian communities, the Lutherans could look upon the New Testament as the document of bygone conditions, which are no longer binding under altered historical circumstances. But Calvin perceived inviolable norms to which the church had to be led back, both in the precepts of the apostles concerning discipline as well as in the first century congregational organization to which the New Testament witnesses.

The manner in which Calvin understood the necessity of the ban and the application of the authority of the New Testament meant that he moved over to the side of the anabaptists to the same degree that he distanced himself from Lutheranism. The point here is not simply the question of discipline, however, although the anabaptists also reproached the Lutheran preachers for neglecting it, according to Bullinger's testimony. In this connection one could assert, rather, that when the two say the same thing, it is not the same thing. For the Calvinist interpretation of the Christian religion and Christian morality differs too much from the anabaptists' legalistic and monastic striving after sanctity to make an actual affinity between the two conceivable. And the similarity that exists between the two in their regard for the ban is simply not strong enough an argument, that it can serve as basis for such an affinity. Even if we suspend this consideration, there is still clear agreement between the two that the authority of the New Testament is to be applied not merely in respect to the religious world view and the image of God, but also in respect to the binding character of certain practical ordinances which occur in the first generation of the church. This agreement is not destroyed by the differences between the two in the scope of their application of that principle. The anabaptists concluded from the authority of the New Testament that Christians as such could not participate in the secular state and that instead they could only be admonished to be patient in the face of injustice from all sides—because such was the situation of the first Christians. Although Calvin was far enough removed from that position, he still asserted the necessity of punitive force in the church and the elimination of all distinctions in rank between the teachers and pastors of the church, only because it had been so in the first generation of Christianity—and the structures of that generation were unconditionally binding upon him since they were documented in holy scripture. As far as we can presently judge, therefore, the normative image for the Christian life-style [*Lebensideal*] which Calvin held is totally different from that of the anabaptists; for that reason, discipline carries a different weight for each of them. For the anabaptists, it is the means for restoring the actual sanctity of the true church. For Calvin, it is, under all circumstances, a means of external order to which one is obligated for the sake of the honor of Christ and the moral well-being of the individual members of the church (*Institutes*, IV, 12, 5). In spite of this, the manner in which this is derived from the New Testament, as though it were an inspired law book, echoes the principle of St. Francis's reformation, namely, that the social order of Christendom is to be referred back to the conditions which obtained during the first generation. On the basis of this formal agreement, it is certainly not likely that Calvinism possesses within itself a particular inclination to accept or reproduce Franciscan or anabaptist forms of life. Calvin's understanding of the Christian structuring of life is identical with the Lutheran position in this respect, that it is linked to the exercise of one's vocation and to one's placement within the civil order. On these grounds, nevertheless, Calvin imparted a moral structure to his church for the maintenance of discipline—a structure which modified considerably the governing image of life-style [*Lebensideal*] which was common to protestantism. In order to make this understandable, we must also take Calvin's personal moral endowments and nationality into consideration at the same time.

It is certainly worth noting that the French who entered actively into the reformation of the sixteenth century were very decidedly intent upon church discipline. Prior to Calvin, in this regard, we may refer to William Farel and Franz Lambert.[81] Especially instruc-

tive, however, is this former Franciscan's [i.e., Lambert's] attempt
to provide the church of Hesse with a disciplinary structure. Luther
had expressed the devout wish for a community of those who earnestly desire to be Christian in his *Deutsche Messe und Ordnung des
Gottesdienstes* [*The German Mass and the Ordering of the Service
of Worship*], which he published in 1526. He meant that these
people would have to designate themselves with the name "Christian" and gather in a particular house for prayer, Bible reading, and
the use of the sacraments. In this community and according to these
conditions, one could discern, punish, reform, exclude, or put under
the ban those who did not comport themselves as Christians. But
Luther added that he could not establish such a community, because
he did not yet have the people for it, and he did not observe many
who would be suited for it. He also feared that there would have
been an uproar if he had carried out the plan for this community on
his own. "For we Germans are a wild, rough, raving people, with
whom it is not easy to begin something new unless there is the most
urgent necessity."[82] This correct, if unflattering, testimony by Luther
about his people, with its prior fear that the implementation of his
plan for forming more restricted communities would bring with it
an uprising, is undoubtedly to be understood as a reasonable assessment of the fact that the Germans as a whole would not have gone
along with his system. Herein an insight is expressed which is
doubtless correct, that the Germans lack the feeling for the equality
and for the involuntary adherence to law which is required for a
system of church discipline. Consequently, the project of forming
such a restricted community, which would condescend voluntarily
to the exercise of discipline, was a fantasy of a devout wish which
did not occupy Luther's thought further in any demonstrable manner. But the Frenchman Lambert had nothing which was more
urgent to him than to incorporate the project of Luther into the
church order which he wanted to use at Homberg as a means of
instituting the reformation of the Hessian church. In the fifteenth
chapter of this church order,[83] he prescribes that after the Sunday
worship service, those men and women should come together who
earnestly practice Christianity and who are to be counted in the
number of the sanctified. They should pledge to place themselves
under excommunication, if it should be necessary, and this pledge

should be written down. This community should pursue all of its concerns under the direction of the bishop; it should not only choose its officers, but should also take in hand the process of excluding persons from the community and receiving them back into it. Everything which is necessary for admonishment should also be communicated to this restricted group. Anyone in the congregation who does not earnestly amend his ways within fourteen days after the protestant preaching begins is to be excluded not only from the Lord's Supper but also from the preaching service and all fraternal relations. Thus, the protestant congregation would be placed on the same basis as a congregation of tertiaries! This man from southern France, a former Franciscan, thought that he could offer such fare to the Hessians without taking warning from Luther's estimate of the German people! It is true that his church order remained, on paper at least, even after the advice which Luther gave, on request, to Landgrave Philip. In his letter[84] to this prince he emphasizes chiefly that laws are useful only when some degree of morality exists to support them; having said this, however, he also confirms the judgment as to why the Germans would not permit the establishment of church discipline. In line with the roughness and intractability that Luther censured among the Germans, there is also the feeling for individual liberty, and, in addition, the feeling for freedom in matters of morals, which are the real reasons why they resist a universal law of church discipline. Since the Frenchman, to the contrary, considers it to be self-evident that the disciplinary prescriptions which seem to be set forth in the New Testament should be put into immediate practice, he counts on that drive for equality and that inclination to permit oneself to be disciplined in all things, which are precisely the factors which differentiate his people from the Germans.

The factors which these men linked with the reformation of the sixteenth century—legal strictness and the task of disciplining the masses—are the characteristics through which the general attitude of the French has distinguished itself in the history of the church. I recall that the monasticism which developed in ancient Egypt was first received with enthusiasm in Gaul, and, further, that in the first half of the Middle Ages the monastic reforms and restorations manifested themselves at Cluny, Chartreux, Citeaux, and Prémontré;

and it is more important to see this fact as a clear testimony to the character of French Christianity than it is to note that the founders of two of these orders were Germans. At the same time, France is the home of the crusades. In the second half of the Middle Ages, the University of Paris was also the center of significant ecclesiastical movements, and that community of learning was always a splendid demonstration of how large numbers of men could be disciplined. Since the epoch of the sixteenth century, the ascetical tendency of the French has burst forth partly in the work of the founding of the order at La Trappe,[85] partly in Jansenism,[86] and not a little in the quietistic mysticism which found its most significant representation among the French, even though it did not originate among them. In addition to these, the work of Vincent de Paul should be recalled.[87] Finally, since the Revolution and the Restoration, French Catholicism has been disciplined ever more intensely as an instrument of the papal efforts at world domination. Moreover, this disposition of the French seems to become all the more distinct as the religious state of affairs becomes more insufficient and weak— a development which presently seems to be linked with the social and political undertakings of the papacy. As representatives of strict church discipline who definitely count on this discipline being carried out, the French reformers of the sixteenth century belong to the tradition of French Christianity, despite their deviations from its doctrine; and they fill in a gap in this tradition since the Roman Catholic spirit did not produce any noteworthy effects in the sixteenth century.

Calvin did impose certain tendencies upon the branch of protestant Christianity which he founded, in the interests of church discipline, which express an unmistakable approximation of the monastic renunciation of the world. In principle, he was indeed in agreement with Luther that the Christian life is to be conducted and tested within the framework of civil vocation, in the state. But, since Calvin needed no personal recreation for his own life, he considered the normal forms of social intercourse and the manifestations of luxury that went along with them to be merely the most pressing temptation for sin. Now it is true that church discipline can assert itself to be churchly only if it is relatively infrequently applied. For this reason, Calvin drew the conclusion that the temptations for immorality which derived from social intercourse, and which therefore would be occasions for ecclesiastical punishment, had to be eliminated. This is the reason that Calvin fought against all that pertains to the cheerful and free enjoyment of life and art; and since he appointed like-minded French immigrants to the governing council in Geneva, he succeeded in imposing upon the patterns of common life which he supervised an attitude of alienation from the world which was similar to that of the Franciscan tertiaries. For among the latter there was a prohibition against participation in social enjoyments, particularly the theater, just as surely as there was among the Calvinists.

Accordingly, we can now determine fully the opposition between Lutheranism and Calvinism in their regard for discipline. The Lutheran formulation goes like this: "If there is a need for church discipline to be carried out, then there is a need for general moral training of the whole society." The Calvinist formulation is expressed thus: "Since church discipline is necessary, the life of the whole society must also be restricted even more, particularly with respect to social intercourse and the public theater." To the extent that Calvinism's governing image of the Christian style of life [*Lebensideal*] is anticatholic, it has sprung from Luther's inspiration. To the extent that it diverges from Luther's point of view, it has turned back to the tradition of the Franciscan image of the style of life [*Lebensideal*]. It seemed to be clear already from our previous analysis that Calvin's application of the authority of the New Testament to the establishing of church discipline was reminiscent of the Franciscan and anabaptist principle: The earliest and most elementary forms of the Christian church should be normative for all time. This formal agreement is now amplified through the aversion to social intercourse and public theater which was common to both groups. Therefore, if pietism has sprung from the same view of the Christian life of the masses that was active in the Franciscan and anabaptism reformation, then it is to be expected that Calvinism is more disposed to accept and reproduce this pietistic tendency than German protestantism, be it of the Lutheran or Zwinglian variety.

It is well known that Calvin could carry out his organization of the church in Geneva only through the authority of the state. Consequently, he also took a number of governmental officials into the agency of church discipline, the consistory. But he also wanted to be certain that the decisions of this ecclesiastical authority would be altogether exempt from the legitimation of the state. In the light of this concern, he struggled for the fundamental autonomy of the church from the state. Differing circumstances proved to be useful for carrying out this principle in different areas of Calvinism. In France, the Reformed church owed its autonomy from the state to the fact that the state opposed the reformation altogether. In Scotland, on the contrary, the essence of that autonomous relation, which was continually striven for and partially achieved, was expressed in a medieval view of the state which the founders of the Reformed church embraced. In particular, John Knox and George Buchanan shared with their teacher, John Major of St. Andrews, the conviction that the state, including, therefore, the monarchy, has its direct basis in the will of the people without any detriment to the divine ordinance, and that the people are justified in deposing an unjust prince.[88] This assertion, which rests on the authority of Thomas Aquinas,[89] depends on the additional argument that the church, representing divine authority directly through its organs and leaders, is of greater worth than the state and for this reason is autonomous, even from a legal point of view. In keeping with this, John Knox implanted the analogous view in the Scottish church, that Christ, as the head of the church, guarantees directly the divine authority of its organization, its liturgical ordinances, and its discipline.[90] Knox borrowed this formulation from John Laski, who, as chairman of the immigrant congregation in London, was pressed by circumstances to establish the church which later came to be called "independentism." The fugitives from the Netherlands and France, whom he served as pastor in London until they fled from Bloody Mary, had to give up, as aliens, all claims to support for their church life by the government; their independent legal constitution placed Laski under the protection of the kingdom of Christ and made his office a direct product of the legislative power of that kingdom. The basis for this view was the harmony of that church's constitution with the ordinances which existed in the primitive church. This image of the church, put into force by these immigrant congregations primarily in response to an emergency, and impressed upon the theory, at least, of the Scottish church, won the upper hand, over the episcopal and presbyterian forms of the church in England, for a time at least, in the seventeenth century. Because, as a consequence of the independentism of Laski, the power of the state was disallowed in respect to the legal ordering of the church, the unity of the state church was also abandoned in favor of the autonomy of every individual congregation. In this manner, a conformity to the church of the primitive period was achieved which extended even beyond Calvin's intention. However, what we have here is evidence of the fact that, to the degree that Calvinism's anticatholic image of the church is consistently followed, that image develops into an independentism which once again approximates the anabaptist congregations. And it is not accidental, either, that the independents' image of the Christian life [*Lebensideal*] also goes back to that of the anabaptists. The congregations of the English independents rested their claims basically on the ascetical sanctity that was revealed in their members, namely, in their strict repudiation of all secular recreation and all games. Since they were for the most part baptists as well, they also came to reject infant baptism. At the same time, theocratic-revolutionary phenomena manifested themselves in their groups in the seventeenth century which were similar to those which appeared among the German anabaptists one hundred years earlier. To be sure, these conditions appeared only in a particular sphere of Calvinism and then under particular circumstances. But they were possible nevertheless only insofar as they were consequences of principles which differentiate Calvinism generally from Lutheranism and state-church forms of Zwinglianism, and which conform, as a whole, to the image of the life-style [*Lebensideal*] which was prevalent in the Franciscan and anabaptist reformation. Since this agreement led to the extensive reversion of independent English Calvinism to the tradition of the anabaptists, we may say that the general inclination of Calvinism has thereby been demonstrated to accept and reproduce anew forms of practical life which correspond to the Franciscan reformation.

This inclination is present in Calvinism in spite of the fact that the founder of this form of protestant Christianity earnestly took precautions that the thrust of his churches toward moral perfection should not result in separatist consequences.[91] In anticipation of this consequence, he insisted that the substance of the church is tied only to the correct teaching of the gospel and the administration of the sacraments; and since he described the imperative of the moral purity of the church as a temptation, he required as virtues which followed from this purity the qualities of forebearance and patience —qualities which are customarily lacking from the virtues of the separatists. It is significant however that he did ascribe the predicate "good" to these strict and impatient persons. Accordingly, these strict and impatient representatives of moral perfection in the church consequently consider themselves to be good people, indeed, the best people in the Reformed church, and, therefore, they treated with contempt all the arguments with which Calvin had opposed them in advance. These arguments are nevertheless worthy of our attention. Calvin appealed first to the fact that Paul viewed the Corinthian church as the church of Christ, even though it was full of moral faults, and also the Galatian Christians who had even abandoned the gospel. He recalled for them, further, that the church was founded on the forgiveness of sins and continued to maintain itself on this foundation. Finally, he characterized as a self-deception the opinion that a person would simply be giving up fellowship with the godless, if he separated himself from the existing church. Such a step was more likely to bring with it the general destruction of the church. Calvin linked these reflections and admonitions against separatism only to the phenomenon of anabaptism in his time. He did not confront similar deviations within the churches he had himself established. However, it is almost as though he anticipated that his intention to develop the legal and disciplinary sanctity of the church would lead the faithful adherents, whom he himself termed good, into the error of separatism. This very thing happened, while these arguments of Calvin, which have just been cited, were fully lost on those people who were precisely the ones who intended to proceed consistently toward the goal which Calvin had set.

VI. THE NECESSITY FOR REFORM IN CHURCHLY PROTESTANTISM

The need for renewed or more extensive reform within protestantism seems to depend first of all on the intensity of the internal and external difficulties which the individual reformers experienced in carrying out their own original ecclesiastical mandates. These difficulties were most significant in the case of Luther and Melanchthon. It was not simply because of their own internal difficulties that they took such great effort and needed more time to break away from their attachment to the given forms of liturgy and church organization; in addition, they experienced particular restraints because of the conditions which the Holy Roman Empire placed upon them. In both of these respects, Zwingli occupied a much more favorable position than the reformers in Saxony. In the first place, he was not hindered by the power of the Holy Roman Empire, not the least because he lacked the devotion to it which animated Luther and Melanchthon. Furthermore, he attained a decided clarity at an early period concerning his religious convictions and their consequences for liturgy and organization. Calvin stood in an even more favorable position in this respect, for as an epigone he had the advantage of being able to take possession of a tradition which had already freed itself from the apron strings of the medieval church. Not only did he take possession of that tradition with his characteristic clarity of reason and strength of will, in that he gave it the most consummate theological expression, but in addition, he yoked that tradition to tasks which had been alien to it up to that time. Furthermore, he found a field for his work of establishing churches which was even further removed from the influence of the empire than Zwingli's area of activity. Through these differences among the reformers, one is able to gauge why the formation of the protestant church in the sphere of the German empire gives the impression of a persisting incompleteness and, at the same time, appears to stand closer to the practice of the catholic church than the churches established by Zwingli and Calvin. Many elements of medieval origin have actually been propagated, or reproduced with modification in the Lutheran church which have disappeared in the other churches. Accordingly, it appears that a need for reform would have manifested itself sooner in the Lutheran church than in the Calvinist-Reformed church. But, of course, this is not the case. The established church of England embodied even more striking compromises with the catholic past, in the ordering of the liturgy as well as in organization. For this reason, the reforming movement of the Puritans began in that church immediately after the external security of the English church was established by Queen Elizabeth. In addition, the imperative for completing the reformation was seized upon in the Reformed church of the Netherlands before the German Lutheran Church could realize the proper conditions for real reformation efforts. In order that one might be prepared to understand pietism's reformation thrust within the Lutheran church, a historical explanation is required of the scholastic restriction of Lutheranism, since, as the well-established assumption has it, it is this restriction which points to the need for reform within that form of church life. I need only add beforehand that Calvinism shares this need equally with Lutheranism. That this fact is customarily overlooked can be explained by the fact that such a characteristic of Calvinism is compensated for and veiled by legalistic tendencies in morals and discipline—characteristics more prominent in Calvinism than in Lutheranism.

But the error we are describing did not make its appearance simply as a later manifestation within the Lutheran or the Reformed church; it is grounded, rather, in the circumstances under which the reformation arrived at its particular church forms. It is well known that the political circumstances in the Holy Roman Empire favored Luther's reformation just as much as they restricted it. The loose character of this political alliance permitted a number of princes not only to protect the reformers, but it also allowed alterations in the liturgy and the actual severing of the new teaching office in their churches from the power of the bishops. But on the other hand the stability of the empire and its association with the Roman church inhibited the autonomy of protestant church life, in contrast, for example, with Switzerland, where the church was established simply by the decision of the municipal authorities to accept the reformation. Since the protestant princes were no less interested in the stability of the empire than those princes who were inclined to the papal church, they felt compelled to retain the substance of the one catholic church to which the political validity of the empire had been linked at one time. Theirs was the task of establishing their evangelical interpretation of the destiny and conditions of the one catholic church in all sections of the empire. As long as they did not succeed in this, and as long as they strove for it through religious negotiations, the protestant princes acknowledged themselves and their church structure, in effect, as a party within the church.

Similarly, they considered the papists to be the other party. This perspective not only dominated the Augsburg Confession of 1530, it also conditioned the religious Peace of Augsburg in 1555, which did not rule out the possibility of a compromise. This political manifestation of parties within the church can be regarded, theologically, only as a difference between schools. The set of doctrines and liturgical principles which were recapitulated as such in the Augsburg Confession (some as noncontroversial and some as controversial) is the direct expression of a scholastic point of view in the church, in which the opponent is also assumed to be a school. No other situation would have been possible, given the conditions which obtained then in the Latin church and in the Holy Roman Empire, since, in the second half of the Middle Ages, an opposition between schools was accepted within the church and in the universities which were legitimated by the church. As long as the assumption was maintained that these parties could come to an understanding through religious negotiations, that is, in a scholastic manner, there could be no official recognition that the controversy of the sixteenth century was concerned with interests much more practical than those which had separated the Thomists and the Nominalists from one another.

In reality, every study of this sort reminds us that the opposition between those parties in the church which were held together by the political forces of the empire cannot be viewed as if it were the opposition between two schools. Moreover, the theologians of the reformation never did restrict themselves to this point of view, but rather interpreted the Roman church to be the false church and the protestant church to be the true one. The Smalcald allies had already adopted this position by 1537, when they refused the invitation to the council.[92] This kind of argumentation was unavoidable, especially since both catholicism and protestantism upheld as Christian world views and images of life style [*Lebensideal*] which were quite different. If their differences were simply of the kind that exists between schools, both parties would subordinate themselves under the same definition of the purpose of Christianity. Therefore, after 1537, the protestants no longer held back their assertion that the church designated by the Augsburg Confession was the catholic church, whereas the papal church was actually a perversion. In one sense, however, the claim that the new church forms should be considered as types of a school was upheld and never excluded. To be sure, it was always asserted that this new church served the purpose of salvation through the gospel it represented, a purpose which was missing from the catholic side because of all sorts of errors. This indicates that the protestant church includes within its self-definition *a total understanding* of the correct world view and proper ordering of the Christian life. But this implication is put aside and overshadowed by the insistence that we possess the correct *doctrine* of the gospel in the Augsburg Confession and that we prove ourselves to be the catholic church by upholding the ancient confessions of that church. It is precisely at this point that the "school" element is asserted as though it were the principal characteristic of the church's existence; and this judgment is confirmed by the fact that Melanchthon, the spokesman in these matters, conceived of the church as a kind of school, in order to uphold his conviction that it was not to be conceived of as a state.[93] Nevertheless, we do not have to hold Melanchthon solely responsible for this fateful assertion. Rather, it is the consequence of the type of struggle through which the reformation had to pass if it were to free itself from medieval ways of church life, and thus it was inevitable that this original form of argumentation would continue to be effective in the self-consciousness of the protestant church.

Whenever it happens that a new form of Christian truth appears, we know that those who find the old wine better tasting than the new exercise their wisdom in the following manner: they pluck out those particulars of the new point of view which offend them, and they vigorously oppose them as though they were individual points of doctrine without first placing themselves in the total context of the new manifestation. In most cases, these premature opponents of the particulars are as incapable as they are unwilling to put themselves in this total context which the new sets forth. Moreover, if the representative of a new point of view permits himself to respond to all such fragmentary attacks, he exposes himself to the danger of fragmenting his accomplishment—whose value consists in the wholeness of its form—into many particularities which, as such, do not retain their recognizable relation to the whole. This is true of Luther who generally gave battle for his convictions which deviated from the traditional opinion before he had established the totality of his view of Christianity in his own mind and put it into organic form. He permitted himself to be forced by his opponents into controversy over individual points, and he never compensated for this by producing a systematic presentation of his interpretation of the gospel. In addition, Melanchthon, after all, was only able to use the loose scheme of the *Loci theologici*,[94] which actually produces the opposite of a theological system. And finally, as much as the character of the Augsburg Confession differs in this respect—to its credit—from the private writings of the reformers, we still confront in this document a disconnectedness in the presentation of the controversial doctrines and ordinances. As a compendium of the controversial doctrines, this legal foundation of the new church serves this end precisely: it assures that the "school" element in the church took on a preponderance over the other necessary functions from the very beginning. There is yet another consideration that intensified this situation. In order to legitimate the protestant church as catholic in the eyes of the emperor and the empire, Melanchthon (as well as Luther) attached major importance to the ancient confessions, and he even granted precedence to them over the new protestant interpretation of the *beneficia Christi* [benefits of Christ].[95] Now the Nicene form of the doctrine of the person of Christ was originally of direct practical consequence for the Greek church and was a vehicle for the soteriology that was distinctive to that church. However, that formulation was no longer normative for the Christian understanding of salvation, even for the Latin church, in the Middle Ages. It had become, much more, a possession of the schools in that epoch and, as such, no longer corresponded to the vital interests of medieval piety. The same is true of the reformation. Thus, Luther could interest himself personally in that dogma only because he reinterpreted it and interpolated his understanding of the love and the grace of God in Christ into the formula concerning the two natures. It was Melanchthon, however, who gave the keynote for his successors, and for him the doctrines of the person of Christ and of the Trinity were only difficult scholastic problems which he did not understand as being directly pertinent for the protestant understanding of salvation.[96] Therefore, if the protestant church were to link its existence and its validity to these doctrines which had become unintelligible, then, in that very act, the school element would be acknowledged as the fundamental condition of protestant church life.

The foregoing will explain the scholastic delimitation of the understanding of salvation in the Lutheran church—it came about through the restrictions which the German reformation experienced from its theological opponents and from the political demands of the Holy Roman Empire. This delimitation made itself manifest through the fact that the Lutheran church expounded its self-consciousness only through a series of doctrinal propositions, rather than by setting forth its perspective in a practical and usefully structured whole. In addition to this, the defective academic disposition which we observe in the sixteenth century theologians who followed Melanchthon's example also made a very distinct impact. This defective disposition consists of the inability or unwillingness, first of all, to consider the Christian religion in terms of its total aim, and then to identify the world, together with God and man, as the only three points through which the course of religion can be viewed as a whole and opened up to human understanding. Frankly, it is shocking that there is no mention of the practical aim of justification by faith[97] in the fourth article [on "justification"] of the Augsburg Confession. And if we explicate this aim in any terms other than those of blessedness, within present experience, and if we do not take the believer's attitude toward the world into consideration, how is it to be understood as distinctively protestant? But these considerations are never asserted as being theologically normative. With such a norm, it is easy to establish the aim of justification by faith on the basis of the Augsburg Confession, namely, that it gives certainty to the human self-consciousness over against the world through God's providence. But the necessity for viewing things in this way was hidden from the theologians of the sixteenth century. Because they were not in the position to place the practical world view of protestantism as such clearly under the above-mentioned categories, the individual doctrines which they formulated remained in a scholastic fragmentation. Thus, if they did not actually hinder the ordering of the Christian life, they certainly did nothing to facilitate it. In addition to this, John Gerhard brought about the direct perversion of protestant teaching through "school theology," in that he adopted—in accordance with an ill-chosen norm of Thomas Aquinas—the so-called natural religion or theology, and he explained faith in God's providence as a conviction that springs from a natural source when, in fact, it is a specific mark of our reconciliation with God through Christ. I have referred elsewhere to the fact that the Lutheran ascetics maintained the truth which John Gerhard's successors, in their acknowledged orthodoxy, placed under a bushel.[98] To be sure, the impact of saving faith upon the believer's attitude toward the world did not wholly sink into oblivion, even among the theologians of this period; but neither was it viewed as being of the first order of importance. Franz Balduin, Gerhard's older contemporary and professor at Wittenberg from 1605 to 1627, puts the question in his work on casuistry thus: "When we ask what, among those things by which the human spirit is cultivated, produces the most excellent faith, what things in man's spiritual activity ought to be considered?" He mentions as marks "of those things that we can point to, by which the human spirit is cultivated to true faith," first of all the love that accompanies spiritual activity; but in addition, secondly, trust in times of calamity; fifthly, prayer, which counts as its fulfillment that which is in accordance with the divine will; sixthly, firmness of hope in times when help vanishes.[99] In between these, however, there appear, thirdly, humility before God and the neighbor; and, fourthly, the confession of faith. Thus we can see that also this theologian did not recognize the full significance of faith for the attitude of the believer toward the world. And although he derives from the examples of David and Job the insight that trust in God overcomes all the billows of misfortune, he nevertheless does not always count on this support for his faith, since he adds apologetically that faith is often weak in similar situations, but that even in its weakness it is a proper faith. But on the contrary and more to the point, it is necessary in such a situation to encourage faith to strong confidence in God rather than to furnish it with a basis for formal correctness in its weakness! That is precisely the scholastic point of view, not the practical one. The former merely provides a support for slackness. And if the faith which experiences justification through Christ must necessarily consist in trust (*fiducia*) in God in order to achieve the result of comfort and a quiet conscience—that is, the restoration of self-confidence from a previous insecurity[100]—then we cannot even clearly perceive what the conditions of faith are unless this trust in God is contrasted with that situation in the world which causes one's self-reliance to be disturbed.

From the very beginning, this clarity and distinctness of principle was never achieved for the Lutheran reformation. By contrast, Calvin's portrayal of the concept of faith achieves the greatest possible fullness since here, as elsewhere, he shows himself to be the most circumspect of Luther's interpreters in regard to the structuring of the order of salvation. If we were to form a synthesis out of the different attempts at defining justification by faith which he sets forth in consecutive manner, we would find that faith consists in the moving, and therefore personal, conviction which is mediated through the feeling [*Gefühl*] of the significance of the grace of God that is apprehended in Christ.[101] Of particular importance is the fact that one must not interpret this statement as though *fiducia* were meant only as an inference from faith. Without a doubt, Calvin intends the derivation of trust from faith mediated through an apostle as an analytical judgment, for he defines the man who really believes as the one who also sets this trust in God against the evils in the world and who extends it to include all of the gifts of life which a person anticipates from God.[102] Should one not expect that this insight would have been ineradicably impressed upon the theologians of Calvin's school? On the contrary, the greatest of these, Gisbert Voet, professor at Utrecht from 1634 to 1676, as well as the entire Calvinist school, did not include *fiducia* in the concept of *fides* but distinguished it, rather, as an inference from faith. Thus he understood Calvin's statement in the fifteenth section of the *Institutes* as synthetic. Accordingly, he understands the principle that man's stance toward the world is discovered through faith as though it were only a different application of faith itself. In his disputation *de praxi fidei* [*Concerning the Practice of Faith*], the matter comes up under the category of "the acts which follow from faith, which are efficacious not in themselves, but in other theological virtues—and such are the acts of elicited hope, love, the new obedience, patience, and renewed repentance."[103] But it is only in the form of patience, cited here, that he asserts that faith maintains its power in favorable as well as in unfavorable conditions of life, in temptation and in death— and not in the form of trust in God. Thus Voet recognizes the thing that matters, but he acknowledges it merely as a postscript to faith in Christ; and he always defines even this by concentrating solely upon the theoretical act of knowing Christ.

All this adds up to the fact that the scholastic aridity of all religious knowledge is even stronger in the Calvinist-Reformed church than in the Lutheran. Calvin gave this impetus, despite his insight into the nature of faith, as cited above, through his rejection of the catholic tolerance of *fides implicita* [implicit faith].[104] Calvin rejected the idea that one might be prepared to believe all that the church prescribes, even without understanding the dogmas, on the grounds that faith does not consist in ignorance but in knowledge, and that of reconciliation through Christ.[105] As he strove to actualize this knowledge among his contemporaries in the church, he asserted that it was to be unfolded clearly and in detail, that it was to emerge from regular reading of the holy scriptures, and that it was to master a body of knowledge that was not insubstantial in scope. In other words, it was to be scholastically precise. Calvin freely admits that the faith of Christians will remain confused in many cases, that much of God's dispensation would remain hidden, and that many passages of scripture would not be understood; in these circumstances, one must simply acknowledge Christ as the best teacher. But in reality, this admission means very little when one considers the high level of religious knowledge which Calvin presupposed and strove after, above all, in his work of establishing churches. For example, when he went to Geneva he required that the citizens subscribe to a confession consisting of twenty-one articles. That was simply not practicable. In spite of this, he attempted all the more zealously to instill in the church members that which he had found missing from the very beginning—a scholastically ordered knowledge of Christian doctrine; and he attempted this through his catechism and public catechizing, imposing upon everyone the obligation to participate. For this reason, even in his church, the intellectual meaning of faith took on such preponderance that actual conviction in the content of faith assumed the position of a postscript, necessary and valuable as that might be. Now, if faith became arid and scholastic in this area also, the basic reason for it lies once again in the need to differentiate the reformation churches from catholicism. Thus, in order to differentiate oneself personally from catholic faith, the body of knowledge of the reformed system had to be appropriated by every member of the church. It was assumed that conviction, with all of its practical effects, would follow. Unfortunately, practical conviction was not necessarily linked even to such a rich deposit of traditional knowledge. For this reason, after a few generations, there were open complaints in the Calvinist areas against the barrenness and the lack of spirituality present in the literalistic faith, just as there were in the Lutheran church.

Nevertheless, it is interesting to see how a theologian from the Netherlands, Hermann Witsius, in Franeker in Frisia, expressed himself on the question of implicit faith 120 years after Calvin.[106] This man shared the complaint about the depravity and lack of spirituality in literalistic Christianity, on the one hand, but, on the other, he is very far from depreciating the scholastic imprint of the same. However, since he was a practical man, in a special sense, at the same time, he could not overlook the fact that those who were uneducated from an intellectual and Christian point of view made liberal use of implicit faith. He justified this on two grounds, one which is catholic in nature, the other, a theoretical self-deception. In other words, he first assumes that these believers grant that holy scripture is, in general, the inerrant source of all the necessary articles of belief, even when those articles are not understood; he then assumes that they hold the fundamental truths firmly in the consciousness, from which other truths are derived as necessary. This is small consolation since we cannot see how it could profit a person to know fundamental truths from which *others* may be able to derive the remaining necessary truths, even though he cannot. And yet Witsius recognizes the situation in which "someone to whom God has measured out a small portion of knowledge might nevertheless be *most firm* in the faith, *even* in *martyrdom.*" And what does he derive from that? That one ought nevertheless not consider ignorance to be the source of faith and piety! And the result? The believer must necessarily know, in general, the divine authority of scripture, and, in particular, that he himself is alienated through sin from the true life in God, that the Lord Christ is full of grace and truth, and that it is necessary to be united with Christ through the Holy Spirit and faith, not simply for justification, but also for sanctification and surrender to his dominion. This amount of theoretical knowledge is prescribed as the minimum that the believer must know! But then, how can even a slight degree of that firmness of faith be based on this knowledge which would be remotely comparable to the decision for martyrdom? Is the structure of the necessary articles of knowledge determined simply by fitting congruent components together? I should have special knowledge that I am alienated from God in sin and, only afterwards, should I know generally the grace of Christ and its possible effects! To that special knowledge of the unworthiness of my own sin must be added the special feeling of my selfhood and my significance, that I am a child of God despite sin. Without this, all the religious knowledge in the world has no meaning for strengthening faith. Therefore, if implicit faith is conceded at this point, as it must be, can we speak about it usefully in any other terms except to say that all things work for the best for those in the Christian church who love God? This knowledge is demonstrable only as personal conviction and, in this case, as the concrete perspective on the world and on life that is mediated specifically through Christ. The most telling confirmation of the fact that the Reformed church also suffered gravely from complacency toward intellectualism and was in need or reform in this respect lies in the fact that this point was not understood by them, even though they had long understood that the intellectual content of their faith was insufficient.

This error, the product of circumstance, would not have asserted itself as strongly as it did, however, if the men of the reformation epoch had not suffered from a distinctively restricted spiritual inclination. What I have in mind is their unfamiliarity with feeling [*Gefühl*]in general and with its particular conditions and relationships in the spiritual life. To be sure, the men of that era did feel, and they also permitted themselves to be moved by desire and aversion in the religious life; but it remained hidden from them that the soul exercises a third activity alongside knowing and desiring. Indeed, even a pietist writer of the seventeenth century, Jodocus van Lodensteyn by name, who took feeling very seriously into consideration, nevertheless recognized only knowing and willing in his scheme for understanding spiritual activities. However, in the sixteenth century, protestantism seems generally to have been little disposed toward religious feeling. Even the asceticism of that

period produced a stiff, doctrinaire discourse, as Stephen Praetorius's *Geistliche Schatzkammer* [*Spiritual Treasury*] indicates.[107]
It almost seems as though protestantism, since it had given up the
life of the cloister, had closed itself off from access to the exercise
of the religious feeling that was indigenous to the cloister. Or was
even the cloister barren in fifteenth century Germany? In short, in
light of the fact that men in reformation circles generally did not give
attention to the life of feeling [*Gefühlsleben*] and did not rightly
esteem it, the doctrinaire portrayal of religion in the sixteenth century
and the tendency to consider this portrayal as the only valid one are
all the more understandable.

The comprehensive view of Christianity which the reformation
assumes is thus not given adequate expression in an exclusively
reason-centered presentation of the doctrines of the gospel. Rather,
it is fragmented on the one hand and muffled and clouded over on the
other. On the contrary, it is only another kind of implicit faith that
is exercised in this doctrinaire interpretation of faith which was
intended to be set against the catholic version of implicit faith. The
reason-centered position which I have described did not enable a
person to possess the feeling of personal worth that accompanies
trust in God in a clear knowledge of the nature and significance of
this feeling itself, even though it is the mark of reconciliation through
Christ; rather, this position confused this feeling with the pride of
possessing pure doctrine or, at best it made the feeling a postscript
to the latter. The distinctiveness of protestantism is still sufficiently
discernible that almost all who count themselves as its adherents
recognize that its original manifestation was stunted or deformed.
All that is pietist and rationalist agrees in *this* judgment; and of
course even those whose ideal futilely consists in the orthodoxy of
the sixteenth and seventeenth centuries are so deeply permeated by
pietism and rationalism that they do not find fault with the scholastic
narrowing of the reformation in that period. But I mean to amplify
this observation through the opposite view—that the reason-centered
narrowing of protestantism, which was unavoidable under the circumstances, was also salutary under those conditions and useful for
maintaining the reformation. I prefer to compare the doctrinaire
narrowing of the reformation to the vestigial leaves which protect the
seed [*Keimblättchen*] as it grows into a young plant; these leaves

must remain until such time as the plant forms and grows its own leaves, which are necessary for its further life. The vestigial leaves are not of the same type as the plant's own leaves, but rather they are adequate to the conditions in which the seed is fertile. In comparison to the plant's own leaves, these protective leaves appear to be stunted or deformed, but at the same time they are indispensable and salutary for the first period of the plant's life. I wish to leave to others the judgment of whether pietism and rationalism are such vestigial organs of protestantism, which correspond to its nature as leaves correspond to the nature of their particular plants; but the efforts of the confessionalists have meant that the plant of protestantism always had to exist with only a modified type of vestigial leaf. I will agree that these comparisons are pertinent only to a limited extent. Protestantism is a common spiritual movement which, until now, has not yet gone under, in spite of the fact that it has also not yet produced an appropriate organizational form, but rather, still more stunting has followed from its original deformation.

In this respect, structures of man's common spiritual life can tolerate more than the forms of organic nature. The rule is always observed that distinctive new thrusts are not appropriated by men directly, especially in their purity and fullness; on the contrary, the habituated thrusts and traditional norms always continue in some relation to that which is new. Such compromises between the new and the old might appear subsequently to be illogical and intolerable; but for the men who are involved, the compromises are not only possible, but they are practicable precisely because they guarantee that continuity of the spiritual life which the majority of men apparently cannot do without. The individual has his continuity, even though his life achieves a meaning which is diametrically opposed to its previous course, be it through the discovery of a new direction in life or through conversion. The masses, who are not spiritually productive, but rather, at the most, are in various degrees receptive, cannot be won over to something new unless accommodations are first made to the old, or unless reversions to the old appear within the new. The masses of those who are simply receptive in nature would be corrupted if they had to experience a rupture in their spiritual life in all clarity and bluntness. But afterwards, it is necessary that these compromises not be solidified again as venerable ordinances, when they have lost their original validity and, in principle, should be disposed of.

The reversions to which I refer have appeared in the various branches of protestantism. In the Lutheran church, the institution of confession belongs under this category. It is simply a modification of the catholic sacrament of penance and, like penance, has the purpose of making the masses sensitive to the moral and religious authority of the church—an authority that they are in need of, even in protestantism. Of course pietism cast doubt on whether the purpose were being realized by this means to the extent which was desirable. At any rate, this institution does not conform to the protestant concern for the doctrine of justification. The insistence upon confession always expresses the idea that God's accepting man is actually and ordinarily dependent upon good works, and that forgiveness of sins is only a substitute because one's good works are defective. In such a context, forgiveness of sins is brought to bear only as the exception, as in catholicism; but in protestantism, the significance of forgiveness is that it is the regular basis of corporate and personal religious life. Be that as it may, this reversion to a catholic institution in the Lutheran church was popular in the sixteenth and seventeenth centuries, and it was probably no obstacle to the assimilation of protestantism's thrust by the masses. This tendency did not occur in the Reformed church. Such a circumstance, along with other factors, is usually used to support the judgment that the Calvinist-Reformed church far surpasses the Lutheran church which remained half catholic, in the purity of its protestant structure. Such is the meaning of the phrase "our church, which has been reformed according to God's word," which is opposed to the Lutheran church, which has been reformed according to God's word, but also with consideration for the Holy Roman Empire and the customs of the "coarse common man." Now this reputation of the two churches is not wholly accurate. Such a phrase seems to infer that Calvinism wishes to imitate the primitive church in organization and in world-renouncing mores to the degree that its existence within the state will allow (see p. 119 above). Calvinism does indeed comport itself so as to exclude all the institutions and cultic forms of the medieval church; but insofar as it was possible within the state, Calvin linked the thrust of the world-renouncing, holy church to Luther's principles. Now this thrust corresponds to a similar drive for reform which existed among the masses at the end of the Middle Ages, as anabaptism demonstrates. Through his personal interpretation of this element and its incorporation in his work of establishing churches, Calvin gave his congregations a power of resistance which was not native to Lutheranism; but this was still simply a reversion of the medieval ideal of reform within the scope of Luther's reformation. In Calvinism, therefore, foreign elements are bound together to a greater extent than in the so-called half catholic Lutheranism. Thus the need for reform in the two branches of protestantism is similar in respect to the doctrinaire narrowing of their understanding of faith, but it is different in respect to their retention of catholic patterns of life. The reform that pietism undertook is therefore similar in both branches of the protestant church as a reaction against an exclusively literalistic, reason-centered Christianity [*Verstandeschristenthum*]; but in spite of this, we should not expect that pietism within the Reformed church would react against the world-renouncing element in that tradition in the same way that it manifested itself in opposition to the institution of confession in the Lutheran church. Rather, in this regard, diametrically opposed phenomena manifested themselves in the two churches. The task of the history which follows [in the three subsequent volumes] is to become acquainted with the complexities of this movement.

If it should seem pertinent to begin by seeking the starting point of pietism, I would observe here that it did not begin with Valentin Weigel (pastor in Zschopau bei Chemnitz; born 1533, died 1588) and Jacob Böhme (born in Görlitz 1575, died 1624). These two men do indeed share pietism's reaction against the dominant rationalism in the Lutheran church, and they did set forth conditions for the Christian life that were of an interior and practical kind. But in all other aspects, they were unlike the pietists. Both men directly forsook the doctrine of justification by faith and therefore stood on ground that is foreign to the Lutheran church; the same is true of their philosophical interests. As followers of Theophrastus Paracelsus (professor of medicine in Basel; born 1493, died 1541), they intertwined the redemptive significance of the Christian religion with a theoretical understanding of the world which was dominated by the correspondence between nature and the spiritual life, and which, at one moment, took a turn toward pantheism and, at the next, toward dualistic materialism. It is obvious that this theosophical tendency does not stand on the same ground as the reformation. Paracelsus, a contemporary of the reformation, was and remained catholic. The fact that his world view deviated from the official pattern of Thomism does not make it either related to or analogous with the reformation. Since, as a nature-philosophy, it provides rather an impulse for referring spiritual phenomena back to powers of nature, it contradicts the tendency of the reformation, which gave practical assurance concerning the superordination of the religious and moral life to all of nature. Apart from the theosophical aspect, which took a totally pantheistic form, Weigel's practical world view stands closest to the movement of the spirituals. He relied on the fact that his view of life would come to completion in the approaching age of the Holy Spirit, when the heavenly kingdom of Christ would exist on earth through the dominion of Christ in us. He believed that the law would be perfectly fulfilled by the believers, and he prescribed the surrender of the will, so that Christ would be allowed to be efficacious within us. He counted on the complete transformation of the civil society; Christ's law rather than Justinian's would be in force; the authorities would be allowed to levy no tax, decree no capital punishment, wage no war. Common ownership of property would prevail; business would be designated as unchristian; procreation of children, and also, therefore, marriage, would be regarded as ordinances of sin. What is to be found here, then, that is not analogous to anabaptism rather than to the Lutheran reformation? The only difference between Weigel's work and the public manifestations of anabaptism is that Weigel quietly entrusted his opinions to paper in writing. And this is also true of the followers whom he found and whom Gottfried Arnold rescued from oblivion in his history of the church and heresy.[108] Weigelism had only a literary existence. Or, as the case of Ezekiel Meth[109] and Isaiah Stiefel[110] in Langensalza demonstrates, there was a circle of family and friends that was interested in Weigel's ideas at one time.

Jacob Böhme differs from Weigel in that he brought only the cosmological speculation into relationship with the Christian idea of redemption, but made no projections about the transformation of civil society. For this reason, his direct influence is also traceable only in the ties of personal friendship among those who shared his temperament. This continued to be true as individual adherents of his were filled at the same time with practical impulses from Weigel. Such was the case with John George Gichtel (1638–1710) and the "community of the brothers of the angels" that took its origin with him, and further, with the English group of the "Philadelphians," Jane Leade (1623–1704), John Pordage (1608–1688), and Thomas Bromley (1629–1691). German pietists, of course, busied themselves a great deal with reading Böhme's writings; individual groups of pietists also took over certain practical principles from Gichtel; but these practical followers of Böhme gave as little direct stimulus for the rise of pietism as did their older relatives from Weigel's party.

NOTES

1. Heinrich Schmid, *Die Geschichte des Pietismus* (Nördling: Beck, 1863).
2. [Philipp Jakob Spener (1635–1705) is considered to be the "Father of Pietism."]
3. [Joachim Lange (1670–1744) was a pietist theologian who is noted for his strong stand against dancing, card-playing, theater, and the like on the grounds of their possible immoral consequences.]
4. [Valentin Loescher (1675–1749) was one of Lange's chief opponents, who insisted that God's creation is to be enjoyed to the fullest.]
5. [Jean de Labadie (1610–1674) was a Spiritual Franciscan who became a Calvinist in 1650. He was active in France, Geneva, and the Netherlands.]
6. Johann Georg Walch, *Historische und theologische Einleitung in die Religionsstreitigkeiten der evangelisch-lutherischen Kirche*, 3 vols. (Jena: Johann Meyers, 1730).
7. [Gottfried Arnold (1666–1714) was an important early protestant historian who recognized the importance of unconventional and heretical movements in Christianity.]
8. [Christian Thomasius (1655–1728) was professor of Law at Leipzig and Halle, a pietist who was close to Spener and Francke.]
9. [In the medieval understanding of religious orders and their congregations, the first order consisted of male religious, the second order of women members, and the third order, or tertiaries, of lay people who remained in their secular occupations while living under the spiritual direction of a religious community.]
10. Max Goebel, *Geschichte des christlichen Lebens in der rheinisch-westphälischen evangelischen Kirche*, 3 vols. (Coblenz: Bädecker, 1849). The third volume was edited by Theodor Link, after the author's death on December 13,

1857. Volumes two and three are pertinent to the task that lies before us; the continuation of the work up to the nineteenth century was made impossible by Goebel's early death.

11. Cf. my *A Critical History of the Christian Doctrine of Justification and Reconciliation*, trans. John S. Black (Edinburgh: Edmonton and Douglas, 1872). [The reference is to Ullmann's *Reformers before the Reformation, principally in Germany and the Netherlands*, trans. Robert Menzies (Edinburgh: T. and T. Clark; London: J. Gladdings, 1855).]

12. [Gotthard Lechler (1811–1888) was a Leipzig professor noted especially for his work on English church history.]

13. Gotthard Lechler, *Johann von Wiclif und die Vorgeschichte der Reformation*, 2 vols. (Leipzig: Hinrichs, 1878), vol. 1. ET, *John Wycliffe and his English Precursors*, 2 vols. (London: C. K. Paul, 1878).

14. [Gregory VII was a great reforming pope of the eleventh century, who impressed celibacy and papal supremacy upon the church.]

15. [The practice whereby the secular authority invested the bishop with his authority was termed lay investiture. Gregory VII challenged this practice, thereby making the church independent of the kings.]

16. [Francis of Assisi (1182–1226) was responsible for one of the most powerful reform movements in western Christendom prior to the sixteenth century, culminating in the establishment of the Franciscan order.]

17. [This translation is from *The Jerusalem Bible*.]

18. [This reference is to *S. Francisci Opuscula sincera*, "Regulae non bullata," 1. In Heinrich Boehmer, *Analekten zur Geschichte des Franciscus von Assisi*, 3rd ed. (Tübingen: J. C. B. Mohr, 1961), p. 1.]

19. [Ibid.]

20. [Peter Waldus was a merchant from Lyons, France, who took the vow of poverty in 1176 and established the Waldensian sect, a peripatetic preaching group, committed to personal repentance.]

21. Jacobus a Vitriaco (died 1244), *Historia occidentalis*, chap. 32: "In those days the Lord added a fourth institution of religion (namely, the Franciscan order). If, however, we diligently heed the circumstances and ordering of the primitive church, we see that he did not add a new rule so much as he renewed the old; he lifted up the falling and he awakened an almost dead religion in the evening of a world traveling towards its death, at the time when the son of perdition was near, so that he might train new athletes to fight against the dangerous times of the Antichrist and so that he might preserve the church by fortifying it."

Ubertinus de Casali (Minorite at about 1312), *Arbor vitae crucifixae*, book V, chap. 3: "Jesus chose the final command for the church at the fifth period of time, awakening the men of noble truth, who by the example of their lives sharply reproved a deformed church and by the words of their preaching aroused the masses to repentance. . . . Among these men, Francis and Dominic singularly exhibited the type of an Elijah and an Enoch. . . . Because in truth, all the evil of the fifth period of time consisted in the corrupting action of a manifold vanity which takes its nourishment from the cupidity and abundance of temporal things, for this very reason that man who separated himself more radically from the temporal things that pertained to himself and his station, that man (Francis) is spoken of as the *principle reformer* of this period." See: Johann Karl Ludwig Gieseler, *Lehrbuch der Kirchengeschichte*, 6 vols. (Bonn: A. Marcus, 1835–57), II/2:325, 350. ET, *A Textbook of Church History*, 5 vols. (New York: Harper and Bros., 1871–80). [The material within the first two sets of parentheses is Ritschl's; the material within the last set is from the source he is quoting.]

22. Cf. Lucius Holstenius, *Codex regularum monasticarum et canonicarum auctus a Mariano Brockie*, 6 vols. (Budapest: Eggenberger, 1759), vol. III. Similar material occurs also in the other monastic rules which St. Francis composed.

23. [Arnold of Brescia was a powerful figure in Rome in the middle of the twelfth century. He was a compelling preacher, enthusiast, and ascetic, who influenced the masses.]

24. See Gieseler, *Kirchengeschichte*, II/2:353. "However far removed all modern religion may be from the form of the primitive church, it can nevertheless be comprehended by many people." Of the sayings of Joachim which the Franciscans applied to themselves, Gieseler's judgment is that the following is genuine (p. 354): "It is necessary that there come into being a true likeness to the apostolic life, in which the possession of an earthly legacy is not acquired, but rather is given up."

25. Johann Herzog, *Die romanischen Waldenser* (Halle: Anton, 1853), pp. 131, 141, 189.

26. Their catholic opponents deny them this claim. See Gieseler, *Kirchengeschichte*, II/2:565.

27. L. Krummel, *Geschichte der böhmischen Reformation in 15. Jahrhundert* (Gotha: F. A. Perthes, 1866), pp. 89 ff.

28. Anton Gindely, *Geschichte der böhmischen Brüder*, 2 vols. (Prague: C. Bellmann, 1857–58), I:21, 26 ff. Cf. A. Ritschl, "Georg Witzels Abkehr vom Luthertum," *Zeitschrift für Kirchengeschichte* II (1878):397.

29. Johannes Gerhardus Rijk Acquoy, *Het klooster te Windesheim en sijn invloed*, 3 vols. (Utrecht: Gebr. Van der Post, 1875–80), II:336, 671.

30. Gieseler, *Kirchengeschichte*, III/2: 675.

31. The Starowerzen [See note 26, above] were excluded from the Russian state church, and the latter manifested a fanatical aversion to them. But this was only an accidental consequence of the refusal of those Old Believers [See note 25, above] to use the reform of the liturgical manuals which had been carried out by the Russian authorities to correct their own corrupted tradition.

32. Heinrich Bullinger, *Der Wiedertaüfer Ursprung, Fürgang, Secten, Wesen* (Zurich: C. Froschauer, 1560).

33. It is not accidental that the first argument for this principle in the sixteenth century stems from Thomas More (in *Utopia*), a man of thoroughly ascetical patterns of life and a martyr for the primacy of the pope.

34. [Conrad Grebel (1498–1526) was one of the earliest anabaptists, and he

is considered to be a founder of the movement. His activity was largely confined to his home city of Zurich.]

35. [See note 25, above.]

36. [See Ritschl's article, "Ueber die beiden Principien des Protestantismus," *Gesammelte Aufsätze* (1893), pp. 234–47.]

37. [Carlstadt (1480–1541) was a co-worker of Luther.]

38. [Hans Denck (1500–1527) was a teacher in Nuremberg who became a spiritualist and anabaptist.]

39. [*LW*, 31.]

40. Karl Adolf Cornelius, in his *Geschichte des Munsterischen Aufruhrs*, 2 vols. (Leipzig: T. D. Weigel, 1855–60), II: 10 ff., seeks the roots of the anabaptists too superficially, namely, in the manner in which the uneducated people appropriated the access to the Bible which was opened to them by Luther. Heinrich Erbkam, in his *Geschichte der Protestantischen Secten im Zeitalter der Reformation* (Hamburg and Gotha: F. and A. Perthes, 1848), p. 485, points, on the contrary, to the substance of medieval sectarianism that existed prior to the reformation and was aroused anew by Luther's activity. Nevertheless, this is not a clear interpretation.

41. [Ritschl refers to an article which embodies the first four sections of this present treatise, "Prolegomena zu einer Geschichte des Pietismus," *Zeitschrift für Kirchengeschichte* II (1878):1–55.]

42. [The Observants were a rigoristic party within the Franciscans which separated into its own congregation during the fifteenth century.]

43. Gieseler, *Kirchengeschichte*, II/4:290–302.

44. Compare my study of him in *Zeitschrift für Kirchengeschichte* II (1878): 390. [See note 28, above.]

45. [*S. Francisci Opuscula sincera*, "Regula non bullata," 14. See p. 9 of the work by Boehmer cited in note 18, above.]

46. [Melchior Hofmann (1500–1543) was one of the early leaders of the anabaptists, who was active in Sweden and the Baltic area.]

47. Cf. Geiseler, *Kirchengeschichte*, II/4:302.

48. Cf. Hermann Reuter, *Geschichte der religiösen Aufklärung im Mittelalter*, 2 vols. (Berlin: W. Hertz, 1875–77), II: 364, note 17.

49. [See note 36, above.]

50. *In primum librum sententiorum*, in *Opera Omnia* (Paris, 1893), VIII, Prologi Qu. III. 14: "Sacred scripture contains sufficiently the doctrine necessary for life."

51. [The Council of Trent (1545–63) embodied the ideals of the counterreformation and led to church reform in the wake of the protestant reformation.]

52. [St. Bernard of Clairvaux (1090–1153) was a Cistercian monk who founded the monastery at Clairvaux and grew to hold great power and widespread influence in the church, because of his asceticism, his preaching, and his mysticism.]

53. See my study "Ueber die beiden Principien des Protestantismus" in Brieger's *Zeitschrift für Kirchengeschichte* I (1877): 397–413. [Reprinted in

Gesammelte Aufsätze (Freiburg, i.B. and Leipzig: J. C. B. Mohr, 1893), pp. 234–47.]

54. "Ueber den eigenthümlichen Werth und das bindende Ansehen symbolischer Bücher" (1819), *Friedrich Schleiermacher's sämmtliche Werke*. Erste Abteilung, zur Theologie, 12 vols. (Berlin: G. Reimer, 1836–49) V:451. See p. 404 in my article cited in the previous note.

55. Cf. my lecture, *Die christliche Vollkommenheit* [Critical edition by Caius Fabricius (Leipzig: J. C. Hinrichs, 1924)] and my *Justification and Reconciliation*.

56. [See note 12, above.]

57. *CA* II, "all men who are propagated according to nature are born in sin. That is to say, they are without fear of God, are without trust in God, and are concupiscent." XVI, "[Our churches] also condemn those who place the perfection of the Gospel not in the fear of God and in faith but in foresaking civil duties." XXVII, 49, 50: "For this is Christian perfection: honestly to fear God and at the same time to have great faith and to trust that for Christ's sake we have a gracious God; to ask of God, and assuredly to expect from him, help in all things which are to be borne in connection with our callings; meanwhile to be diligent in the performance of good works for others and to attend to our calling. True perfection and true service of God consist of these things and not of celibacy, mendicancy, or humble attire."

58. *De votis monasticis* (1522) *WA* VIII, 573–669. *LW* (ed. James Atkinson), 44, 245–400: "The state of perfection consists of disdaining—with spirited faith—death, life, glory, and the whole world, and serving all with fer rent love." 344: "The obedience of sons, husbands, slaves, captives is better and more perfect than the obedience of monks. . . . Therefore, if one must make the transition from imperfect to perfect, he must make the transition from monastic obedience to the obedience to parents, masters, friends, rulers, adversaries, and all others." "Temporal Authority" (1523), *WA* II, 245–80; *LW* (ed. Walther Brandt), 45: "Perfection or imperfection does not consist in works, nor does it confer external status among Christians; rather, it resides in the heart, causing one to believe more and love more; that man is perfect, whether he is externally husband or wife, prince or peasant, monk or laity." *Hauspostille über Matthäus 22:34–46, WA* 52, 489–93: "A Christian says: 'To be perfect is to fear God and love and do all possible good to the neighbor; for God has commanded nothing else.' "

59. [The *Apology* was written to answer objections to the *Augsburg Confession*.]

60. *Apology*, XXVII, 37: "All men, whatever their calling, ought to seek perfection, that is, growth in the fear of God, in faith, in the love of their neighbor, and similar spiritual virtues." [Ritschl lists other references to the *Apology*, but, due to typographical errors in the original, it is impossible to ascertain just which passages he was referring to. He may have been referring to IV, 71, 232; XII, 25, 61. See also *CA* XXVII, 49–50.]

61. *CA* XX, 24–25: "Whoever knows that in Christ he has a gracious God, truly knows God, calls upon him, and is not, like the heathen, without God. For the devil and the ungodly do not believe this article concerning the for-

giveness of sin, and so they are at enmity with God, cannot call upon him, and have no hope of receiving good from him." *Apology* IV, 4, 46, 180–82. XII, 73, 74. [References to *Apology* are misprints, corrected by editor.]

62. In *Sermons on the Song of Songs*, XLVI, 2: "In the cloisters, we live quietly, far from the impulses of the world and the worrisome cares of life."

63. In respect to Calvin, one might compare briefly, *Institutes of the Christian Religion* [ed. John T. McNeill, Library of Christian Classics 20 (Philadelphia: Westminster, 1960)], III, 2:10, 10:6.

64. Martin Kähler's review of P. Lobstein's *Die Ethik Calvins*, in *Theologische Literaturzeitung* III (1878):295–97.

65. Luther's Commentary on Genesis 1:26; 2:17, 21. *WA* 42, 41–51. *LW* (ed. Jaroslav Pelikan), 1, 55–68. Calvin, *Institutes*, I, 2.

66. [Georg Witzel (1501–1573) was a Lutheran pastor who became a Roman Catholic.]

67. See my study, "Georg Witzels Abkehr vom Lutherthum," *Zeitschrift für Kirchengeschichte* II (1878):386–417.

68. [This group emerged in the Netherlands in the 1380s, as a society of both clergy and lay, around the person of Gerhard Groote.]

69. [The Brothers of the Common Life was a movement that emerged in the mid-fifteenth century as a result of the impulse for a nonmonastic Christian form of life engendered by the *devotio moderna*. The movement flourished in the Netherlands and western Germany, where it formed numerous communities, of which the central one was at Hildesheim. Communities of Sisters were also formed.]

70. [Saint Bernard, *On the Song of Songs: Sermones in Cantica Canticorum*, trans. and ed. by A Religious of C.S.M.V. (New York: Morehouse-Gorham Co., 1951).]

71. Among Bernard's hymns, the one which is devoted to this idea is *Rhythmica oratio ad unumquodlibet membrorum Christi patientis a cruce pendentia.*

72. In *Sermons on the Song of Songs*, VI, 3. [Here Ritschl cites a long section in which Bernard speaks of Christ's human nature.]

73. [Hans Hut (ca. 1490–1527) was a chiliast and anabaptist who worked in southeast Germany.]

74. I might adduce here that Schmid, *Die Geschichte des Pietismus*, p. 442, had the insight that there was a difference between Lutheranism and Calvinism at this point; but he did not interpret it clearly, because he assumed from Goebel the concept of the church which he imputed to the Reformed churches, as if there were no Reformed confessions which in their own circles had as great value as the Lutheran confessions to which Schmid was obligated.

75. Richter, *Evangelische Kirchenordnungen* (Weimar: Verlag des Landes-Industrie comptoire, 1846), I, 158.

76. Calvin, *Institutes*, IV, 12, 1. Brenz's church-order for Schwäbisch-Hall (1526), in Richter, *Evangelische Kirchenordnungen*, I, 45.

77. [See note 26, above.]

78. Richter, *Evangelische Kirchenordnungen*, I, 25: "Two things are neces-

sary for Christianity to exist, that one hear God's word and believe in it and that one love his neighbor. The preacher's office is to preach the word of God clearly and purely; to the secular authority belongs the task of governing in an orderly fashion, that Christian love and harmony may be maintained and what is forbidden by God's word may be hindered, yea even punished." [Ritschl adduces an entire page of quotations from Richter which elaborate on this same point.]

79. This writing is not taken into account in the study by Moritz Frhr. von Engelhardt (currently professor at Erlangen), "Erasmus Sarcerius in seinem Verhältnis zur Geschichte der Kirchenzucht und des Kirchenregiments in der lutherischen Kirche," *Zeitschrift für die historische Theologie* XX (1850): 70–142. Nevertheless, the dominant thinking of Sarcerius himself is suggested on p. 89.

80. *Opera latina*, Wittenberg, IV, 514b. Walch, VI, 1632–33.

81. [Farel (1489–1565) was a leading Reformed preacher and organizer in Switzerland. Lambert (1486–1530) worked in Germany, where he was professor of theology at Marburg in his last years.]

82. Richter, *Evangelische Kirchenordnungen*, I, 36.

83. Ibid., I, 62.

84. January 1527, *WA Br.*, 4, 157–58.

85. [The Cistercian cloister in Normandy, where the Trappists emerged in 1664, was founded by Jean le Bouthillier de Rancé.]

86. [A rigorist Catholicism that attracted the upper classes in France during the seventeenth century. The movement grew up around Cornelius Jansen, but was repressed by the Jesuits and the curia.]

87. [Vincent de Paul (1576–1660) founded the Sisters of Charity, the Lazarists, and other charitable groups, as well as the *caritas* movement.]

88. Julius Köstlin, *Die Schottische Kirche, ihr inneres Leben und ihr Verhältnis zum Staat* (Gotha:Perthes, 1852), pp. 26 ff.

89. Johann Baumann, *Die Staatslehre des Thomas von Aquino* (Leipzig: Hirzel, 1873), pp. 23 ff., 141.

90. *R.u.V.*, III, 368. *ET*, section 44.

91. Calvin, *Institutes*, IV, 1, 13–27.

92. See my study, "Die Entstehung der altkatholischen Kirche," in *Gesammelte Aufsätze* (Freiburg and Leipzig: J. C. B. Mohr, 1893), pp. 186–87.

93. Ibid., p. 201.

94. [Melanchthon's *Loci communes rerum theologicarum* was his theological magnum opus. The first Lutheran textbook in Christian doctrine, this work ran through sixty editions, of which the 1521 edition was the first. Its organization features a series of propositions, rather than a logical or theological system.]

95. "Entstehung der altkatholischen Kirche," pp. 191–92.

96. Ibid., pp. 179–80.

97. [Tappert, pp. 31 f.]

98. *R.u.V.*, III, 158. *ET*, section 24, pp. 159–60.

99. Franz Balduin, *De casibus conscientiae, Opus posthumum* (Frankfurt a. Main, 1654), p. 670.

100. *Apology*, III, 178–84.

101. *Institutes*, III, 2, 7 (McNeill, 551): "Now we shall possess a right definition of faith if we call it a firm and certain knowledge of God's benevolence toward us, founded upon the truth of the freely given promise in Christ, both revealed to our minds and sealed upon our hearts through the Holy Spirit." III, 2, 8 (McNeill, 552): "that very assent itself—as I have already partially suggested, and will reiterate more fully—is more of the heart than of the brain, and more of the disposition than of the understanding. For this reason, it is called 'obedience of faith.'" III, 2, 14 (McNeill, 559 f.): "When we call faith 'knowledge' we do not mean comprehension of the sort that is commonly concerned with those things which fall under human sense perception. . . . But while it is persuaded of what it does not grasp, by the very certainty of its persuasion it understands more than if it perceived anything human by its own capacity. . . . From this we conclude that the knowledge of faith consists in assurance rather than in comprehension." III, 2, 15 (McNeill, 561): "But there is a far different feeling of full assurance that in the Scriptures is always attributed to faith. It is this which puts beyond doubt God's goodness clearly manifested for us. But that cannot happen without our truly feeling its sweetness and experiencing it in ourselves. For this reason, the apostle derives confidence from faith. . . . By these words he obviously shows that there is no right faith except when we dare with tranquil hearts to stand in God's sight."

102. Ibid., III, 2, 16 (McNeill, 562): "Briefly, he alone is truly a believer who, convinced by a firm conviction that God is a kindly and well-disposed Father toward him, promises himself all things on the basis of his generosity. . . . No man is a believer, I say, except him who, leaning upon the assurance of his salvation, confidently triumphs over the devil and death; as we are taught from that masterly summation of Paul (Rom. 8:38)." III, 2, 28 (McNeill, 573 f.): "Now, in the divine benevolence, which faith is said to look to, we understand the possession of salvation and eternal life is obtained. For if, while God is favorable, no good can be lacking. . . . By this they intimate that when God is reconciled to us no danger remains to prevent all things from prospering for us. Faith, therefore, having grasped the love of God, has promises of the present life and of that to come. . . .'"

103. *Selectae disputationes*, II, 501.

104. [*Implicit faith* refers to the readiness with which a person, especially an unsophisticated or unlearned person, may assent to propositions of belief on authority even when he does not understand them.]

105. *Institutes*, chap. 2: "Is believing, therefore, to know nothing, but only to submit your mind obediently to the church? Faith does not arise in ignorance, but rather in knowledge. . . . For we do not find salvation in that which we are prepared to embrace as true whatsoever the church prescribes, but rather when we know God the father to be our propitiation by the reconciliation worked through Christ, the Christ truly given to us for justification, sanctification, and life." Chap. 3: "Faith in God and Christ rests on knowledge, not on reverence for the church."

106. *Exercitationes in symbolum apostolorum* (Franeker, 1681), Ex. III, 9, 10.

107. [Stephan Praetorius (1536–1603) was an author of devotional literature.]

108. [See note 7, above.]

109. [Ezekiel Meth was a nephew of Isaiah Stiefel (see note 110, below), whose ideas he propagandized.]

110. [Isaiah Stiefel (1560–1626) was a disciple of Thomas Müntzer. He separated himself from the Lutheran church and actively propagated what are now considered to be anabaptist beliefs, in the province of Saxony, for which he was frequently persecuted and imprisoned.]

THEOLOGY AND

METAPHYSICS

THEOLOGY AND METAPHYSICS

Ritschl finished his magnum opus, the three volumes on justification and reconciliation, in 1874, followed in the next year by *Instruction in the Christian Religion*. This meant that his theological system was complete and in the public eye, with the result that it was fair game for the critics. After 1875, Ritschl and his disciples came under increasing fire in the journals, and beginning in the 1880s, his critics among the confessionalist Lutherans and the pietists began to attack him in pastoral conferences and provincial synods. Ritschl himself felt that he had been extraordinarily patient in the face of attacks, scarcely responding in public. In 1881, however, the attacks on his own work, as well as those on *The Doctrine of Christ's Divinity*, by a friend and disciple, Hermann Schultz, moved him to action. He was convinced that his opponents were blinded by adherence to an outmoded metaphysics which they confused with their Christian faith, and when in April a journal appeared with three articles that intensified his opinions, he interrupted his work on the *History of Pietism* to write a rejoinder. He wrote this essay between April 15 and June 6 of 1881, aiming it specifically against Luthardt of Leipzig, Frank of Erlangen, and Hermann Weiss of Tübingen. The first two were confessionalists, the third a pietist. The essay shows some signs of hasty writing, and it is acknowledged that Ritschl tends to obscure the fact that he is relying on Kant as much as on Lotze in his attack on metaphysics, just as he is vague on some of his own problems of methodology. Nevertheless, the piece gives a clear insight into what Ritschl thought was at stake in his rejection of metaphysics and what he considered to be the foundations of dogmatic theology.

The first edition appeared in 1881, from Adolph Marcus in Bonn, in the same volume with the second edition of *Instruction*. A second edition in 1887 is virtually unchanged from the first. This translation is the first to appear in English.

Theology and

Metaphysics

Towards Rapprochement and Defense

I

Christoph Ernst Luthardt,[1] on page 62 of his *Compendium der Dogmatik* (5th ed., 1878), expresses the opinion that my theology, "since it eliminates all metaphysics, places Christianity exclusively within that framework in which we concern ourselves with the value which every particular thing holds for the moral determination of man's will; this moralizing evaluation of Christianity cheapens it because it constitutes a rationalistic misunderstanding of Christianity's divine nature." This judgment, which serves as the Leipzig professor's introduction of me to his students, has caused Professor Wilhelm Herrmann to doubt whether this "censor" has ever read my *Christliche Lehre von der Rechtfertigung und Versöhnung* [*Christian Doctrine of Justification and Reconciliation*] or whether he had read it thoroughly and with the care it deserves.[2] Herrmann, on my behalf, attests to Luthardt that I have devoted the utmost diligence precisely to the effort to differentiate between the specifically religious element of Christianity (justification by faith) and the other element that stands together with it, namely, that which is attainable through moral striving. Furthermore, he stresses the fact that I have sought to insure that this differentiation would not be overlooked. With regard to this [Luthardt's] judgment upon my work, there are several further points with which I find fault. According to Luthardt (p. 11), "Restricting religion to feeling engenders mysticism; restricting it to knowing, rationalism; and restricting it to human willing or doing, moralism." If his opinion holds true, that I have cheapened Christianity itself through a moralizing evaluation, then, by his own formulation, it is not possible for me to have misinterpreted Christianity rationalistically at the same time. Finally, if it were a mistake to eliminate all metaphysics (from what? from theology, that is all I have said!) I would expect some instruction in the *Compendium* as to what metaphysical knowledge is necessary for theology. But I have looked in vain for such information, everywhere it might be given, even for the word "metaphysics." This judgment lacks the care which would have been helpful for Luthardt in opposing me, his disclosed intention being to warn others about me, *Hic niger est, hunc tu Romane caveto*[3] ["A very shady customer is he. Roman, beware of him!"].

So be it. I take Luthardt's first accusation as occasion for examining what claim metaphysical knowledge has to make in theology. This very question is the source, I find, for all possible kinds of misunderstandings among my colleagues in theology. In the hope of getting this discussion off to a good start, I have the good fortune of being able to call upon Luthardt himself who, three pages after the opinion ascribed to me, surprises me most pleasantly with the following assertion. He begins the doctrine of God in section 22 as follows: "The Christian doctrine of God is the doctrine of God as the revelation of redemption." He also adds in a note: "On this point Luther expresses himself repeatedly in opposition to the scholastics, as, for example, in his commentary on John 17:3,

> Notice how Christ, in this saying, weaves and binds together his knowledge and his Father's, with the result that therefore one knows the Father only in and through Christ. I have often said, and I say it continually, that even after I am dead, one should meditate thereupon and guard himself from *all teachers (as if they were driven and led by the devil) who begin to teach and preach from the pulpit about God alone in isolation from Christ, as, up to this time, men have speculated in the schools and have played* with his works above in heaven, as to *what he might be and think and do alone by himself.*[4]

On the basis of these statements, one would be entitled to certain expectations. They are: that the author would thereupon sketch, according to the biblical-theological method, a picture of the person or work of Christ; that he would establish upon the principle of knowledge so derived all the parts of the Christian view of the world and life, giving preeminence to the necessary concept of God. We would expect him to build his dogmatics upon the principle of knowledge derived from Christ, because it is the authoritative revelation of God for the Christian church. But this expectation is not fulfilled by the said dogmatician. On the contrary, section 23 deals with the natural revelation of God: ·

> All knowledge of God rests on revelation. There is, first of all, the general self-revelation of God the Creator within men and through the world. The consciousness of God that is thus established finds its truth fulfilled, however, only in that which is mediated through the history of salvation [*heilsgeschichtlich*].

This paragraph stands on the same page as Luther's assertion, but it is on the reverse side and thus, analogically and in fact, it turns its back on Luther's utterance. This coincidence imposed on the long-suffering page constitutes the only rational relationship to be found between the two assertions. Rather, if one has experienced the fact that he knows God in Christ and only in Christ—and this fact arises from his existence within the Christian community that theology is to serve—then other revelations of God are, at the most, only of interest when one can measure them against the revelation that is mediated by the Son. And if this revelation is not set forth within an orderly biography of Christ, the only result is a confusion produced in dogmatics by the misrepresentation of a "natural" revelation of God. As a result, the character of all the assertions in section 23 is thoughtlessness compounded by confusion.

"All knowledge of God rests upon revelation." The apostle Paul knows a widespread knowledge of God which rests upon a perversion of revelation. "Revelation is, *first of all*, the general self-revelation of God the Creator within man and through the world." In many religions, men do not believe in God as creator of the world; but all religions do believe in God or gods as the helpers and defenders of man. What the dogmatician expresses in this second assertion is not at all *close* to the first assertion but is, on the contrary, quite removed from it. This is true even when we grant its validity within the Pauline limitations just cited. In fact, the second assertion stands *close* only to Luthardt's own resolve to copy the books of certain authorities in order to bring a *Compendium of Dogmatics* into existence. "The consciousness of God that is thus established finds its truth fulfilled, however, only in that which is mediated through the history of salvation [*heilsgeschichtlich*]." If this so-called natural consciousness of God finds its truth fulfilled only through something else, then, in itself, it has no truth. Thus, in itself, it is a false doctrine of God. Or, should this natural theology stand somehow as a half-truth until it is augmented by the revelation of redemption to full truth? Unfortunately, falsity would nevertheless cling to this proposition, because the truth is not to be found by adding together the heterogeneous halves.

Nevertheless, this natural revelation of God and a part of the "Proofs for God" (section 24) form the nest in which metaphysical knowledge of God has been nurtured in the past. But, since Luthardt has not acknowledged this fact directly, I shall attempt to prove that the cosmological and teleological proofs for the existence of God belong to metaphysics and that, on that account, they do fall short of their goal. Indeed, in this manner, I shall have also justified the fact that I refrain from this use of metaphysics in theology.

"Metaphysics" is familiar as the quite fortuitous title of Aristotle's "First Philosophy." This discipline devotes itself to the investigation of the universal foundations of all being. Now the things that our cognition concerns itself with are differentiated as nature and spiritual life [*geistiges Leben*[5]]. Therefore, any investigation of the common foundations of all being must set aside the particular characteristics by which one represents the difference between nature and spirit and the means by which one knows that these groups of things are dissimilar entities. Thus natural and spiritual manifestations or entities occupy the attention of metaphysical knowing only insofar as they are to be grasped generally as "things." For the conditions of knowing that are common to the manifestations of both nature and spirit are established in this concept of "thing." The "First Philosophy," therefore, indicates the knowledge which may temporally precede or follow the preoccupation with the particular circumstances in which things are partly nature and partly spirit, but metaphysics does not surpass the philosophy of nature and spirit in value.

For either all parts of philosophy are of equal value in a formal sense, or those parts of philosophy which explain reality more exhaustively are of more value than others. According to this latter standard, however, the philosophical cognition of nature and spirit surpasses metaphysical cognition in value since, when metaphysical cognition investigates both nature and spirit, these entities are treated only generally and, therefore, superficially under the general concept of "thing." But metaphysical cognition of nature and spiritual life as "things" is *a priori*; it establishes the forms which originate in the cognizing spirit of man. These forms alone enable the spirit to rise above the flow of impressions and perceptions in order to proceed to the fixing of conceptual objects. Thus, metaphysical concepts do indeed embrace and dominate all other concepts that are directed toward the particularity of nature and spirit, and these metaphysical concepts clarify the fact that through experience the human spirit fixes its specific perceptions on things and differentiates them accordingly as natural things and as spiritual entities. However, it does not follow from the superordination of metaphysics to knowledge based on experience that one arrives through metaphysical concepts at a more basic and more valuable cognition of spiritual entities than would be the case through psychology and ethical examination of those entities. For it is only these latter forms of cognition that succeed in reaching to the reality of spiritual life. By itself, metaphysical analysis of a spiritual entity is not capable of differentiating that entity from natural entities. Such an analysis is inadequate for grasping the form and peculiarity of the spirit, and in that sense is without value.

Within the boundaries just described as thinking about things, metaphysics is ontology. In addition, it encompasses *a priori* concepts in which the manifold of perceived and presented things is ordered again into the unity of the world (be this conceived necessarily as limitless or as a whole); that is, metaphysics is also cosmology. From the concept of the "thing" which is neutral or blind toward the distinction between nature and spirit, it follows however that metaphysical cosmology is also neutral toward this distinction. Furthermore, metaphysical thought about the world is indifferent to the distinction in value by which the metaphysician, as spirit, knows himself to be set off from all nature and feels superior to it. It is at this very point that the disparity between metaphysical cosmology and every religious world view emerges. In all of its forms, the religious world view is established on the principle that the human spirit differentiates itself to some degree in value from the phenomena within its environment and from the workings of nature that press in upon it. All religion is interpretation of that course of the world which is always perceived, in whatever circumstances, an interpretation in the sense that the sublime power which holds sway in or over that course of the world sustains or confirms for the personal spirit its own value over against the limitations imposed by nature or by the natural workings of human society.

In opposition to these conclusions, the most widely circulated assumption is that religion and metaphysics either belong close together or that they are related to each other in the most intimate way. This assumption finds its most characteristic expression in the assertion, met often enough, that religion is the metaphysics of the masses! Now this combination of religion and metaphysics rests historically on the fact that Aristotle regarded it as suitable to link the word of God with the concept of the final end of the world. The fragmentary perception which orders things through the concepts of means and end, which he broadened to become the law of the cosmos, demands augmentation through the assumption of a final end according to which all things move themselves. For the final end moves all things indirectly, in that as the unmoved and self-originating conception of itself, it claims the perfection of being pure reality. Aristotle calls this end or destiny of the cosmos "God," although the final end of things does not transcend the concept of the cosmos itself. But it is devious to entitle this metaphysical postulate "God." The idea of the final end of the world does have a certain similarity with God conceived as unique in his kind; and that which Aristotle calls "God" does bear comparison with the monotheistic thrust which accompanied Hellenic polytheism. But the difference between the Aristotelian idea of God and the view of the divine being in Hellenic religion is greater than the similarity. The compassion for men in the midst of the difficulties of life, which even the Hellenic religion acknowledged was demonstrated by the gods, is excluded in the unmoved *actus purus* which the philosopher conceives of as the destiny and ordering ground of the world in general.

No veneration of God can attach itself to this idea. Similarly, the Aristotelian God is only the representation of the fate that governs even the gods. Still, this idea does indeed have a monotheistic appearance even though it is the denial of religion altogether. Where it gained validity among the Greeks, it expresses a skepticism concerning the religion practiced among them, that is, the irrepressible misgiving that the gods, who were so involved in nature, did not possess the power to fulfill the expectations that their votaries entertained concerning them. The result was fate, to which the Hellenic gods themselves were as subject as the men who prayed to them. Fate can no more be venerated as the true God than the entity in the world, which Aristotle calls God, can attract religious veneration to itself, because fate leaves men caught in their misery.[6] This entity therefore cannot rightly carry the title God. Or, if the title God does seem justified for the Aristotelian concept of the final end of the world, this is so only for heathen circles in which the specific differentiation between the world and God has not yet arisen. This state of affairs must also be taken into account in the concept of God in later Platonism, represented by Philo and the neoplatonists, which was accepted by the Christian Apologists as valid. The illimitable Being which they call God because it exists in a realm beyond the appearance of a world that is itself divided and ordered in antitheses, the entity which embraces all and excludes from itself all determinations—this entity, although it is represented as the ground of the world, is indeed merely the idea of the world itself and nothing more. Only on the level of heathenism, however, is it possible to entertain the idea of the world as God since it knows only divine beings who are involved in nature.

Two conclusions follow from this discussion. If God is the power in or over the world, venerated by man because it sustains his spiritual self-consciousness [*Selbstgefühl*] against the limitations of nature, then the idea of God does not belong to metaphysics since metaphysical knowledge is indifferent toward the distinctions of kind and value that exist between spirit and nature. In addition, when Aristotle and the Platonists (though in a different manner) set forth an idea of God which is really the correlate to their philosophical evaluation of the world in general, they manage to come to this view only within the same horizon of ideas which Hellenic religion incorporates when it commingles the divine essence with the natural world. That is, their idea of God either does not transcend the world or it merely represents the idea of the world. From this it follows that if one is able to differentiate the conditions of the religious world view from those of a metaphysical cosmology, then as a Christian, he cannot grant a metaphysical knowledge of God on which one believes for his salvation. Or if a Christian commits himself to metaphysical knowledge of God he thereby relinquishes his Christian orientation and moves to a position corresponding in general to the level of paganism. For paganism asserts as divine, entities which in the judgment of Christians properly belong to the world.

The cosmological and teleological proofs for God are metaphysical because they disregard the difference between nature and spirit, since they regard the content of the world as a chain of effects and causes. Illustrations of these proofs indeed are normally taken from the analysis of objects of nature and major attention is directed to these objects, only in respect to their general character as neutral things. Now it is remarkable indeed that the author of the *Compendium* excuses himself from working out these proofs, and is content, rather, to direct his students to all sorts of references and citations which here and there demonstrate the argument of the cosmological proof. Finally, when he does mention that in Kant's judgment the concept of causality does not reach beyond the boundaries of the sensible world, he adds: "And indeed this argument leads *chiefly* only to a 'world-ground' which can also be an immanent 'ground' in the pantheistic sense." Luthardt himself, then, as the representative of the opinion that metaphysics is an essential and valuable element of theology, agrees with me at this point: the cosmological argument is no proof for the existence of a God who is the originator of the world. For *if* one *postulates*, from a subjective standard of knowledge, that the nexus of objects is a *closed* nexus of causes and effects or that it is *a whole*, and if he proceeds correctly, then he can arrive at no other point but the knowledge that the world is one substance, one thing. The usual thrust of the argument, that the *causa sui* [the self-originating cause] which forms the end of all *res causatae* [caused things] is God, is false. The *causa sui* is each thing in itself, since at the same time, *in another relation*, it is conceived of as the *res causata.* One reaches the end of the causal nexus only by assuming a *causa sui* which is under *the same circumstances* also *causa omnium* [cause of all things]. Therefore, this "cause" is the expression of the oneness of the world which we attain on this level of reflection both at the outset and as the end result of our thinking. But insofar as this reflection is metaphysical, it has no further relation at all to the Christian religion and therefore also no specific significance in theology—and Luthardt is rather clearly aware of this. He shows that he has decided to forget this *especially* when he says that it is only *possibly* the case that the conclusion of such metaphysical reflection can be understood in "a pantheistic sense." However, this characterization of the matter is already an evasion and this agreed-upon concept of a unified world ground does not by any means enable us to arrive at a representation of God. The world ground is the representation of the world which is posited as the ground or, rather, as the causative unity of the otherwise endless number of imaginable things. Anyone who clothes this representation in terms of a "pantheistic sense" is not thinking metaphysically, but rather in Brahmanic terms. He does not, in any case, hold to the scholarly precision that is demanded in a compendium. Luthardt continues:

> But that which obtrudes urgently upon our immediate sensibilities, namely that the observation of the world in itself engenders the idea of God, also validates itself in our thinking (cf. Matthias Claudius, in his *Chrie*).[7] The finite world cannot be its own ground; *nor can nature engender spirit, nor the spirit nature.* Therefore, this world calls for a cause outside itself and not simply for a world-substance.

This would be another possible way of elaborating the cosmological argument, but how does he carry out this elaboration? Even Luthardt should recognize that "immediate sensibilities" only correspond to individual manifestations and impressions as the elemental spiritual activity and that the sensibility which accompanies our representation of the world is very much a mediated one. However, even when the consideration of the world does engender the idea of God—as in the case of Matthias Claudius—we do not construct a metaphysical argument in order to discover the idea for the first time. Rather, it is the case that an acquired and nurtured *religious*

faith in God the maker of heaven and earth is brought into primary
relationship with one's consideration of the world. This is quite
different from the cosmological argument, and Luthardt abandons
the field of this argument when he finally postulates God as being
over the world, because neither nature nor the spirit that resides in
the world permits itself to be derived from the other. Indeed, the
essential character of the cosmological argument lies precisely in its
ability to comprehend things as causes and effects, irrespective of
their differentiation as nature or spirit. As a metaphysical line of
thought, this argument actually leads only to the idea that the world
is the substance of all things, the one thing that subsists in all appearances. Insofar as Luthardt entertains the possibility that the cosmological argument leads to the supramundane God—in addition to
what I have just mentioned—he places upon that same argument
the task of differentiating between spirit and nature and the task
of clarifying the distinction between things according to these qualities, and from this thrust he concludes with the postulate of the
supramundane God. However, this differentiation is not the thrust
of the cosmological argument, but rather it is a reflection that emerges
out of the regard for the spirit that is based on the Christian religion.
And if, therefore, Luthardt attains his proof, or rather, his postulate,
for the existence of God on the basis of this presupposition, then he
himself accomplishes at this point the very thing for which he
reproaches me—the elimination of metaphysics from theology. It
has taken only a little effort to clarify his opinion of the cosmological
argument. I find that this work is permeated by an unmistakable
carelessness and this appears precisely in regard to that object which
alone makes a compendium desirable. I will let others judge how a
novice in theology would find the right path through the blinding
variation of assumptions that come together on this point.

The paragraph of section 24 which deals with the teleological argument also omits the necessary information about the form of this
argument and a clear judgment as to its possibilities for success. "The
inference from the purposefulness of the world to a highest Intelligence" is by no means a proof for the existence of the supramundane
God that we believe in as Christians. Just as we consider ourselves
justified in forming the concept of a world-whole on the assumption
of an ultimate purpose as the result of our observation of the pur-

poseful relations between things, so also we find that Aristotle has already clothed this concept with the idea of highest Intelligence. When we turn to this side of the matter, the ultimate purpose of the world is to be represented as the world soul. But if one proceeds with the teleological induction in a statistically precise fashion (others have already shown that one can substantiate innumerable cases where purposeless relationships and purposeful relationships between things exist side by side), then one reaches no goal at all in this metaphysical view of the world, least of all the safe inference of a supramundane God. The result, rather, like the familiar natural reason of the Buddhists, is that the world which embraces so many purposeless relationships within itself cannot be referred to a rational Source at all but, on the contrary, one can only conclude that it ought not to exist at all. But if the opposite seems true (namely, that the world is purposeful), the validity of that truth for us Christians is not based on a more correct metaphysical knowledge, since such knowledge is indemonstrable, but rather on an opposite religious world view. Moreover, the exclusive claim of this religious world view is certified by a totally different point of view, to which a Buddhist can scarcely be open, rather than by some reasonableness that is common to all men. The following quotation, "Insofar as *man* reflects upon the world and upon himself, he finds God in both and through this justifies for himself his immediate consciousness of God," expresses the totally hollow argumentation of section 24. I decline the task of judging the oraclelike comments on the so-called ontological and moral proofs for the existence of God which occur in these sections, since they are not pertinent to metaphysics. These arguments do not at all portray a possession common to all human reason. Rather, the ontological argument merely serves to dispel a doubt which the representatives of Platonic idealism have felt under certain circumstances concerning the success of their way of thinking. Kant's moral argument, however, stands under the unmistakable influence of the Christian world view.

II

I shall now proceed to another investigation of metaphysics in the Christian doctrine of God. Franz Hermann Reinhold Frank of Erlangen has written a curious essay[8] in which he aims to show

the error of a portrayal of the *Christian* concept of God which I
attempted in my doctrine of reconciliation, and, in the same essay,
he also strives to maintain intact the necessity of a metaphysical
origin of the doctrine of God in dogmatics. I affirmed that as a
dogmatician one has to assert the idea of God which takes its place
in the Christian view of life and the world; that one has to define
God fundamentally as he is revealed in Christ; and that one is permitted, accordingly, to take the brief Johannine assertion, "God is
love," as a theme of the doctrine of God. On these points I certainly
did not expect opposition from a Lutheran theologian. Even though
my enterprise might not be a common one for such a theologian, I
nevertheless thought that its correctness and obligatory nature would
have occurred to him as a Christian and would have been clear to
him as a Lutheran, especially since Luther so decisively rejected the
opposite enterprise and so clearly stigmatized it, as the passage cited
by Luthardt to which I referred above indicates. In my work on
justification I amplified the opinion that the assertion of the personal
character (*Persönlichkeit*) of God can only be firmly established
upon the substance of love and in the directing of the will [which is
implied in that love] toward the kingdom of God; in other words,
the world view of the Christian church is fully established upon the
Son whom God loves eternally. Everything else that pertains to the
concept of God must be demonstrated within this framework. I
assumed that everyone would recognize the appropriate substance
which amplifies the name of God in this concept of love, a concept
which entails within itself the relationship between Father and Son,
as well as the purpose which embraces the world. Furthermore, in
the will to love so defined, everyone could perceive the differentiation between God and the spiritual creatures who, according to their
form and limitations (i.e., as members of God's kingdom), become
subjects of that will to love. I interpreted John's words with this
understanding and I thought that I would be so understood by every
theologian who seeks to establish the Christian concept of God and
no other. But, on the contrary, Frank holds fast to the beginning
point of my discussion without paying attention to the way in which
I established the essential relations of the concept of love as the
title for God. Accordingly, he explains (p. 308):

God is neither exhausted nor even conceptualized when one simply assumes such a concept [i.e. Ritschl's concept of God] to be a positive concept of the divine being; for one finds, since [Ritschl] never brings it to expression, that he must always add 'the specifically divine' *since Ritschl's concept, per se, does not clarify the difference between God and the creaturely.* It is love, indeed, but divine love; personhood indeed, but divine personhood.

I reject this censure as thoroughly pointless. Because, as I explained at the end of the section to which the preceding comments refer:

God is love insofar as he establishes his own inner purpose [*Selbstzweck*] in drawing mankind into the kingdom of God as the supramundane purposiveness of man himself. . . . The kingdom of God which is formed of men is, therefore, the correlate to the divine inner purpose, and it is the goal of the creation and ordering of the world.[9]

Frank indicates where he wants to come out on this matter in the following sentences.

The predicate of absoluteness is always present where man, i.e., *a Christian*, perceives God. By means of this predicate, he distinguishes what God is from all of the factors that make up the world, not merely as an empty denial of the world, devoid of substance, but as a thoroughly positive concept, namely, as the only position which can support the *Christian* in the world and the world as concomitant with the Christian, the rock that begot us, the God who gave birth to us (Deut. 32:18). There is *nothing that is more positive than the expression of that which exists through itself [Durchsichselbstsein], in itself [Insichselbstsein], and which is in full possession of itself [Seinselbstsein].* This expression of the *absolute* is the form in which man experiences God practically, not a means of rendering God dialectically accessible. On this basis the God who was before the mountains were formed is our refuge and on this basis when we are with him, the rock of our hearts, we do not inquire after heaven and earth, or about the ultimate fate of our flesh and hearts. This *positive concept of absoluteness* is the fundamental one in all expressions of the *Christian* consciousness of God. Through this concept, to be sure, the distinction between God and the world is maintained while, at the same time, however, the other predicates like personhood [*Persönlichkeit*] and love are elevated into the sphere of the divine. (Pp. 309, 310.)

It is a shame that so much pathos is lavished on a totally false assertion! What is asserted here is not true, in any case not demonstrable,
even though these assertions are made with direct reference to the
religious reflection of Christians and, through Old Testament catch-
words, with indirect reference to the pious ones of Israel. Much
more, rather, the Christian affirms with Paul: "If God is for us, who
is against us? He who did not spare his own Son but gave him up
for us all, will he not also give us all things with him? In all these
things, we are more than conquerors through him who loved us"
(Rom. 8:31–32, 37). And the Old Testament believer acknowledged
Jehovah as his rock, because he knew him as the covenant God of his
people. But, I hear the opponent contradicting, behind the love of
the Father of Jesus Christ and behind the covenant grace of Jehovah,
the Christian, like the Hebrew, must nevertheless think of the God
of his salvation as the absolute, as the subject of the love and of the
covenant grace!

I can see in Frank's postulate, however, nothing but an unseemly
mingling of metaphysics with revealed religion. Still, one would
remain on the ground of religious reflection if he commented thusly
on the Pauline passage just cited: That One must indeed be thought
of first of all as the all-powerful One who, as the father of Jesus
Christ, shows us his love through Jesus' sacrifice in death for our
sake, and who thereby establishes the certainty that he procures for
us all good gifts; therefore we believe in him as the all-powerful One
who possesses in himself the characteristic of love for the community
of his son. We would have to believe that behind his love God stands
as the subject of all-powerfulness. But this line of thought is not the
only possible one. In contradistinction, it is also possible to conceive
of God as loving will—and this arises from his orientation toward
that community which he elected before the creation of the world,
that it might adore him. To this community his loving will appears
to encompass the world and, for this reason, is recognized as the love
that possesses the characteristic of all-powerfulness. I think that I
may assume that this latter line of thought stands closer than the
other to the pattern of thought that dominates the New Testament
sources, but enough of that for now. Frank does not make the concept of all-powerfulness the valid one for referring to the bearer of
love; rather, he stresses the concept of the absolute (*sensu neutro*)

—even though he grants that when this concept is understood as a divine predicate, it should be interpreted by reference to the same phenomenon among created beings, to which it stands in contradistinction. The absolute! How exalted that sounds! I can still recall, if only dimly, how that word occupied me in my youth, when the Hegelian terminology threatened to draw me, too, into its vortex. But that was long ago. Now, since I do not find any far-reaching ideas designated by it, the word has become largely alien to me. Literally, it means that which has been severed, which stands in no relation to another. Frank understands it thus, since he substitutes for it the expressions "to exist through oneself" [*Durchsichselbstsein*], "to exist in oneself" [*Insichselbstsein*], and "to exist in full possession of oneself" [*Seinselbstsein*]. On this basis, my opponent asserts that this concept, "is the form in which man experiences God practically, not a means of rendering God dialectically accessible." If that is correct, then at the very least the man in whom God dwells is a different subject from the Christian in general, to whom the earlier comments pertained.

The absolute, as Frank defines it, is indeed something similar to what the Brahmins assert, and the mystics in Islam and in the Christian church experience and explore it practically in that they temporarily lose themselves and their self-consciousness in universal being, but not in order to place their trust in it as the Christian does in his Father in Christ. But if the absolute is conceived as existing only for itself, outside all relationships to others, it cannot rightly be designated as "the rock which has begotten us, the God who has given us birth." For these words designate a being who does enter into relationships with others, and if these relationships are correct predicates, they are either excluded from the concept of the absolute or they call into question the definition established above. In both cases it is clear that the absolute is not a product of religious reflection, but rather is a metaphysical concept which is entirely foreign to the Christian and is current only among the mystics in the religious groups we have mentioned. In metaphysics, however, the concept of the absolute (as Frank defines it) does not possess the highest place or the most comprehensive breadth, but rather it enjoys a severely restricted realm of operation. In the explanation that Frank includes in his work, the word "absolute" designates that which can be conceived of only in terms of the unity of its internal relationships. It is something, therefore, that is represented as being incomplete since we recognize an autonomous entity as being complete, first of all, in its qualities, that is, in its effects upon our perception and upon other things. When appearances are perceived within a restricted realm in a position or in a series that remains constant and whose changes are perceived within certain limits and order, these appearances focus our thought, so that we conceive of the unity of the thing in analogy to the perceiving soul, which feels and remembers itself to be an enduring unity in the midst of the alterations which correspond to its sensibilities.[10] Accordingly, the thing that we represent to ourselves exists in and of itself. And as the soul asserts itself as the source of its changing sensibilities under the stimulation of the appearance of an object and also perceives itself, in these perceptions, as the purpose of its own self, so also the soul represents the isolated object in its characteristics as both *causa sui* and *finis sui* [cause and goal of itself]. Accordingly, the isolated object is thought of as existing through and for itself. But when it is so conceived, the object is deprived of all specific qualities. It is a purely formal concept without content. Thus we see how trivial the concept of the absolute is— the very concept which Frank proclaims as God with such gravity! But when we designate for ourselves the position that this idea rightly holds, then another factor must be taken into consideration. Namely, the absolute is not at all conceived of as complete, except in a preliminary way, when we visualize it across the boundaries of our cognition as an isolated object outside of the relationship to us which makes it possible for us to sense its qualities and represent its unity in itself. And if we wanted to deny this obvious relationship, even in regard to the isolated object, we would be talking nonsense, because an object in and of itself would be inaccessible to our perception and representation. And, finally, if we were to affix the predicates of personhood and love to the absolute which Frank designates as the basic representation of God—in order that one could raise the concept "into the sphere of the divine"—we would discover that this cannot be easily done. Both of these predicates express relationships to another. Love is conceivable only with an object, and personhood only as a distinctive relationship of the spiritual life to the world or to other persons. If the absolute, isolated and without qualities, is conceived of with such predicates, then either these predicates contradict their subject, or it is not possible for us to infer the assumed subject from these predicates. One can say all he wants, therefore, about the object which stands outside all relationships to another possessing love for others or even indeed being that love—but such talk has no useful meaning. And with his absolute, Frank really establishes nothing else but a metaphysical idol which, moreover, cannot support the distinction between creator and creature.

For many men there must be a singular attraction in the prospect of knowing something about God *a priori*. Frank sacrifices every other consideration to this attraction; the unclear, confused idea of God that he forms is set forth as the foundation of religion. But at the same time he freely grants that this idea does not exhaust the necessary religious knowledge of God. But he does have to take account of the familiar representations such as personhood and love, which arise from positive religion and to which the metaphysical concept of the absolute cannot relate itself. Consequently, he has attached them quite externally to the metaphysical concept, with the result that the concept of God is expressly established as an aggre-gate, as an edifice of several stories whose foundation is incapable of sustaining the superstructure. Friedrich Adolf Philippi's *Kirch-liche Dogmatik*[11] has already set forth such an aggregate, whose parts are layered one upon another and which is characterized by numbered parts, like a column of figures to be added. In this work, the attri-butes of God are ordered according to the "three phases in which the divine being discloses itself to us, in ascending stages": God (1) as absolute substance, (a) eternity, (b) omnipresence; (2) as abso-lute subject, (a) omnipotence, (b) omniscience; (3) as holy love, (a) wisdom, (b) righteousness, (c) goodness. This is a clear renun-ciation of the proper concept of God, namely, one that articulates his unity. This error, however, stands in direct relationship to the fact that the individual "phases" of the divine being are derived from differing epistemological bases which do not enjoy equal validity in theology.

I have still another claim to establish in this matter. Frank, since he chooses a metaphysical construct to be the vehicle of his Chris-tian cognition of God, thereby permits himself to be led astray into a peculiar error, when he judges my thinking which is contrary to his. He deceives himself in thinking that I go astray by defining the will of God, as it is revealed in Christianity, in an *a priori* fashion with the concept of love—as if I proceeded in the same way he does in his definition of the absolute. He analyzes a formulation of mine, which he had previously left unnoticed, that God is recognized as love in that he actualizes his purpose for himself [*Selbstzweck*] and his purpose for the world in the kingdom of God. In an attempt to demonstrate once again his concept of the absolute, he makes the following comments against this statement:

> The execution of this purpose (of the kingdom of God as God's purpose for himself) cannot actualize itself save in a way that is commensurate with the nature of man, namely, that man comes into communion with God as a person with free choice. God can determine man to such communion, and he can create him and equip him accordingly; he can also guarantee to man, as a sinner, the possibility of returning to this communion, but always under the condition that man will accomplish this actualization of his will as a person in free autonomy, since he has intended man to be a person and created him thus. However, if one conceives things in such a way that God, out of love, makes the purpose of his kingdom the correlate of his own purpose for himself, without adding absoluteness to love as its basis, then one of two things will happen: *either* God will carry through this correlate of his self-purpose under any and all circumstances, *or* if he does not carry it through, then when he abandons the correlate he abandons his purpose for himself at the same time. The one alternative is as impossible as the other. God cannot compel man to take part in his community. . . . It is just as impossible, however, to conceive that God should cease to be himself, which would logically follow upon his abandoning his purpose for himself. This unacceptable consequence is the result, therefore, of the unacceptable presupposition.[12]

True! Except that the unacceptable presupposition is my opponent's and not mine! If he had read my presentation fully, instead of reading only one paragraph and stopping before he got to the following comments, then he could have seen (cf. *R.u.V.*, III (2nd ed.), 265. *ET*, section 34) that (in accordance with the testimony of Christ and the well-established experience that rests on faith in him) I presuppose the kingdom of God in the community of Christ as being in some sense real when I speak of the relation between the

love of God and the men who are united in the kingdom of God.
For I have derived the description of God as love only from the
knowledge which Christ has mediated to his community. If my
opponent deceives himself that I spoke in this connection *a priori*, in
the sense of a hypothesis, then he subsumes me under a heading
diametrically opposed to that which I truly represent. These two
absurd alternatives, which he wishes to place upon me, grow only
out of his presupposition that I choose a starting point for my theology as untenable as the one he has chosen for his.

And what does he gain from his own hypothesis of the absolute
by way of contributing a resolution of the difficulty which he has
fashioned from the two impossible consequences of his misunderstanding of my teaching? He says:

> Things take on an entirely different form when we take the creation's
> being-for-God up into God's being-for-himself as an expression of his
> absoluteness and then establish on this basis the love of God which is
> included in the divine being. For here, then, there is an implicit insist-
> ence that man's being-for-God can and must actualize itself even when
> he sets himself against *the loving will of God, which itself exists in
> man's being created for God.* For even the repression of the sinner
> under the divine ordinance against his will is the realization of his
> being-for-God; this being-for-God must come to the fore, for the sake
> of God's absoluteness, even when it cannot do so in the form of a
> .voluntary being-for-God to which God's loving will relate itself.

When one grasps this line of reasoning, he may indeed be astonished.
Frank attempts to incorporate the thrust of mankind's tendency
toward the absolute within the concept of the absolute as that concept serves as the basic formulation for God. But how is this possible, since every relationship to another is excluded from the concept
of the absolute, including also every relationship of another to the
absolute itself? For in this case a reciprocal relationship is indicated
over against which the absolute excludes itself. This is no exercise in
consistency but merely a play on words. But let us go on! Is it possible for my opponent to think that the loving will of God lies in the
thrust of mankind toward the absolute? What a strange way to
express oneself! What expectations this lays on the powers of the
imagination! Is the attribute of love for God equivalent to the concept of mankind's thrust toward God? Or is it set forth as a direct

correlate of this thrust? I do not know. Toward what kind of a theologian is this assertion directed? I take the liberty simply to reject such theological instruction. What it amounts to for my opponent, however, is this. He combines the thrust of mankind toward the absolute with the absolute itself, that is, with the isolated object (that possesses no qualities) which he equates with God. He does this in order to make the attributes of love and legal righteousness into correlates of equal value with the freedom of the created spirits, so that he can hang them like alternately coordinated characteristics on both arms of the great "X" which is the appropriate image of his idea of the absolute. With this, he opens our eyes to another chapter of natural theology which really does not exist. I decline this opportunity, however, to go into the question of God's recompensing righteousness and the covenant of works.

III

It is understandable that one would make use of metaphysical concepts, assigning to them the highest priority in systematic theology, if he understands the task of systematic theology to be the harmonization of Christian revelation, that is, the Christian world view, with that comprehensive secular world view which is thought to be preeminent because it claims to be both universal and rational. But the preceding discussion has shown that such an attempt in systematic theology is, by its very nature, a rationalistic misuse of reason in theology which diminished the value of the knowledge of God that we obtain from revelation—even though both Luthardt and Frank may affirm or demand such an attempt. Moreover, this is Luther's judgment also, as may be seen in the above-cited passage from Luthardt. It is more difficult to understand the supposition of metaphysical concepts in the interpretation of certain Johannine passages where Christ speaks of his unity with God the Father (cf. John 10:30; 17:11; 21:22). I am not referring to the interpreters old and new who impose dogmatic propositions upon every passage that even faintly echoes them as they expound the biblical writings. Calvin has already protested such practices, in comments on John 10:30:

> The ancients misuse this passage when they prove that Christ was consubstantial with the Father. For Christ did not dispute about the unity

of substance, but rather, concerning the unity of mind that he had with the Father; whatever is clearly performed by Christ is confirmed by the goodness of the Father.[13]

Heeding this admonition, Friedrich Lücke, August Meyer,[14] and Luthardt understood the meaning of Jesus' saying in accordance with its context, that Jesus here clarified the equality of his power with God's, and, as Meyer rightly adds, in qualification, this equality lies in the unity of activity in carrying out the redemptive will of God. But this exposition of Meyer is accompanied by another comment which reintroduces the interpretation just discarded: "The homoousion is *presupposed* as the essential basis of this communion between the Son and the Father, because of the metaphysical relationship of the Son to the Father which is clearly attested, particularly by John." Luthardt considers this postscript to be correct, inasmuch as he attaches similar reflections to his interpretation of the text. These two also agree in their exposition of John 17:11, 21, 22, that the unity between the Father and the Son, as it is compared with the unity of the faithful among themselves, pertains not only to the will and disposition but designates beyond that something that is different and higher. As Luthardt expresses it:

The Father and the Son should be the element in which the faithful live and move in a mystical union (*unio mystica*). . . . The faithful are not only united with the Father and the Son in their will and disposition, but rather, in their *own actual being*, without ceasing nevertheless to be creaturely and sinful.

It is very easy to write such a thing and let it be published, but it is very difficult for others to understand it and more difficult still to accept it as a true representation of the ideas Jesus had in mind. These few statements of Luthardt appear to me as so many unbearable burdens which the author himself will not even lift a finger to help us carry. I am to imagine that my will—that is, my disposition in which I form my purposes and designs and which calls forth and directs my activity in the community of the faithful, my will which moves itself in the direction of God and his purpose—I am to imagine that all of these are not actually my own being, but are really only a derived and apparent being! Indeed, in the light of this

being which is unreal and not my own (according to Luthardt) I
know myself, exercise my responsibility, have the feeling of my own
distinctiveness and worth. And, in relationship to this being, I rebuke
myself before God or experience my blessedness. But I know nothing
about this thing Luthardt calls my "actual and authentic being," that
is, my metaphysical being. I experience nothing of it and cannot
orient myself according to it. And Luthardt himself cannot teach me
anything about it, since he too knows nothing of it. Further, it is
said that "the Father and the Son are the *element* in which the faithful live and move: *unio mystica.*" I would demand an explanation of
the word "element," if I were not further enlightened as to his
meaning by the term *unio mystica,* which Luthardt attaches as a
synonym. As a "repristinating theologian,"[15] he undoubtedly intends
the concept, a feature of seventeenth century Lutheran dogmatics,
to be predicated of every individual believer. Thus, after justification,
the Trinity takes residence in the believer with the proviso that this
unio cum patre, filio et spiritu sancto [union with the Father, Son,
and Holy Spirit] is neither *substantialis* [substantial] nor *personalis*
[personal] but, rather, *mystica* [mystical], which is to say, indeterminable. This means that one should not think of this unity, as did
Philipp Nicolai,[16] as one in which the believer is amalgamated with
God into one cake or lump and thus partakes of divine nature, nor
should one assume, as did Stephen Praetorius,[17] that the believer is
divinized and therefore can rightly say that he is Christ. I assume that
I am dealing, in these distinctions, pertinently with the idea Luthardt expresses in *unio mystica.*[18] According to his view, therefore,
our Lord Christ had in mind this concept of *unio mystica,* as we have
defined it, since he did not apply the unity of the believers to their
disposition as such, analogous to his substantial unity with the Father,
but rather to their actual and authentic being and only by implication from that to their disposition. If these remarks do not deal pertinently with the author's meaning, then I can only complain that he
does not speak clearly.

Therefore, I shall recapitulate here Luthardt's probable meaning
on the basis of the two assertions which are not fully in accord
with each other but, rather, which are ranged against each other. The
will, even though it is orderly and stable in its disposition, whether
for good or evil, and is necessarily accompanied by a corresponding

cognition and governing self-consciousness, still does not set forth the actual and authentic being of a man. Since this is true of the will, we must also say that the unity of the believer with the Son and the Father, patterned after the unity between God the Father and his Son, is not to be understood in terms of the unity of will that exists among all men in the purpose which the Son (and in him, the Father) carries out in establishing the redemption of the believers. Rather, this unity between the believer and the Son and the Father is to be understood as a more significant reciprocity between these parties, and this reciprocity, which lies behind the volitional unity, is neither an identity of essence nor of personal life but an identity which, according to its nature, is indeterminable, that is, the *unio mystica*. In this line of reasoning we observe that a metaphysical distinction is placed between the unreal, inauthentic being of spiritual persons (which is equated with will and disposition) and their real being which is posited only for the sake of the concept which Luthardt esteems so highly, the *unio mystica cum tota sancta trinitate* [mystical union with the complete Holy Trinity]. The saying of Christ is explained on the basis of the religious concept of the *unio mystica* and not directly in a metaphysical manner even though the explanation is analogous to the metaphysical distinction between the authentic and inauthentic reality of man. These ideas of the metaphysical and the religious are ranged against each other but they share one common ground, they are both totally unclear. The only thing we experience in the "real and authentic being" of man is that it does not consist in his disposition. What can we say of the *unio mystica*? I can only assume—in line with the older dogmaticians—that our proponent means that the *unio mystica* is to be conceived of neither as *substantialis* nor as *personalis*. Therefore, if the *unio mystica* is the key to understanding this saying of Christ, then metaphysics is not the direct criterion of Luthardt's interpretation of it at all. Thus one cannot perceive here a misuse of metaphysics which compares to that noted in earlier examples of his theology.

Indeed, there is such a close relationship between mysticism and *this kind* of metaphysics that it is immaterial whether one counts certain affirmations as mysticism or as false metaphysics. In order to perceive this one must define mysticism in its original sense and scope as a method of religious life and yearning, rather than in the special formulas of the later Lutheran dogmaticians. In the mystical method, the important thing is to go beyond the individuality of the spiritual life which maintains itself in discursive knowledge and in ethical action that contributes to the common good. Rather, one must transport oneself to the realm of one's real and authentic being. This is to be achieved when one loses himself, either through theoretical intuition or through the negation of one's own will, in the universal being which is considered to be God. The only conceptual scheme in which this process is intelligible is the neoplatonic with its deprecation of all particular, determinate being and life in favor of universal being. Thus, according to the criterion of universal being, the particular and determinate are predominately deceptive and unreal whereas the universal being is the real, with the added meaning of being authentic. Therefore, a manner of life which bases itself on this understanding will consequently lead one to conclude that his goal is the dissolution of his own distinctiveness into universal being. Hence, mysticism is the practice of the neoplatonic metaphysics, and this metaphysics is the theoretical norm of the so-called mystical enjoyment of God. But it is a deception to believe that the universal being into which the mystic wants to melt is God. For the only consonance between the idea of God and the concept of the universal, indeterminate being lies in this, that God is not the world and that the universal, indeterminate being is the negation of all those characteristics by means of which we know the world which fills our perceptions. At the same time, we may say that the neoplatonic God is also the idea of the world; and as such it is the universal, colorless scheme in which all particularities and interrelations of things are eliminated but which, as an idea in the Platonic sense, is nevertheless set forth as the real, authentic being.

Gottfried Arnold has rendered a most noteworthy witness to the collapsing of this sort of metaphysics into practical mysticism.[19] For example, at one point, he shows in parallel columns the three paths to the secret knowledge of God according to the instructions of the books of the most all-wise King Solomon.

The secret learning of God, belonging to the *path* which unites, illumines, and *reconciles*, is taught, respectively, in Proverbs, Ecclesiastes, and *Song of Songs*. . . . In like manner, there is a threefold love of wisdom, *Ethica, Physica,* and *Metaphysica* which deals with morals or external works, with natural things, and with *spiritual matters.* In such a manner Solomon would teach love of wisdom in his position as an ethical teacher who deals with virtues and would instruct his children as a father; as a teacher of natural things he would differentiate things according to their natures and as a physician would heal the sick; similarly, as a teacher of supernatural things *he points to the divine and as a learned man of God would lead men to God.* . . . That teaching which Solomon considered most necessary was how to live peacefully in the world, despise the vain and unworthy, *and through love to enter into communion with God.* . . . So that man might know how to live well in the world and to subject the world, after he had recognized it, to himself, *that he might ascend to the embrace of the bridegroom.*

These juxtapositions continue for ten pages. Nevertheless, I have the following comments to add to the statements just cited. Metaphysics and mysticism were identified by Arnold; and ethics was subordinated to them as the most elementary and least valuable stage of knowledge and practice. Indeed, even physics was placed above ethics. Meanwhile, one also recognizes that the combination of the second stage of wisdom with the Preacher Solomon is related to the rejection of the natural world in asceticism in accordance with his saying, "All is folly." Therefore, if the first stage is meant to be *natural* morality, then it is clear why he ranks asceticism above it, since asceticism is the rejection of the natural. Then the second stage is, at the same time, characterized by man's *knowing how to subordinate the world to himself,* since this ascetical predicate is excluded from the ethical life of the first stage. I would here refer incidentally to my description of the ethical determination of man in Christianity. In keeping with the concept of the kingdom of God, I emphasize the supernatural and supramundane character of man's ethical calling, and I have expressly shown how the believer exercises spiritual dominion over the world in accordance with his justification through faith.[20] Thus I deplore the fact that Luthardt, in his reproach of my "moralizing interpretation" of Christianity which he considers erroneous, thereby also loses the ability to distinguish between natural morality on the one hand and supernatural, world-dominating piety and ethical action on the other. In comparison, however, I do not find the so-called higher metaphysical path to mystical union a more valuable method than this ethical life-style [*Lebensführung*] which I characterize as Christian, nor do I recognize the mandate of Christianity in the goal of mystical union.

I return now to Christ's saying whose exposition gave rise to these controversies. Why have Meyer and Luthardt not simply contented themselves to explicate the unity of the apostolic community (identical with the unity of the Son with the Father) in terms of its basis in a common purpose of the will or disposition? Why have they deliberately made its meaning unclear by mixing a metaphysical distinction and an unintelligible mystical formula? Because a mixing of metaphysical concepts is at hand in the Nicene definition of the relationship between the logos of God and God. This mixture rings in their ears and dominates all the impressions which they might have gotten from the scriptural manner of viewing things, even though they are obligated to expound this point of view in the context of scripture's own terms. Thus, when less clear sayings present themselves in a piece of scripture, as in the Johannine witness to the unity of Christ with God, then these passages are to be clarified by comparing them with parallel sayings which are clear in their own way. Meyer has done this with John 10:30, where he explains the unity of Christ with God in terms of the identity of their working for man's salvation. But it is interesting to note that he fails, at the same time, to go into the passage in which this thought first appears, namely, 4:34, and he only notes the later expression in 17:4. Meyer's interpretation of 4:34 transposes the metaphorical expression "food" in the following sense: "It is my pleasure to carry out the work of God." But it is much more appropriate to the context if one says: "Carrying out the work of God *is the means by which I maintain myself.*" Luthardt has not interpreted this passage at all; he has simply designated it as full of meaning. He can hardly hold it against me, therefore, if I use it as the key for the interpretation of the less clear sayings of the Lord. For the Son's unity with the Father, or the coinherence of both [*Ineinandersein*] should indeed designate something real. Within a person's life, however, reality cleaves to his spiritual activity and to nothing else. And he who can honestly say of himself that the total activity of his vocation is the work of God can demonstrate this alleged unity with God in his life-work [*Lebens-werk*]. Therefore, the ethical perspective still obtains here. If any-

one recognizes in what I have just said something that is unworthy
of the divine level of Christ's self-consciousness, then he must hold
to Arnold's understanding of the conditions of the will; namely, that
the will can be conceived only as the bearer of natural morality.
Meanwhile, it is precisely from Christ himself as he appears in all
of the Gospels, that we learn that under his guidance the human will
is destined to grasp the supramundane goal which corresponds to
the cosmic purpose of God as he set it forth in Christ, namely, the
salvation of man. The overcoming of the world which Christ designates as the accomplishment of his own life is the proof that his
solidary unity with God is actual in his will, to which he holds fast
even under the opposition of the God-defying tendency of the world.
This conclusion corresponds to the exposition of Christ's words in
John and it takes as its criterion the context itself.

What would it mean if one understood the passages in question
metaphysically? Metaphysical concepts are the elementary cognitions
in which one determines the objects of cognition as such, as things in
general, in their isolation and moreover in their given positions vis-
à-vis each other. In this way of looking at things, one avoids the task
of distinguishing whether objects of cognition are nature or spirit.
Therefore, the metaphysical method only allows one to perceive
spiritual entities superficially, incompletely, and not in their distinctiveness. If Christ, therefore, in the sayings which lie before us,
designates the unity he shares with God as that which actually exists
between him, a spiritual person, and God, who is spirit and will,
then (of necessity) he did not practice a metaphysical way of thinking. Nor should we think that Christ was capable of ordering his
self-consciousness according to the categories of metaphysical and
ethical knowledge; for he was certainly not a philosopher. And
even if he were such, or were to be compared with philosophers, it
would be absurd to attribute such distinctions to him. For even a
philosopher, if he is a wise man, will not express the distinctive
self-awareness, by which he knows himself, in metaphysical concepts as such, nor will he express himself by blending the images by
which he designates himself as a spiritual person with metaphysical
concepts.

From the point of view I am representing here, that classification
is also valid which includes the unity among the disciples with the

unity that exists between the Son and the Father. Both of those interpreters note Johann Bengel's saying in reference to John 17:11: *Illa
unitas est ex natura, haec ex gratia; igitur illi haec similis est, non
aequalis* [That unity is one of nature, this one, of grace; therefore,
this one is similar to that unity, not equal].[21] Neither interpreter
could understand this comment to mean that the one unity is metaphysical, whereas the other is ethical; for both are metaphysical
according to Meyer and Luthardt. But I would be able to appropriate
Bengel's comment when I interpret both instances of the unity
ethically. That which pertains to Christ is *ex natura* ["of nature"]
insofar as Christ is presented to our cognition in that communion
with God which remains constant and without change; so that what
he performs in his life (*sein Lebenswerk*) is the work of God. To
the degree that a man wants to be a Christian, he has this datum
which he must acknowledge as given: the relationship to God which
is expressed by Christ and sustained by him through his death and
resurrection. One must avoid all attempts *to go behind this datum*,
that is, to determine in detail how it has come into being and
empirically how it has come to be what it is. These attempts are
superfluous because they are ineffectual; and it is dangerous to give
oneself to these attempts since they are superfluous. The corresponding unity of the community with Christ and God, however, is *ex
gratia* ["of grace"] because in the community we only see men who,
in themselves, cannot give testimony to this unity with God. Moreover, in themselves, these men give the appearance of changeableness
which is not present in the given appearance of Christ, thereby indicating that this unity can only be accounted for through God's grace.

IV

In their presentation of the dogmatic teaching about God and
in their exegesis of the Johannine Gospel, I have shown that my
opponents are guilty of an improper and unsuitable use of metaphysics. Their exegetical work also brought before us the use of a
false metaphysics. This false metaphysics was mixed in with their
exegesis only because my opponents dispersed it over the entire
range of their theological perception. I do not think that Luthardt
has paid attention to this fact, since he has counted it an error in
my work that I eliminate all metaphysics from theology. But his

aversion to my theology and his inability to judge it justly arises from the fact that I use a different epistemology and the way I grasp the object of knowledge is different from his work, which represents what has been established and handed down. Because I determine the contents of theology in a manner to which he is not accustomed, he cannot understand why I teach many things that have not occurred to him, and why I leave many things aside on which he sets great value. And my relationship with him is similar to my relationships with many others. Therefore I am all the more interested in demonstrating that the metaphysics and, specifically, the ontology (i.e., the use which one makes of the concept of that which is the object of knowledge) which I use differ from that of my opponents. And, at the same time, I will also demonstrate that my opponents, in that they represent the theological tradition, utilize a false epistemology. In addition, it will hopefully become clear that when they allege that they surpass me in their concern for Christianity, it is only a deception which mirrors their unexamined faith in a false epistemology.

There is a commonplace view of the things we know which, upon closer examination, is shown to suffer from an error, namely, that it is uncertain in its ability to make distinctions as well as premature in its tendency to unify things. In this commonplace view, the impressions [Empfindungen] mediated through our senses [Sinne] are the first and last guarantee that the things we perceive through the sensations [Empfindung] they excite are actually present or real. And this view is held in spite of the fact that we deceive ourselves in many of the perceptions which accompany our sensory experience [Empfindungen] and which subsequently even confirm these deceptions. We consider that things we perceive and sense are real even when we can only recollect our sense-impressions [Empfindungen] of them from our memory, because we justifiably assume that others have had perceptions just like ours in the meantime. And it is precisely at this point that the commonplace view draws the conclusion that the things which are present to us can be grasped as they are *in themselves* through subsequent precise representation and study. This fixed distinction between things as they are in themselves outside any relation to our sense-impressions [Empfindung] and perception and their existence *for us* is the first error of the commonplace view. Because things are separated here which, in the light of the origin of the process of knowing, belong together.

In addition to the relationships in which we perceive the existence of things generally, there also belongs (necessarily and unfailingly) the relation of those things to us as subjects of the acts of receiving sense-impressions, perceptions, and mental images. And even though a person can forget this additional relationship in many instances, it should never go unheeded in scientific reflections, i.e., precise and complete reflections. For things which we might posit and define for experimental purposes, in and of themselves but not in their relation to us, are necessarily unknowable to us. Yet a person conceals this truth from himself when he thinks that in the relationship of things to us there is only a mass of false, deceiving appearances, and when he tries to guard himself from these appearances by grasping things in and of themselves, as they exist for themselves. But indeed, by this procedure, one is really only yielding again to the appearance, namely, that in the relationship of things to us, there is always deception and only false appearance.

Now even if it were taken for granted that the above were correct, it could not be verified; there could be no criterion for judging the matter. But one quickly ascertains the reliability of appearance (admittedly, a limited reliability) when, in several different instances, the consensus of many persons' perceptions establishes that things are indeed what they have appeared to be to us. And if God belongs to the objects of cognition of scientific theology, then there is no satisfactory basis for the claim that one can teach something about God in himself, something that is allegedly knowable for us apart from his revelation which, however it is fashioned, is sensed and perceived by us. Yet this claim is made by my opponents. By Frank when he pretends to think of God as the absolute; by Luthardt (in section 29 of the work referred to above) when he teaches about the characteristics of God's nature *in itself* which, he thinks, can be known prior to those attributes of God that are efficacious for us. In these instances, therefore, they adhere to the false metaphysics of the commonplace level of human reason, a metaphysics which is not scientific truth, even though it has found its place in the textbooks of metaphysics since the time of Christian Wolff.[22]

The second error of the commonplace view of things lies in the fact that the image we form in our memory, in which we fix the repeated perceptions of a thing, does not take into account certain alterations which we have subsequently perceived from time to time in that very thing. The recollected image [*Erinnerungsbild*] is attached to the thing through intentional abstraction from the changing appearances of the thing. Under such circumstances, the recollected image asserts a solidity and clarity in the ordering of its characteristics which does not correspond precisely to any of the individual observations in which the thing was originally given to our perceptions. Yet the essential characteristics of the thing, characteristics in which it exists as actual in distinction from the accidental characteristics in which it appears as changeable, are ascribed to this recollected image. In our original sense-impressions we persuaded ourselves both of the reality of the thing itself and of the reality of its changing appearances [*Affectionen*]; the sense-impressions are aroused within us by these appearances, and we compensate for their changeableness by means of the continuity of our own self-consciousness. Now the placid image of a thing in one's memory certainly does not stimulate the kind of sense-impressions that we actually receive from the appearances themselves as they strike our senses. Yet an interest, a feeling for the value of the thing, attaches itself to the recollection. The recollected image preserves this interest so that it directs, abbreviates, and facilitates future observations of the recollected thing. This feeling for the value of a thing, in one's recollection of it, is then made equal with the sense-impression which originally authenticated the reality of the thing in its immediate perception. And so ordinary human reason carries with it two kinds of impressions of the reality of a thing; and as long as this reason continues in its conventional manner, it does not take time to scrutinize them precisely and fully. But if on this level of cognition one is led to undertake a comparison between the immediate perception of a thing and the image of that thing in one's memory, that is, between the perceptible changeableness of the thing in its appearances and the solid and clear delineations of the recollected image, then the way is open, under such circumstances, for him to observe an error in his cognition. A person entertains the recollected image in a dimension which lies behind the circumstances in which the immediate perception of the thing unfolds. Thus he separates all those aspects of the perceived object which stimulate our senses directly from the characteristics which make our recollection firm and clear. We can conceive of that which stimulates our sensibilities in no other way except as the relationship, movement, and activity of the thing itself. Therefore, we can justifiably posit a thing as real only as it stands before us in the realm of appearance. We must judge our recollected image—which we have placed in a realm "behind" the thing—to be unreal to the extent and in the sense that its placidity and indifference hold it aloof from the activity of our senses. Yet, in these circumstances, ordinary reason makes its judgments as if the thing whose recollected image carries with it both placidity and indifference were actually presented in that fashion to us in the *moment* that our sensibilities were stimulated by the movements which we perceive in the "front realm." Nevertheless, the discrepancy between the "back realm" position of the recollected image and the "front realm" position of the thing as it stands in the flux of time does not at all permit us to transfer the characteristics of the thing to its recollected image. For in the arrangement of the momentary and the lasting realms, one behind the other, the two images of the same thing are bound to be opposed to each other despite all their similarities. Thus the one realm is dynamic, changeable, and possessed of efficacy, while the other is placid, indifferent, and without relationship to anything else. Therefore a contradiction results when a thing, presupposed to be placid, indifferent, and powerless in our recollection, is at the same time represented as moved and moving, changing and alterable. Such inconsistencies do not matter to unscientific thought. But it is insidious when this false combination of recollected image and direct perception of things is also found in scientific metaphysics. For the assumption that one can know things in themselves, i.e., spatially "behind" and temporally "before" their appearance, is nothing but a deceptive distortion of the recollected image which one acquires "behind" the first observations and which he carries with him "before" subsequent observations. The recollected image is overvalued or improperly cherished when a person substitutes it for the actual reality of a thing, even though we rightly treasure it because it serves to simplify and stabilize our cognition. I will grant that the solidity and clarity which the image bears in itself seem to justify themselves since these characteristics bid fair to satisfy the drive for cognition. But there are, on the other hand, other aspects of the recollected image, namely pallor and indeterminacy, which stand over against the apparent solidity and clarity and frustrate them as warrants of its reality.

What I have been designating here is that element of cognition whose generalization forms Plato's doctrine of ideas. In his meaning of the term "idea," the recollected image is the generic concept for a multiplicity of things that are similar in most of their characteristics and are, therefore, of the same kind. Nevertheless, these generic concepts that we form are held to be the real things. In relation to these concepts, the things of sense-perception exist only insofar as they participate in the ideas. These eternal primal images of all individual existence exist purely for themselves, in the locus of the mind, accessible only to thought, and untouched by the alterations of those things that only participate in them. Individual things are only the shadow-images of the ideas. The ordering of the ideas (only hinted at and yet maintained as a postulate) expressed Plato's difference from the Eleatic philosophy which held that the being which was most real was constituted by a plurality within unity rather than by an undifferentiated unity. However, the idea of the good, which orders the plurality of ideas, does not refer to the morally good but rather to the first cause and final purpose. This world view perpetuates the same errors that are indicated in our treatment of ordinary human reason. Plato leads us precisely to the point of thinking about the thing in itself, quite apart from its individual appearance for us. He posits further that these things-in-themselves are the causes of the behavior which attaches to the individual things since the individual things exist only insofar as they participate in the ideas. Granted, this is quite unclear, but lack of clarity is not in contradiction to the tendency of this entire world view. Historically, this world view grew out of the challenge to guide cognition between the sophistical assertions of the Eleatics that all reality is only simple being and the principle of the Heracliteans that all reality is only the flux of appearances. But Plato's answer to this problem does not precisely determine the relation between cognition and being. For we must amplify the statement that ideas are only generalized images of the memory by observing that these images become more and more dim and imprecise and even, in themselves, uncertain, to the extent that they are called upon to include more and more specimens or subspecies. Is the idea of an apple a solid and clear representation? The generic characteristics of size, shape, color, taste, inner structure, etc., must always be represented in a limited but sliding scale. It is self-deception therefore to expect that one can achieve a solid and clear cognition in the concept of genus. To the extent, however, that a person purifies a generic concept of the fluctuation within it and gives to it contours that are solid and clear—to that extent one can be certain that the concept is only a shadow-image of the actual thing in our memory and that no reality belongs to it. But this understanding is just the opposite of the Platonic assertion that individual things are the shadow-images of the ideas. Accordingly, the concept of universal, undifferentiated, indeterminate, and boundless being which Plutarch, Philo, and the neoplatonists posit as God is nothing but the shadow of the world. This confusion is to be attributed to the Greeks, since they were never able to differentiate with certainty between the mundane and the divine. To a lesser extent, the confusion can be attributed to Philo the Jew. I shall not comment again here on the fact that Christian theologians persist in this same confusion as warrant for the Christian cognition of God.

The representation of a thing arises out of the different sense-impressions which attach themselves in a certain order to something which fixes perception in a limited space. We posit the apple as round, red, and sweet because the impressions of the senses of touch, sight, and taste attach themselves to the place where the corresponding relationships of form, color, and taste are perceived. It is precisely from these relationships which converge in the same place in repeated perceptions that we focus the representation of a thing. A thing "exists" in its relationships and it is only in them that we can know the thing and only by them that we can name it. The significance of the relation of these characteristics, ascertained through sense-impressions and expressed in the judgment, "This thing is round, red, and sweet," is that we get to know the subject of this sentence only in its predicates. If it were possible for us to let these predicates drop from our sight or for us to forget them, then the thing with which we were acquainted under these characteristics would also fall out of our cognition. There is no reason at this elementary level of the formation of the concept of a "thing" for us to posit the thing and its characteristics (sensed and perceived together) in two dimensions, one behind the other and separate from each other; nor is it necessary to assert that it is possible to know the thing "behind" its characteristics or "before" the naming of those characteristics. But, there is also no occasion for attempting to amplify the concept of "thing," by saying that we learn to understand the characteristics of a thing as the apparent functions of a cause [*Ursache*] and as instruments of a purpose [*Zweck*], or that even though a thing's characteristics are perceived as variable up to a certain point the whole is seen as functioning in the orderly variation of its qualities, or that, finally, a law can be conjectured from the perceived history of a thing. Rather, the thing is the cause of its functions and the purpose governing the orderly succession of its apparent variations.

The impression that the perceived thing is one despite the variation of its characteristics arises from the continuity of the self-consciousness within the succession of sense-impressions which the thing arouses in us (cf. above, p. 166). Furthermore, the comprehension of a thing as cause and purpose of itself emerges from the certainty that I am cause and purpose of the functions that I myself originate. We would do no violence to the evidence that is obtained from perceiving a thing in its characteristics and recognizing its reality in its effects upon us (in accordance with which we judge the thing in itself) and upon other things with which its effects stand in reciprocal relations—to repeat, we would do no violence to this evidence unless we indulge in an improper use (described above) of the individual recollected image of a thing and its universalization in the concept of genus. But a person teaches something that is contrary to the evidence and incomprehensible when he uses the analogy which the common understanding is wont to use. When he does use that analogy, he follows the direction of Plato's thought by positing the thing as pure being or as a reality without properties, to which one only accidentally and subsequently attaches its relations and its specific properties, in order to establish the thing clearly and solidly and to guard it against the disturbances of the variations which are perceived in it by our senses. Furthermore, such thinking introduces a kind of conception which is akin to myth. Myth represents things

of nature as bearers of spiritual life. False metaphysics holds that pale
and wavering recollected images of generic concepts are real. And
even though these images and concepts have been relegated to a state
of motionlessness through the scaling off of all the conditioning elements associated with concrete functioning, a kind of intentionality is
attributed to them under indeterminable circumstances in order to
ascribe a functioning to these images and concepts that was previously
expressly denied to them. And this functioning is to be understood
as constituting no variation in the things, since it is posited as accidentally related to the things that are motionless in themselves, since
they always remain in themselves the same. This whole line of reasoning is neither consistent nor clear. It is completely foreign to our concrete behavior in regard to things of nature and spiritual persons. This
behavior is never guided by such abstractions but always by the
evidence that the individual apple we eat is real and that the man
we get to know through the direction of his will and the states of his
self-consciousness is himself. There is no being "behind" these
appearances of the man that is somehow more authentic to him or
more real, which has to be taken into consideration in order for us
to understand him and assume a meaningful relation to him. Nevertheless, the false metaphysics to which this distinction of Luthardt
(between a thing and its appearances) belongs, carries within itself
a force of prejudgment, a fact to be considered in view of the presentation of ontology in the *Metaphysics* of Lotze, which proceeds in
a constant refutation of that assumption. I will use the following
quotation from this work as a conclusion to my effort to clarify the
issue:

> Metaphysics does not have the task of making reality, but, rather, of
> acknowledging it; it is the task of probing the inner ordering of what
> is given, not of deriving the given from what is not given. In order to
> meet this task, metaphysics must guard itself against the misunder-
> standing which regards the abstractions, through which metaphysics
> fixes the specific determinations of what is real for its own purposes, as
> positive and independent elements which can be used again, as they are,
> to construct the structure of reality. We have seen metaphysics fre-
> quently caught up in this misunderstanding: it formed a concept of
> pure being and gave a meaning to this concept that is cut off from all
> the relationships which alone show forth reality; it ascribed to a con-
> cept of reality, *per se*, which is without properties the reality that can

only belong to that which is fully conditioned; it spoke of laws which would stand as an imperious power between or outside the very things and events in which alone laws have real validity.[23]

V

Apart from the doctrine of God, Christian dogmatics offers no opportunity to set forth directly a metaphysical concept as if it were theological. All of the remaining theological themes are so specifically spiritual in nature that metaphysics can only come into play as the formal pattern for the cognition of religious entities or relationships. In view of this, every theologian, as a scientific worker, is under the necessity or obligation to proceed according to a certain epistemology of which he is himself aware and whose correctness he must demonstrate. Thus it would be ill-considered and unthinkable to assert that I would eliminate all metaphysics from theology. For if I am capable of working in theology in a scientific manner—and in general no one has yet contested that—then I must follow an epistemology which proceeds according to a concept of "things" in its determination of the objects of knowledge; that is, it proceeds metaphysically. Therefore, the question at issue between Luthardt and me can be formulated correctly only in the following manner: "Which metaphysics is justified in theology?"

The theory of knowledge which can claim to hold a dominant place in the theological tradition is the Platonic, in which everything is deduced from above by means of general concepts. My opponent represents this position whereas I have given it up. The above discussions against Frank have demonstrated adequately that he and Luthardt have subordinated the knowledge of the God and Father of our Lord Jesus Christ to an idea, to a general concept which is called the Absolute, Substance, that is, Thing or Object. The conventional form of dogmatics teaches that one knows God as the subject of characteristics that are in and of themselves inert; this, in turn, enables them to focus their attention next on a presentation of God in his actions toward the world. Knowledge of Christ is subordinated to a general concept of his preexistent divinity, whose incongruity with the corresponding Johannine train of thought is clear; and then the futile attempt is made to authenticate the divinity of Christ in his historical existence. Furthermore, this dogmatics sets forth the

concept of Christ's full person before it even brings that person to
our attention through his distinctive works. When this dogmatics
deals with the doctrine of sin, its general concept of sin is put forth
as the passive, inherited corruption of human nature and afterwards
actual sin is judged and clarified. Finally, the entire structure of this
dogmatics is not oriented upon Christ as the bearer of revelation but,
rather, upon the perfection of Adam; for sin is judged in reference
to Adam's nature and the redeemer from sin is judged in reference
to sin itself. Once again, the first men before the fall are understood
only as the idea of man which is brought into existence through
God's creation.

Within this method that I have outlined, we can account for the
fact that Professor Hermann Weiss[24] of Tübingen recently rebuked
me because I do not allow room in my theology for the *unio mystica*,
that is, that I omit a demonstration of the direct personal unity of
the believer with God.[25] For, he asserts, "the spirit is indeed not
simple (that must mean: simply) will, but also a certain kind of
being and living, and certainly herein it possesses an objective side
that is akin to nature" (p. 410). In response to this assertion, intelligible to me in spite of its confusion, I can refer to what I have said
concerning the same assertion by Luthardt in regard to John 17.
This most recent opponent continually misinterprets or distorts my
assertions, despite his efforts to understand me, since, as a quasi
platonist, he wants to understand the issues "from above" through
general concepts before he gives himself to the scrutiny of individual
entities as they actually exist. In an article published a few years
ago, "The Christian Idea of the Good," he dealt first with the idea
of the Good in general and only subsequently with the Christian
idea of Good. I remember very clearly the error into which the
author fell because of this approach. The "Good in general" cannot
be described except, perhaps, in a pale, indeterminate fashion which
stands neutrally over against all determinate forms and stages of
ethical communities that have appeared in the course of history.
Since Weiss needed to bring more concrete phenomena into this
part of his article, he transposed a mass of Christian interpretations
of the Good into the framework of the Good in general. I cannot
trust the author of such a theological work to have the necessary
predisposition to understand my own style of theology since it

rejects the method of proceeding from the realm of the universal which exists "up above." Accordingly, the picture of my position that he draws with his peculiar reasoning is only a caricature. Weiss always seeks only the conventional categories, and it is into these that he wants to squeeze me through his critique. He asserts that my presentation is inherently contradictory since I alternate in my description of the subjective religious processes between the perspective of divine grace and that of free human action (as if there were any other way!). He intimates that something like an objective nature can be identified behind free human action; a nature to which God can be directly and immediately present. It is upon precisely this metaphysical peg in the human spirit that he hangs the concept, determinative for him, of the *unio mystica*. He further alleges that this concept of the immediate personal relation of the believer to Christ is the truth which I deny. My reply to this is that the concept of the *unio mystica* is either unintelligible and impractical, as in the older dogmatics, or else it blots out the normal protestant confidence in salvation, as in pietism. Weiss asserts that it is evident that the well-known Pauline formulations and the Johannine farewell discourses compel a theologian to affirm the *unio mystica* as a truth necessary for salvation! I contest the evidence upon which this presupposition rests. I reject this use of scripture—a literalistic notation of certain passages without any attempt to interpret them, in order to stamp a favorite truth as necessary for salvation. In the light of such a procedure by an academic theologian, I cannot see how one could criticize or even be amazed at the way the anabaptists or the Russian Old Believers use the holy scriptures.[26] Indeed, it is clearly written: "What you hear whispered, proclaim upon the housetops" (Matt. 10:27); "If anyone comes to me and does not hate his own father and mother and wife and children . . . he cannot be my disciple" (Luke 15:26). Therefore, the anabaptists preached from the housetops, abandoned their families, and wandered about. It also stands written: "What comes out of the mouth, this defiles a man" (Matt. 15:11), and that we should "attain to the measure of the stature of the fullness of Christ" (Eph. 4:13). Therefore, the Starowerzen[27] refrained from smoking tobacco as a great sin and cared for their beards as if it were a command from Christ. I find the New Testament passages that Weiss applies literalistically as proof

of the *unio mystica* no more compelling than the justification of these
sectarian principles on the basis of the New Testament passages just
cited.

It is either a remarkable coincidence that the same issue of
Studien und Kritiken which contains Weiss's attack on me also
presents an essay by C. F. Georg Heinrici[28] entitled *Zum genos-
senschaftlichen Charakter der paulinischen Christengemeinden*
["Concerning the Character of the Pauline Communities as Fellow-
ships"], or else it is a testimony that my friend, the editor, follows
no particular "party." For in this essay, following a contrary interpretation, the same controversy appears which figures in Weiss's
objections to me, the controversy between a judgment based on
universal concepts and the derivation of a broad perspective that
emerges from the observation of the individual and the particular.
Carl Christian Johann Holsten[29] is the representative of universal
concepts in comprehending the situation of the Corinthian church,
and Heinrici refutes both his method and his conclusions. Weiss and
Holsten stand together harmoniously; and the same epistemology
with which Weiss thought he could win the victory over me suffers
a defeat at the hands of Heinrici. Holsten holds the following concept of the church:

> The nature of God should be brought to expression in the church; the
> transcendent power of God's spirit shapes the plurality of the believers
> in the church of God into an organic unity; therefore the church of
> God is an organism of God's spirit.[30]

But when Holsten undertakes to interpret the evidences contained
in the Pauline letters concerning the situation in the Corinthian
church according to this universal concept he finds, in Heinrici's
estimate, that that church has asserted a formlessness which stands
diametrically opposed to the unity which was asserted in principle.
From the heights of his universal concept he has not recognized in
which functions of the church's life the Holy Spirit is active and,
therefore, present. As Heinrici (p. 515) summarizes his opponent's
opinion, Holsten seems to be saying that it is much more important
to understand that transcendent and ideal powers hover over a
formless and unorganized aggregate of believers since "where the
Spirit dwells in the hearts of the faithful, he also remains as a

transcendent power." In opposition to such a position, Heinrici introduces the argument that if the Holy Spirit is not authenticated concretely in the harmonious and corporate movements and activities of the faithful, then his transcendent presence is fruitless and worthless. Weiss's argument against me is similar to Holsten's argument about the Corinthian church. He goes so far as to assert that I have simply wrenched the Holy Spirit out of the organic whole of Christian doctrine. Indeed, as he further alleges, I have conceived of the Holy Spirit as the ground of the common consciousness of God's sonship, as the motive and divine power of the church's supramundane religious and ethical life, and therefore as the necessary concrete determinant of Christian personhood! That is not enough for Weiss, and he misses the significance of these assertions for precisely the same reasons that Holsten does not recognize the functions of God's spirit in the church at Corinth: a preoccupation with the transcendence of that Spirit. Weiss triumphantly draws his conclusion out of my interpretation of the Holy Spirit: "Therefore, the Holy Spirit is in no sense something real or actual," etc. Naturally! What is real, in his sense, must be *asserted* before and quite apart from all its particular functioning. The Holy Spirit in man is set forth as real according to the same standard as that which asserts that "the human spirit is not just will, but, rather, also a certain kind of being and living, and, in this sense, possesses an objective side which it shares with nature." In this fog, spun out of the metaphysics and the physics of human spiritual life, one is supposed to be able to recognize the reality of the Holy Spirit. Furthermore, this fog is supposedly the place where the *unio mystica* is to be found *quite apart* from the given functions of the Christian life in which the Holy Spirit is grasped as something active and real. The Tübingen professor ought to test the order of his own concepts first before he criticizes someone else; particularly before he insinuates that I have deprived Christianity of one of the essential parts of its world view.

My opponents' charge (whether direct or indirect) that my theology devaluates Christianity is based on nothing else than their conviction that their own modes of knowledge are in solid agreement with Christianity. Their claim contains the indirect suggestion that I ought to accustom myself to their platonizing and mystical-

metaphysical epistemology if my reputation as a theologian and my
salvation are dear to me, since one cannot be saved in a Christianity
that is devalued and mutilated. I reply that I have protected myself
from the implied consequences of their reproaches by my continual
willingness to criticize myself. Therefore, if my opponents are right
in attacking me in the interest of Christianity, then I would have
to resolve to acknowledge the customary universal concepts of
theology and the derivation of particular perceptions from these
concepts—terrible as that might sound—since those universal concepts authenticate at the same time the reality of the relationships
which they designate. If I did not acknowledge those universal concepts, then I would not be a reliable theologian and Christian. But
I find such a demand to be a deadly analogy to the talk of those men
who in their own time came from Judea to Antioch saying, "If you
do not permit yourself to be circumcised, you cannot be saved." For
just as, in that instance, the particularity of a national custom was
forced upon Christianity as a condition of its validity, so now the
particularity of an epistemology is held up to me as the condition
of the integrity and correctness of a theological presentation of
Christianity and, as a consequence, a condition also of my own personal character as a theologian and a Christian. But the sacrifice
which the Judaistic Christians demanded of the Gentiles and the
sacrificium intellectus [sacrifice of the intellect] which I am supposed to offer have equally little in common with Christianity. For
Christianity is neutral over against the differences between Jewish
and Hellenistic customs, just as it is religiously neutral over against
the different epistemologies through which its intellectual content
might be scientifically ordered. Consequently, the collision between
the different epistemologies which has occurred in the objections my
opponents make against me can only be correctly judged as a scientific controversy, and this is the way I myself have understood it.
The only result of Weiss's critique is to show that I theologize differently from the manner to which he is accustomed and that my
theology is absurd when judged by the criteria of his beloved universal concepts. His efforts in this connection remind me of the
treatment which the famous Procrustes gave his guests. Therefore I
cannot acknowledge the comfortable bed of universal concepts as
the rightful norm of my theological knowledge; rather, I find that

Weiss's treatment of my work is a kind of torture by which he succeeds in making my assertions give *him* a meaning different from that which I intended and expressed. His example, Procrustes, was manifestly and without doubt gifted, but he was brutal at the same time; in the realm of scientific knowledge these two characteristics flow together to form sophistry.

Weiss and Luthardt give evidence of their metaphysical inclination in their joint assertion that the reality of the human spirit is not to be grasped in its volition which, naturally, includes knowing and the dominant feeling of self-consciousness but, rather, that one must conceive of man's real and authentic being "behind," "under" or "over" these functions in an objective form that is also proper to nature. These two gentlemen have not clarified their thoughts any more than this. They have not demonstrated that this conception of man, this hovering mist, is reality; and, further, that it is a reality of more persuasive power than the concrete functions in which every man knows his own actuality, partly as experienced by him (i.e., passively) and partly as his own activity (i.e., actively). I do not level any particular reproach against them for this; the circumstances in which my own controverted assertions emerged did not allow me to furnish any such proof either. Moreover, both of these men intend only to assert the firm deposit of faith contained in tradition. But the kind of proof I demand is one that they can never produce. Such a proof would have to be carried out in a manner somewhat analogous to the ontological proof for the existence of God. That is, it would have to be a proof that representations of the nature of man that are formed quite apart from all experience do nevertheless correspond to reality by virtue of their universal and ambiguous content. I do not wish to take the lead over my opponents in formulating such a proof; rather, I put the challenge before them here and now. But before they try to put off this responsibility in some proper fashion, I will add this on the basis of the conditions that I have already set forth for metaphysical knowledge: The elementary knowledge that spiritual life is something real is only preparatory to the knowledge of the distinctive character of spirit in the functions of feeling, knowing, and willing—chiefly, however, in willing. Furthermore, one cannot authenticate the impact of others upon the human spirit except in the context of active and conscious sense-impressions [*Empfinden*] which comprise the raw material for the articulate self-consciousness of the "I." This raw material is the key to all knowing and the occasion for recognizing the motives of the will. Only in this realm of the actuality of the spiritual life can one understand the actions of God which furnish the basis for religion. But since we can only perceive God in his actions toward us, which correspond to his public revelation, so it is that we perceive God's presence for us precisely in these actions. Of course the evidence for this is different than it would be for individual sense-perceptions [*Sinneswahrnehmung*]. But this difference does not lie in the fact that sense-perceptions are immediate whereas the religious evidence of God's presence is frequently mediated. For even the simplest sense-perception which appears to common sense as immediate is actually a complex of sense-impressions and the faculty of judgment mediated through habit. Rather, the religious evidence for God's presence depends upon a connection of religious community and education with ethical self-formation and self-criticism. I shall not describe them here since my opponents can authenticate this for themselves if *they* wish. The historical side of this connection in religious experience also has its perceptible characteristics but these are so far removed from the act that I have in mind that they come into view as of secondary importance, even when one analyzes the matter in detail.

But it is precisely at this point that I encounter the sharpest criticism of my opponents. In their opinion, it is a defect of Christian conviction that I and others with me refer only to the effects of God or Christ[31] which the believer experiences in himself as a member of the community through the mediation of the preaching of the gospel. They say, rather, that one must be in possession of an unmediated personal relation to Christ our redeemer.[32] Against this opinion I dare to adduce the following in my defense. If one correctly conceives of effects, he conceives the cause in the effects. It is only the false judgment of popular common sense which asserts that a person places the causes in an imagined space "behind" the space in which he sees the appearances which he believes to be the effects of those causes or that he places the causes at an earlier point in time than the effects themselves. In these schemes, one does not really conceive of the perceived appearances as effects of those causes because these two concepts (i.e., cause and effect) properly stand in such a relation to each other that they can be referred to one another only within a unity of space or time. Our separation of these concepts in time and space is only a provisional operation of thought in which we establish firmly for ourselves the order of the relationships we have differentiated in our observation of the thing. Indeed, when we have once grasped the unity of a thing or the connections between things, we do away with the scheme which separates these elements spatially. Therefore, what we substantiate religiously as the activity of God or Christ within us authenticates the presence rather than the distance of the author of our salvation. And it does this according to the model of the relation that exists between persons. For God punishes me in remorse; Christ consoles me and gives me courage when I sense the worth of his example or when I direct myself toward the motives which, since they are focused and made actual for me in his person, make him the originator and perfecter of my salvation. If, in spite of this, my opponents should ascribe this admission simply to my subjective fancy, because it does not fall within the formulae of reality that are familiar to them, then things must rest as follows: They themselves posit pale and wavering images from their memory as the reality of things, and from them they have abstracted their universal concepts without any sort of proof, even when these universal concepts are themselves borrowed from some tradition.

On the contrary, when the human spirit orients itself toward those effective and worthwhile motives which give distinctive substance to its life, it appropriates those motives in the form of a precise and detailed recollection. This is a better way to understand the phenomenon of recollection. The self-consciousness of our actual spiritual life is thereby the sufficient ground for knowing the reality of all that which contributes to our reality, that is, to our worthwhile and effective existence in the world. The personal interrelationships of life are mediated, in particular, through precise recollection. Thus, for example, one person continues to be efficacious in the life of others and is therefore present to them when they act on the basis of education or other stimulation which they have derived from him. In the broadest sense, this is the case with the religious bond between our lives and God—mediated through the precise recollection of

Christ. But one should not consider such relationships to be immediate ones—particularly the relationship to God—else he is really
suggesting that they are imagined. For without mediation, nothing
is real. The personal relationship of God or Christ to us, however, is
and remains mediated through our precise recollection of the word,
i.e., of the law and the promise of God. And God works upon us
only through the one or the other of these revelations. The basic
assertion of the immediacy of certain perceptions and relationships
raises the question of distinguishing between reality and hallucina-
tion. Those who maintain the pretension of having an immediate
personal relationship to Christ or God are apparently not well-read
in the literature of mysticism. They could, for example, learn from
the nun Catherine of Genoa and from her description of her life
what sort of content is possible in the immediacy of relationship to
Christ which they maintain![33] Therefore, without the means of the
word of God as law and gospel and without the precise recollection
of this personal revelation of God in Christ, there is no personal
relation between a Christian and God. I want to clarify and justify
this correct and useful insight of the reformers by my comments. I
am not obligated to any other doctrine, nor am I justified in holding
to any other. Nevertheless, it is remarkable that a theologian like
Weiss should dare to judge me at this point according to his pietistic
pretensions whereas I should maintain my position along the line
laid down in the teachings of the reformation. It is even more
instructive, in the present confusion between pietistic and orthodox
tendencies, when a person can observe in a Lutheran who is considered to be correct that he lays considerable weight on his immediate personal relationship to Christ and that when he permits
himself to be greatly persuaded by it, he consequently betrays
Lutheranism and becomes an enthusiast.[34] This is precisely what is
so distressing and offensive about the contemporary situation of
theology and the church—that the flag of churchliness and confessional loyalty flies over so much pietistic cargo which does not belong
under that flag because it is of an opposing and conflicting nature.

The subtitle of Weiss's treatise, "Critical Survey, with Particular
Relationship to Ritschl's Theology," provides me a further opportunity to confirm that he himself has only cursorily surveyed the
emergence and structure of the later Lutheran doctrine of the *unio*

mystica, a doctrine which he wishes to retain and which I hold to be impractical. He recalls the conclusion of Matthias Schneckenburger (pp. 409–10), "who has recently fallen into a shameful obscurity and not been appreciated," that the Reformed and the Lutherans understood *unio mystica* in different ways. While it is true that I am not one of those who has forgotten Schneckenburger, I have nevertheless shown (*Geschichte des Pietismus,* I:167) that the Reformed theologian Jodocus van Lodensteyn[35] represented the same position which was first introduced into Lutheran theology by Justus Feuerborn[36] and Johann Hülsemann,[37] in the same way that Philipp Nicolai[38] and also Johann Arndt[39] and Balthasar Meisner[40] had previously enunciated it. Lucas Osiander the Younger[41] testified quite to the contrary in his writing against Arndt (1624), that up to that time Lutherans had understood the *unio mystica* to apply only to the image of the body and the members of Christ; that is, to the framework of the religious community, within which they conceive of the rebirth and continuance of faith in the individual believer. This means that before Arndt the Lutherans explained this matter exactly as Calvin did in the *Institutes* III, 1, 1 and 2, 30, 35.[42] And I know a few ascetical books before and after which confirm the same opinion. Thus it is precisely at this point that Schneckenburger's observation is neither complete nor correct. Rather, both explanations of the *unio mystica* (i.e., as referring to the believer's relationship with God and to his relationship with the church) appear in both Reformed and Lutheran understandings, and the Lutheran Meisner puts them in his academic lecture: "We are Christian together"—but he did not make it clear that the different perspectives do not coincide with each other. The *inhabitatio totius trinitatis* [the presence of the entire Trinity] as it is used for example in the Formula of Concord[43] and by Johann Gerhard[44] means nothing more than regeneration as a way of understanding good works. It is not until the work of Philipp Nicolai and Balthasar Meisner that the concept of this *unio mystica* took on the meaning of being the basis for the joyous mood of the faithful and for their royal and priestly character. Thus the effects which inherently correspond to justification by faith were carried over to the concept of the *unio mystica* and these same combinations of ideas were repeated by Johann Andreas Quenstedt[45] and Abraham Calov.[46]

This is the basis for asserting that this new doctrine was only later brought into competition with the doctrine of justification. For when one attends to Philipp Nicolai and Johann Arndt, he is persuaded that the original doctrine of the reformation was set aside and rendered practically ineffectual, in order to glorify the ambiguous and apocryphal concept of this *unio mystica*, which was supposed to authenticate blessedness. One can judge accordingly whether Luther's occasional use of mystical formulae establishes—as Weiss would have it—an attitude toward those formulae which is characteristic of the reformation. Did Luther base his reformation on the doctrine of justification by faith or on the doctrine of the *unio mystica*? The original formula of the *inhabitatio trinitatis* is without a doubt to be traced back to the thought of Andreas Osiander[47] where it is made the basis of active sanctification. It also has found a place in the Formula of Concord, III, 54 and, in the same sense, Philip Melanchthon[48] already acknowledged it in his *Postille*. Naturally, one could not acknowledge that this formula is the correct expression for justification; however, the image which it calls to mind of God's dwelling in believers seemed to be important enough that a formula which corresponds to this notion of God's indwelling should be permitted as an explanation of how sanctification follows upon the decree of justification. This tendency appeared first in the seventeenth century when Nicolai and Arndt, disregarding and opposing the Formula of Concord and reviving medieval modes of thought, appended the kinds of relationships to the *unio mystica* through which it was finally made into the doublet of the doctrine of justification, with the result that justification became simply a theoretical presupposition for it. Finally, Johann Arndt and, later, Christian Hoburg[49] and others explained the actuality of this union with God as referring to the tender relationship of love between the soul and its bridegroom. Since I am defending the doctrine of justification in its original formulation and for its well-known practical relation to belief in providence, humility, patience, and prayer, I must reject the aforementioned doctrine of the *unio mystica* which arose only in the seventeenth century. I hope I have answered Professor Weiss's insinuation that it is not a Kantian moralist antipathy which leads me to this position; and I hope I have also shown that the naïveté on this matter which he boasts of (p. 408) grows out of a defect in historical knowledge which renders his advice to me unusable.

Finally, I cannot resist touching upon still one more characteristic point in my opponent's deductions. As one might expect, Weiss brings Friedrich Schleiermacher[50] into the concerns which he represents. He is said to be so liberal that he forsakes the scholastic form in which the Lutheran dogmaticians *developed the details* of the doctrine of the *unio mystica*. One might also ask whether Weiss has ever looked at Quenstedt's or Calov's treatment of this doctrine. I observed only a concise delimitation of the doctrine in their work rather than a more or less detailed development. But everything in Weiss's work is unclear and imprecise. He disclaims the scholastic form and he

> holds fast only to the kernel of the matter, as it is indubitably witnessed to in the New Testament, and, *in his own way*, reproduced also by Schleiermacher—that through faith there is formed a personal and therein real spiritual union between God and the believer, a union which provides the lasting foundation for a real spiritual union between them, that is, a meaningful common life.

Now the fact of the matter is that Schleiermacher did indeed use these expressions which were current for him out of his Herrnhut[51] background, but he reinterpreted them to refer to the *effects* which extend from the redeemer to the believers within the church. In addition, he analyzes all of the circumstances that are here suggested within the framework of the subjective life. With respect to method, therefore, he is my forerunner; I have learned my method partly from him and partly from Schneckenburger! Weiss apparently has not perceived or retained this in his recollection of Schleiermacher's theology—a recollection which is probably already somewhat obsolete. Therefore, out of regard for his faded recollection, I must add that Schleiermacher is also opposed to me. Thus it is that theologians like my opponent, who desire what is old but not in the superannuated costume of the scholastic forms; who always guard themselves in every possible way from heretical deviations; who thus narrow their scope until they finally revolve only about themselves; who always criticize and never get along with others—these unfruitful theologians, I must say, always claim Schleiermacher's patronage

for themselves. But it is not Schleiermacher as he really was but
rather their idea of him, their dull recollection (which they have
"dressed up") of the great theologian's teaching, to which they
ascribe at the same time all their own intentions and merits. Thus
he is idealized according to a flaccid "mediating theology,"[52] set
upon the scene, and claimed to be in harmony with the views of
men who have taken their roots in places other than his and whose
thought is projected from methods quite opposed to his. To the
many amenities which one is accorded when he tries to make his way
independently as a theologian must be added this, that he is trumped
by the Schleiermacher who has been accommodated to the needs of
these men. But that is a dishonest game.

VI

The controversy over original sin which Victorinus Strigel, Jacob
Andreae, Tilemann Hesshus, and Johann Wigand[53] carried on
against Matthias Flacius[54] furnishes an instructive example of the
value of judging theological assertions metaphysically. To the utterance that original sin is *accidens* [accidental] to man, made by
Strigel in the Disputation at Weimar (1560), Flacius responded
with the opposing assertion that original sin is of man's *substantia*
[substance]. It was only in 1567 that he published the tractate *De
peccati originalis aut veteris Adami appellationibus et essentia*
["Concerning original sin, or the names and essence of the old
Adam"], in the *Clavis scripturae sacrae* [Key to the Holy Scrip-
tures], which explained and preserved that familiar concept. Flacius's
assertion was not intended to be as offensive and exaggerated as it
appears. For one thing, it is directly related to the framework of
ideas in which Luther used to portray original sin and in which he
taught that it should be abhorred. In addition, Flacius did not wish
to ascribe a simple diabolicalness to Adam's progeny but, on the
contrary, he wanted to ascribe some good to them, in spite of his
assertion. To this end, he differentiated two meanings of the concept
substantia: substantia materialis [material substance] and *forma
substantialis* [substantial form]. In respect to the former meaning,
he allows that despite corruption it remains the bearer of some good;
in respect to the latter, the substantial form, he makes the judgment
that without exception it has become the bearer of evil, just as

through creation it had been the bearer of the divine image. Even in respect to this first distinction, Flacius's meaning remains ambiguous because it is spelled out only in metaphysical concepts. That is, what he says about the material substance is unintelligible:

> The mass of mankind established at the beginning, although it is deeply corrupted, has nevertheless remained to this day, in the same way as with wine and spices, when their airy and fiery substance evaporates, only an earthy, watery substance remains.[55]

This example from chemistry does not make the metaphysical notion any clearer. What Flacius strove for in this connection becomes clear when one understands that sin is to be conceived within the structure of volition. For it is in the conscious will that sin appears as an effect. Thus the law of the will consists in the power, either to convert the propensity of its drives toward lust into actual intentions, projects, resolutions and transactions, or through these means to moderate and divert that propensity. The will is evil, however, insofar as it sets its projected *course* on unrestrained lust or on lust that has been intentionally limited so that its pleasure might be intensified accordingly. The will is good insofar as it circumscribes its drives through the good intention which it holds, that is, converting those impulses into means for doing good. This formal law of the will corresponds to the *substantia materialis* [material substance]; that course of the will which is specified by a purpose with a certain content corresponds to the *forma substantialis* [substantial form]. When the nature of character is to be judged by the criterion of which values in life [*Lebensinhalt*] the will directs itself toward, then the judgment that the character is evil must include the same appraisal of the negative value of sin which Flacius certainly meant to imply in his assertion. But none of this is clear in the inadequate metaphysical categories in which Flacius and his opponents expressed themselves. In other words, it never became explicit that the controversy dealt with the appraisal of the value of sin—and it could not become explicit because this insight is based on feeling, which stands between the concrete course of the will and the presentiment or knowledge of man's destiny.

Hence the controversy revolved around the question of whether sin is the *substantia* of man or *accidens* upon his *substantia*. The

Aristotelian traditions preserved in Melanchthon's *Erotemata dialectices* (1547)[56] served to facilitate the decision. This work describes substance in the following manner: "Substance is a thing which has the property of being and which sustains accidents." Accident is thus defined: "An accident is that which does not subsist through itself, nor is it a part of substance, but it is changeable into something else" or "that which is present or absent over and above the corruption of the subject." However, it depends on how the characteristics under which a thing manifests itself are classified between the categories of "substance" and "accident." According to the way this is done, the concept of substance becomes either fuller or emptier. The tendency Melanchthon followed was toward emptying the concept, since he did not reckon the qualities as substance, but placed them with the accidents. He says: "Quality is the form through which a substance makes itself efficacious, or that which stimulates the senses." He assumed that *habitus, potentiae, naturales, affectus,* and *figura* were qualities.[57] These *forms of the efficacy and perceptibility of things* were therefore *excluded from the concept of the thing*. To take an example, that would mean that the characteristics under which a thing is perceived as round, triangular, or square are irrelevant to its existence as a thing! Flacius rejected this differentiation between substance and accident. He reckoned the qualities, particularly the shape, to things and to their substance. Accordingly, in his opinion, the will belongs to the substance of man. For the good will was established through creation as the essence of the first man; therefore the evil will in Adam's progeny is of their substance. Now it is interesting that of Flacius's opponents, two (namely Strigel and Andreae) join with him in rejecting Melanchthon's distinction,[58] even though they distinguish between substance and accident differently from Flacius in their interpretation of the will. They posit the will, generally, as the substance of man; its constitution as good or bad is, however, accident in their opinion. Wigand came to the same result much more simply and, finally, Hesshus did too. They reckoned that on the whole neither reason nor will was man's substance, but rather accidents *quae in substantia sunt mutabilitar* [which, in substance, are changeable]! Naturally, then, original sin is also accident. But as what, then, is the essence of man to be known? As an indeterminate thing without relations, without effects, the doublet of Frank's "absolute," differing from that "absolute" only in the indemonstrable assertion that that absolute is God, whereas the soul is created. The assertion that original sin is accidental to man's essence is every bit as intolerable as the opposite, that it is the substance of contemporary humanity. But even more fatal is the fact that the assertion of Flacius's opponents found a place in the Formula of Concord, Solid Declaration I, 57.[59] For that would mean that there is a contradiction in the interpretation of original sin as *corruptio totius naturae et virium* [corruption of all nature and of men] and, at the same time, as something *quod adest praeter subiecti corruptionem* [which is present over and above the corruption of the subject]. At the same time, it is this formula of the corruption of nature which prevented the original, intended deviation from catholic teaching, a teaching which included the substance of man's essence, the *liberum arbitrium* [free will] under original sin (Council of Trent, session VI, 1), thus holding that original sin should be thought of as *accidens praeter corruptionem subiecti* [accident over and above the corruption of the subject]. This all came forth because someone undertook to define this point of Christian teaching with metaphysical concepts, but its application had already made a correct formulation of the question impossible since such an application could not possibly correspond to the religious and ethical appraisal of sin.

The conceptual definitions and distinctions which extend throughout the Formula of Concord demonstrate how influential the tradition of the popular metaphysics which Melanchthon favored was upon the formation of the second generation of reformation theologians. But Luther's conscious intention follows just the opposite method, since his intention was embodied in his comprehension of the total task of theology as oriented toward our salvation. I would call to attention some of his sayings: that knowledge of God's essence, as such, as it is undertaken by the scholastics, is without redemptive value and ruinous; that knowledge of God's gracious will can only be understood as the correlate of knowledge of Christ; that Christ's divinity can only be understood in his activity to fulfill his vocation. Hermann Schultz has brought these sayings together recently.[60] All of these ideas follow the rule for knowledge that a thing is known through effects which manifest themselves and that, therefore, a spiritual person exists in his volition as it is visible and present to us. This idea dominates as well the total reformation usage of terms such as *evangelium* [gospel], *promissiones* [promises], *fides evangelii* [faith of the gospel], and *fides promissionum* [faith of the promises]. Pietism erroneously judged the value of these formulae. Wilhelm Brakel and Friedrich Adolf Lampe[61] overlooked the security of Christ's presence that is in these formulae, and they believed that they themselves offered promises so great that, if they were right, they surpassed the promises of the Lord himself. In this instance, however, the impulse toward out-of-the-ordinary piety can oppose the idea of the reformers only because it misunderstands the correct epistemology.[62]

Furthermore, the formula in which Melanchthon defined the task of theology generally in the first edition of the *Loci theologici* (1521) corresponds to this correct epistemology. Thus: *Hoc est Christum cognoscere, beneficia eius cognoscere non quod isti (scholastici) docent, eius naturas, modos incarnationis contueri* ["This is what it is to know Christ—to know his benefits, not what those (scholastics) teach, to survey his natures, his modes of incarnation."].[63] Therefore the substance and worth of Christ should be understood in the beneficent actions upon us Christians, in the gift of the blessedness which we sought in vain under the law—not in a previously held general concept of his divinity. For we will never be able to make this concept coincide with our necessary contemplation of the man Jesus. Moreover, the theory of kenosis,[64] which is currently in vogue, expresses the same thing as the Platonic formula concerning the individual, namely, that Jesus only partakes of divinity. What Melanchthon says about sin is no less characteristic: "Scripture does not call this original sin and that actual sin. For even original sin is plainly a certain perverse lust which is actual."[65] This perspective is also expressed in the first half of the second article of the Augsburg Confession, whereas the second half of that same article presents again the general concept of passively inherited sinfulness. Melanchthon's original intention is to conceive of the sin that is common to all as an active indifference to and mistrust of God and, also, as a self-seeking desire. His intention was not, however, to posit as real a general concept of sin behind those rebellious acts, a concept which is unintelligible. For a passively inherited circumstance cannot be thought of as sin. In respect to the doctrine of sin, as well as in the doctrine of Christ, Melanchthon did not carry things out to a proper development of the theme.

He applied this principle of knowledge more clearly in the sketch of the doctrine of God, where the corresponding explanations of Luther guided him. As is well known, he passed over these in the first edition of the *Loci*. Contrariwise, in the second edition of 1535, the doctrine of God is found, where it is linked to the doctrine of the Trinity. This amplification was certainly occasioned as much by the inner necessity of the theological task as it was by the outward position of the protestants vis-à-vis the Roman church or by Servetus's argument against the doctrine of the Trinity. This amplification was already present in the lectures of 1533, and out of this vividly presented statement I extract the following. Melanchthon begins by saying that one must proceed from the saying of Christ in John 14:9, "He who sees me sees the Father."

> Let us hold to this admonition, that we may learn to seek God in Christ; for in him he wishes to be disclosed, to become known and to be apprehended. . . . For if we allow ourselves to be drawn away from Christ, as if we could know either the nature or will of God without Christ, our souls fall into fearful darkness, because nature is not able to perceive God. . . . The human mind does not comprehend the nature of God by speculations, nor in fact is it able to judge the mercy of God toward us; but when the mercy of God is apprehended in Christ, then it begins to discern the goodness and presence of God, and to understand God in some way. And that does not happen by speculative knowledge, with the result that I may speak with common words, but it happens in practical meditation, that is, when hearts terrified by the knowledge of sin, throw themselves back upon Christ and in him apprehend the promised mercy. Then they know consolation and life, and they know that their lives are returned to God, they know in truth that God is present and merciful. This is the wisdom of Christians. This method does not proceed *a priori*, that is, from the hidden nature of God to knowledge of God's will, but from knowledge of Christ and of the mercy revealed in him to the knowledge of God. To strengthen and confirm souls in this knowledge is far better than to philosophize about the hidden nature of God.[66]

This is an unambiguous position and a candid definition of the doctrine of God. However, the methodological execution of the position does not follow from the task which is here set forth. Rather, on the very next page, Melanchthon frustrates the reshaping of the doctrine of God which he himself lays down by a formula which he describes as the summation of the biblical affirmations about God, but which, in reality, represents a capitulation to the neoplatonic and scholastic position.

> Scripture testifies that God is a spiritual substance. It assigns to him eternity, infinite power, etc. Moreover, this substance is perceived not as that which sustains accidents but, rather, it signifies most properly the essence that subsists in and through itself. Wisdom, goodness, justice, mercy, are not accidents of God, but, just as we do not sunder power from its substance, so we separate neither wisdom nor goodness from their substance. For power is itself wisdom, goodness, etc.[67]

Since the beginning of his service in Wittenberg, Melanchthon had cultivated the dialectic with success, that is, the Aristotelian doctrine of categories and logic. He busied himself with these matters in three treatises, carrying different titles, in 1520, 1528, and 1547. In the last of these, *Erotemata Dialectices* [Dialectical Inquiries] which is published in *Corpus Reformatorum*, XIII, we find the same definition of God as in the *Loci*, with the explanation: "Human minds learn this description from demonstrations *outside the church and without special revelation.*"[68] Could one speak more clearly? This description is simply to be augmented in the church through the application of the name and structures of the Trinity. Although this realm of knowledge is amplified through the customary proofs from scripture and the traditional formulae, even so, the contrary point of view also assumes a certain validity here, namely, that the divinity of Christ and that of the Holy Spirit is recognized in the effects and demands which they exercise upon the believers.

> Thus scripture teaches us, concerning the divinity of the Son, not so much speculatively as practically; this it commands so that we might invoke Christ, so that we might have confidence in him—for in that way the honor and divinity is truly given to him—and thus scripture wishes us to know the divinity of the Holy Spirit in that same consolation and vivification. . . . It is useful for us to consider these offices of the Holy Spirit. . . . These offices intend for us to contemplate rather than dispute concerning the Spirit's nature. . . . In this invocation, in

these exercises of faith, it is better to know the Trinity than to engage in otiose speculations which dispute concerning what the persons of the Trinity do among themselves, but not what they do with us.[69]

The situation is such, in the second edition of the Loci (1535), that the two opposing epistemologies within the doctrine of God carry equal weight. In the third edition, the doctrine of God drawn from theoretical knowledge (*firmae demonstrationes*) and ecclesiastical tradition carries the preponderant weight. While it is true that the reference to John 14:9 remains, the protest based thereon, against *a priori* knowledge of God, has fallen to the side. And it corresponds to the move from the demonstrable and therefore generally rational concept of God to a concern for the structure of his revelation in Christ that now the first question raised concerns the essence of God and secondly concerns his will.[70] These indicators are but another test of the fact that Melanchthon, to the extent that he was or became independent over against Luther, did not keep in force the characteristic thrusts which Luther set in motion. I will say that I do not reproach him for this, nor do I derive a judgment of disrespect from it. *Ultra posse nemo obligatur.* [No man is required to do more than he is able.] But since it is the current fashion to overestimate Melanchthon, it appears to be incumbent upon me to curb this trend in the interest of truth. Thus he relinquished the new epistemology which Luther had set forth, and he led theology back again into the old channels of scholastic apriorism to whose deductions the positive data of revelation are attached in a loosely structured manner. So it has remained, and the new wine was handled to such an extent that it could no longer burst the old wine skins. I am not in the least surprised that the outline of the new theology which Luther drew up eluded the patrons of the old skins completely; nevertheless, I will let this example work to my own advantage. Now, if one is inclined to compare the thrust of Melanchthon's doctrine of God in the texts of 1533 and 1535, he will soon see that the controversy between Frank and me is, actually, the open controversy of Melanchthon versus Melanchthon. This is possible since the one Melanchthon is the representative of Luther's thought, whereas the other Melanchthon is the representative of himself, the Aristotelian, the metaphysician, and, at the same time, the representative of unexamined tradition. As I have already shown, Luthardt is still in the same position of acknowledging the two opposing methods simultaneously on one page of his *Compendium*. Between me and Frank, these two methods are handled as opposites which exclude each other and I consider this controversy to be a gain.

Calvin's *Institutes of the Christian Religion*, in its full form of 1539–59, is so laid out that he progresses from natural religion to revealed religion, from God as creator to God as redeemer. This is precisely a sketch, similar to the scholastic, which holds to the path on which Melanchthon once again guided the theology of the reformation. But that does not hinder Calvin from giving unambiguous expression, on occasion, to the contradictory viewpoints of Luther and Melanchthon. Insofar as he specifies the structure of faith he teaches that God is known as a gracious will in Christ, and Christ is known in the picture of his beneficial deeds and gifts which accompanies the word.

> This, then, is the true knowledge of Christ, if we receive him as he is offered by the Father: namely, clothed with his gospel. For just as he has been appointed as the goal of our faith, so we cannot take the right road to him unless the gospel goes before us. And there, surely, the treasures of grace are opened to us; for if they had been closed, Christ would have benefited us little. . . . He [Paul] understands by this term ["doctrine of faith" in I Tim. 4:6] the new and extraordinary kind of teaching by which Christ, after he became our teacher, has more clearly set forth the mercy of the Father, and has more surely testified to our salvation. . . . First, we must be reminded that there is a permanent relationship between faith and the Word. He could not separate one from the other any more than we could separate the rays from the sun from which they come. (Therefore, there is no immediate relation to Christ!) . . . In understanding faith it is not merely a question of knowing that God exists, but also—and this especially—of knowing what is his will toward us. For it is not so much our concern to know who he is in himself, as what he wills to be toward us . . . for it is after we have learned that our salvation rests with God that we are attracted to seek him. . . . Accordingly, we need the promise of grace, which can testify to us that the Father is merciful. . . . Now we shall possess a right definition of faith if we call it a firm and certain knowledge of God's benevolence toward us, founded upon the truth of the freely given promise in Christ, both revealed to our minds and sealed upon our hearts through the Holy Spirit.[71]

A theology which was laid out as an analysis of this assertion would distinguish itself very favorably in comparison with the traditional form which is analogous to the scholastic.

But also, on yet another point, Calvin follows the method of authenticating a thing in the manifestation of its appearances, that is, a specific action of God in the sequence of the human acts which correspond to it. In contrast to the reproaches of Weiss, it is very interesting to me how Calvin judges the "repentance that for the Christian man ought to extend throughout his life" (Chap. 3, par. 2). Concerning this human life-style [*Lebensführung*] which is conceived of as expressing itself spontaneously in mortification and vivification, he says in paragraph 9:

> I interpret repentance as regeneration, whose sole end is to restore in us the image of God. . . . And indeed, this restoration does not take place in one moment or one day or one year; but through continual and sometimes even slow advances God wipes out in his elect the corruptions of the flesh . . . consecrates them to himself as temples renewing all their minds to true purity that they may practice repentance throughout their lives. . . .[72]

Weiss, therefore, does not need to adduce this chapter of Calvin as yet another testimony for *his unio mystica*.

*　　*　　*　　*　　*

In what I have written here, I have shown that the epistemology which I use in theology corresponds to the actual intention of Luther, in particular, his aim to break with the scholastic methodology. He was not able to perform this task. Melanchthon, for his part, was not equal to it either. On the contrary, this leader of theology in the church of the reformation set out on a return trip to the scholastic methodology—slowly but with progressively greater decisiveness. Up to now, at least methodologically, our theology has remained, as a whole, in the channels of scholasticism. Even Schleiermacher shares in the fundamental error of this mode of theology, in that he portrays the pious self-consciousness as the first part of theology, which is presupposed in every excitation of Christian sensibilities and yet, at the same time, is also always contained within it. That is, as with Melanchthon, his general doctrine of God is natural theology. I know of only one theologian who has broken with this whole tradition: Gottfried Menken.[73] He opens his *Versuch einer Anleitung zum eigenen Unterricht in den Wahrheiten der heiligen Schrift* ["An Attempt at an Introduction to My Own Instruction in the Truths of Holy Scriptures"] with the following assertion:

> A people has never been found, indeed, not even a single man has been found, who had a natural religion—i.e., such a religion whose concepts, truths, commands, usages, and hopes were innate to him, or who had come upon his religion prior to all instruction, all education and intercourse with men, who had come upon his religion through reflection and speculation without any teaching, tradition, or history. No man has been found who wanted to consider his religion as the result of his own speculation rather than as holy teaching of divine origin.[74]

Logically, the rejection of natural religion means, at the same time, a rejection of all universal concepts which one might possess prior to the particular structures of revealed religion or apart from the actuality of those structures in the founder and in the community.

These are the viewpoints by which my attempt at theology is guided. In general, it does not amaze me that this attempt has encountered misunderstanding and hostile misinterpretations. Specifically, however, the range and the kind of distortions in which men have brought me to exhibition and made me a horrible example has exceeded my furthest expectations.[75] And, worst of all, in their zeal to degrade me, my opponents have left themselves in a most vulnerable position without thinking that a corresponding judgment could follow upon the heels of their criticism. Many of them really appear to me to be very much like the Corinthian speakers in tongues. I have been silent for six years in the face of the slanders of my doctrine of atonement, and even now I have decided not to change my behavior. This present writing intends neither to make retaliation nor to advance the scandal. Rather, first of all, it aims at rapprochement and it makes defense only to the extent that it seems necessary to explain the matter itself in the light of my opponents' assertions. Whether I will achieve my goal, I do not know. Up to now, I have simply reconciled myself to the fact that the worst distortions of my viewpoint will be reckoned to me as my own work, and I have no direct means of cutting off the water to the mill of accusation in which I am constantly being ground to powder. My patience even endured the attacks of Frank and Luthardt for a long time. But one day, at the beginning of April, the controversy over metaphysics in theology was carried on so close to me, at the same time, though from different sides, that I decided to discuss the topic openly. Having entered the battle, I could not resist settling accounts with my opponents in Erlangen and Leipzig, even at this late date. At the same time, Weiss's discussions came into my hands, and they showed so much agreement with the prejudices of the theologians just named that I could only regard it as providence to take this opponent into my discussion as well. Besides, I do not wish to conceal the fact that, under these circumstances, I owe him a certain debt of gratitude, because he gave me so many opportunities to defend my convictions which were offensive to him.

Now, in order to bring this to a good end, I beg my opponents' indulgence as I recall still another man who handled metaphysics in a manner such as theirs and with the same unclear results—and that 200 years ago. Philipp Jakob Spener expressed things correctly,[76] saying that metaphysics is the doctrine of universal concepts which are used in all disciplines. But, at the same time and in the same sentence, he also pronounced the true metaphysics (which was not yet in existence) to be "a solid knowledge of the *doctrinae spiritum* [doctrine of the spirits]." Is it not true that this could only refer to the doctrine of angels? And one can understand Spener only with this presupposition, that metaphysics is the specific knowledge of divine things. But how is this assumption related to the correct definition of metaphysics, of which Spener is also sure? He evidences this same confusion in still other places.[77] In the controversy over the conditions necessary for theology, whether the theologian could be unregenerate or must be regenerate, he grants to his opponent George Conrad Dilfeld[78] his first assertion that the true knowledge of God is to be understood in a logical sense. But he nevertheless denies his opponent's assertion that the true knowledge of God is to be understood in a metaphysical sense. For in that case he would mean that the criterion for true knowledge of God is that *such knowledge must include everything which belongs to divine knowledge*. This would not be intelligible unless metaphysical knowledge were meant here to be equivalent to knowledge that takes its origin from religious interests, and this confusion is possible only if metaphysics is taken to be identical with the knowledge of God and of divine things. One can see that the nest of confusions which I have attempted to resolve is of fairly ancient standing. May I permit myself the hope that I have not merely shaken it up, but that I have destroyed it, so that no more barren and deformed theological eggs can be laid in it?

Written on the second day of Pentecost, June 6, 1881.

NOTES

1. [Christoph Ernst Luthardt (1823–1902) was an orthodox "neo-Lutheran," who was professor of New Testament and Systematic Theology at Leipzig. Ritschl's references to his *Compendium* are from the fifth edition (Leipzig: Döffling und Franke, 1878).]

2. Wilhelm Herrmann, *Die Religion im Verhältnis zum Welterkennen und zur Sittlichkeit* (Halle: M. Niemeyer, 1879), p. 14. [Herrmann (1846–1922) was one of Ritschl's greatest students.]

3. [Horace, *Satires*, Bk. I, 4; lines 155–56. Trans. by Henry H. Chamberlin, *Horace Talks* (Norwood, Mass.: The Plimpton Press, 1940).]

4. In J. G. Walch, *Dr. Martin Luthers Sämmtliche Schriften*, 23 vols. (Saint Louis: Concordia Publishing House, 1880–1910), VIII, 697.

5. [The German term *Geist* and its various forms are translated generally throughout this essay as "spirit." The term refers to the psychic life of man, and it is not necessarily religious in its meaning, although the connotations deriving from German Idealism which relate man's spirit to the Absolute Spirit cannot be set aside completely. The term often emphasizes man's intellectual or mental activity and in some instances it is translated with the word "mental." In the present passage, Ritschl provides an excellent description of *Geist*.]

6. Cf. Herrmann, *Die Religion im Verhältnis*, pp. 123 ff.

7. [Matthias Claudius (1740–1815) was a noted literary figure who emphasized the inner awakening of the human spirit.]

8. Franz Hermann Reinhold Frank, "Aus der neueren Dogmatik," *Zeitschrift für Protestantismus und Kirche*, n. s. LXXI (1876):301–22. [Frank (1827–1894) was prominent in the "Erlangen school" of theology, which was more confessional and conservative than Ritschl.]

9. *R.u.V.* III, 242–43. See *ET*, 282, 283.

10. Rudolf Hermann Lotze, *Metaphysik*, 2nd ed. (Leipzig: S. Hirzel, 1884), p. 185. *ET: Metaphysic*, trans. B. Bosanquet (Oxford: Clarendon Press, 1884), p. 168. [Lotze (1817–1881), a philosopher, was Ritschl's colleague at Göttingen.]

11. Friedrich Adolf Philippi, *Kirchliche Glaubenslehre*, 3rd ed. (Gütersloh: Bertelsmann, 1883), II:20 ff. [Philippi (1809–1882) was a confessional theologian associated with "neo-Lutheran" movements. Ritschl erroneously refers to this work as *Kirchliche Dogmatik*.]

12. Frank, "Aus der neueren Dogmatik," p. 319.

13. John Calvin, *Commentary on the Gospel According to John*, 2 vols. (Grand Rapids: Eerdmans, 1949), I:417.

14. [Friedrich Lücke (1791–1855) was a middle-of-the-road theologian at Bonn. Ritschl probably refers to Heinrich August Wilhelm Meyer (1800–1873), a Hannover church official who founded a celebrated commentary series on the New Testament.]

15. ["Repristinating theology" refers to a nineteenth century German Lutheran theological trend which emphasized adherence to the Lutheran confessional documents, with special opposition to rationalism and to "union" attempts which aimed at uniting the Lutheran and Reformed churches in Prussia.]

16. [Philipp Nicolai (1556–1608) was a Lutheran theologian and hymn writer.]

17. [Stephen Praetorius (1536–1603) was a pastor who wrote devotional tracts during the period of the reformation.]

18. See my *Geschichte des Pietismus*, II: 19, 23, 32.

19. Gottfried Arnold, *Historie und Beschreibung der mystischen Theologie oder geheimen Gottesgelehrtheit* (Frankfurt: Thomas Fritschen, 1703), pp. 132 ff. [Arnold (1666–1714) was an important early protestant historian, who recognized the importance of unconventional and heretical movements in Christianity.]

20. [See, for example, Ritschl's comments in *Die christliche Vollkommenheit*, critical edition by Cajus Fabricius (Leipzig: J. C. Hinrichs, 1924), pp. 8 ff. Also *R.u.V.*, III, 343–45, 472–73, 489–90, and section 49; *ET*, 362–64, 501–2, 519–21.]

21. [Johann Albert Bengel, *Gnomon of the New Testament* (Philadelphia: Perkinpine and Higgins, 1888), I:705. Bengel (1687–1752) was a noted pietist biblical scholar.]

22. [Christian Wolff (1679–1754) was an Enlightenment metaphysician who attempted to synthesize science and ontology.]

23. Lotze, *Metaphysik*, p. 163.

24. [Hermann Weiss, a contemporary of Ritschl, was professor of theology at Tübingen.]

25. Hermann Weiss, "Ueber das Wesen des persönlichen Christenstandes; Eine Kritische Orientierung mit besonderer Beziehung auf die Theologie Ritschls" in *Studien und Kritiken* LIV, 3 (1881):377–417.

26. [The anabaptists comprise a movement within the reformation, generally termed "left-wing," which emphasized a second birth for Christians. Luther and Calvin were very critical of the anabaptists, an attitude which their followers maintained in Ritschl's time. The Old Believers is a sectarian movement which originated within the Russian church in the seventeenth century, in protest against ecclesiastical and civil authority. The movement included broad sections of the common people, and it tended toward fanaticism.]

27. [Starowerzen refers to the Russian Old Believers.]

28. [C. F. Georg Heinrici (1844–1915) was professor of New Testament in Marburg and Leipzig.]

29. [Carl Christian Johann Holsten (1825–1897) was professor of New Testament in Heidelberg.]

30. [The citation is quoted from the article by Heinrici, p. 510.]

31. Perhaps it would be interesting to examine Spener on this point. *Theologisches Bedenken* (Halle: Wäysen-Hauses, 1702), Vol. 1, chap. 1, section 34: "What is the actual *formal element* of the spiritual life in the soul of the regenerate? Grace or Christ or faith or the powers granted us? Christ himself is not the *formal element*, rather he belongs much more to the *efficient cause*; and the spiritual life is something that, as it were, flows from him. And if on the basis of Gal. 2:20 ("It is no longer I who live, but Christ who lives in me") or Col. 3:4 ("Christ who is our life") it should be said that Christ is made the *form* of our life, that is nevertheless not the intention of those passages; rather, they only show that our spiritual life comes from Christ, that he—far more than we—is efficacious in it. . . . Again the grace of God is not the *formal element,* but rather belongs to the efficacious cause; for just as we are reborn because of the grace of God, so also, therefore, our life flows out of that same grace. . . . Therefore, I do not know how to characterize the *formal element* other than as the new manner of the new man or new divine nature in him (II Peter 1:4); this new manner consists in a divine light of a lively knowledge of God and in the divine power, out of which the regenerate person is not only able to do good, but he also has a drive toward the good and is like-minded with the divine will."

32. See, for example, Hartung's review of Hartmann's *Die Krisis des Christenthums in der modernen Theologie*, in *Theologische Literaturzeitung* VI, 8 (1881):191–92.

33. [Catherine of Genoa (1447–1510), daughter of a wealthy family, became a mystic, noted for her writings.]

34. ["Enthusiasm" refers to the ecstatic phenomena associated with the anabaptists.]

35. [Jodocus van Lodensteyn (1620–1677) was a Reformed theologian and revival preacher.]

36. [Justus Feuerborn (1587–1656) was professor of theology at Giessen.]

37. [Johann Hülsemann (1602–1661) was professor of theology in Wittenberg and Leipzig, noted for his Lutheran orthodoxy.]

38. [See note 16 above.]

39. [Johann Arndt (1555–1621) was one of the principal figures in the emergence of pietism.]

40. [Balthasar Meisner (1587–1626] was an important theologian of orthodox Lutheranism in the century after Luther.]

41. [Lucas Osiander the Younger (1571–1638), together with his father, represented the strong Swabian theological tradition after the reformation.]

42. [John T. McNeill (ed.), Calvin: *Institutes of the Christian Religion*, Library of Christian Classics 20 (Philadelphia: Westminster, 1960), pp. 537, 576, 582–83.]

43. [The *Formula of Concord* of 1580 is one of the chief confessional documents of the Lutheran tradition. It was the last of these documents in time, coming after a period of bitter controversy among Luther's followers. The standard text is found in Tappert.]

44. [Johann Gerhard (1582–1637) was one of the most significant Lutheran theologians in the century after Luther.]

45. [Johann Andreas Quenstedt (1617–1688) was a major orthodox Lutheran theologian.]

46. [Abraham Calov (1612–1686) was a major orthodox Lutheran theologian.]

47. [Andreas Osiander (1498–1552) was a contemporary of Melanchthon who was a leading force for conservatism and strict orthodoxy, although in the issue discussed here by Ritschl, Osiander was considered unorthodox because of his insistence that justification must mean that Christ dwells within the believer, since it is not enough to say (as the more orthodox did say) that the believer is *declared* righteous. In this connection he used the concept of *unio mystica* to express the indwelling of Christ.]

48. [Philip Melanchthon (1497–1560) was Luther's co-worker and chief disciple. See also Ritschl's essay from 1878, "Die Entstehung der lutherischen Kirche" ("The Emergence of the Lutheran Church") in Gesammelte Aufsätze (Freiburg and Leipzig: J. C. B. Mohr, 1893).]

49. [Christian Hoburg (1607–1665) was a pietist and appreciative of mysticism.]

50. [Friedrich Schleiermacher (1786–1834) is often termed the greatest modern protestant theologian. He was strongly influenced by pietism and romanticism.]

51. [Herrnhut is the site of a famous Moravian pietist community where Schleiermacher lived for some years during his youth.]

52. ["Mediating theology" refers to a nineteenth century German protestant theological tendency which attempted to hold the rising scientific liberal spirit and traditional Christianity together—thus mediating between repristinating theologians and liberals.]

53. [Victorinus Strigel (1524–1569), Jacob Andreae (1528–1590), Tilemann Hesshus (1488–1540), and Johann Wigand (1523–1587) were all strict orthodox Lutheran theologians who were active during the reformation period.]

54. Cf. Johann Wilhelm Preger, *Matthias Flacius Illyricus und seine Zeit*, 2 vols. (Erlangen, 1859–61), II:310 ff., 395 ff. [Matthias Flacius (1520–1575) was a co-worker and contemporary of Melanchthon and Luther. See also "The Emergence of the Lutheran Church," cited above, note 48.]

55. Ibid., p. 313: "massam hominis initio conditam adhuc utcunque remansisse, tametsi valde vitiatam, sicut si in vino et aromatibus, exspirante aerea et ignea substantia, remaneret tantum terrena et aquea."

56. [Cf. *CR* XIII, 507–752. The discussion of substance and accidents is taken from pp. 522, 528–29.]

57. Ibid., pp. 534–35. [These five philosophical categories are difficult to translate. Ritschl's point is that Melanchthon did not reckon a person's empirically observable actions and appearance as a part of his essential self.

Thus, we may render the terms as actions of habit (*habitus*), possibilities of action (*potentiae*), necessary action by which we adjust to our world (*naturales*), action aroused by the effects of others upon us (*affectus*), and our physical appearance (*figura*).

58. Preger, *Matthias Flacius*, pp. 397 ff.

59. [Ritschl erroneously cites Section II, paragraph 57, in his text. See Tappert, p. 518.]

60. Hermann Schultz, "Luther's Ansicht von der Methode und den Grenzen der dogmatischen Aussagen über Gott," *Zeitschrift für Kirchengeschichte* IV, 1 (1880):77–104. Also, "Lehre von der Gottheit Christi," pp. 195 ff.

61. Ritschl, *Geschichte des Pietismus*, I:296, 299, 436.

62. Weiss proceeds quite analogously, since he is intent upon demonstrating that I set God aside in a deistic manner. Simply because I do not—on every page where the complex relationships of the Christian life are being examined in light of the inescapable form of spontaneity [*Selbstthätigkeit*]—buttress his memory with the reminder that this all has its present basis in the love and gracious will of God—because of this, he asserts that the concepts of love and grace hold no place in my work. Immediately thereupon (p. 397), he reproaches me: "The idea, however, that individuals obtain the basis and content of their religious life *totally only* from the community is, despite Ritschl's assurances to the contrary, catholicizing." I want to come to the assistance of the Herr Professor's memory with (Luther's) *Large Catechism*, part II, 40–42: "I believe that the Holy Spirit makes me holy. . . . How does he do this? By what means? Answer: Through the *Christian church*, the forgiveness of sins. . . . In the first place, he has a unique community in the world. *It is the mother that begets and bears every Christian through the Word of God*, etc." Yet I do not conceal the fact that this enterprise, in its attempt to fasten upon me, in one breath, the opposite error has momentarily shattered my equanimity. But I regain it through reflection upon the probable basis on which Weiss made his judgment of me. To begin with, he is a pietist, or at least he sees everything through the pietist glasses, and therefore he has no idea of and no concern for the practical interests of the reformation. Further, as a disciple of Max Landerer (Cf. my review of Landerer's *Neueste Dogmengeschichte* in *Theologische Literaturzeitung* VI, 4 (1881):77–81), he has learned to investigate other persons for all possible heresies. Finally, however, he betrays the source of his virtuosity and violence in this way, that also a drop of critical oil from Baur's legacy has gone to his head.

63. *CR* XXI, 85.

64. ["Kenosis" comes from the Greek "emptying," and it refers to a theory concerning Christ, that he emptied himself of his divinity, in order to become incarnate redeemer. Cf. Phil. 2:7.]

65. *CR* XXI, 97.

66. Ibid., 255.

67. Ibid., 256.

68. Ibid., 530.

69. Ibid., 366, 367.

70. Ibid., 607–10.

71. [Calvin, *Institutes,* III, 2, 6, 7 (McNeill, 548–51). Material in parentheses is Ritschl's.]

72. [Ibid., 601.]

73. [Gottfried Menken (1768–1831) was a pietist theologian.]

74. Gottfried Menken, *Versuch einer Anleitung zum eigenen Unterricht in den Wahrheiten der heiligen Schrift,* 2nd ed. (Bremen: W. Kaiser, 1825).

75. Spener already had his experience with this theological evil. He writes in 1680 in *Die Allgemeine Gottesgelehrtheit aller gläubigen Christen und rechtschaffenen Theologen* (Frankfurt, 1680), I:326: "It is a grievous rudeness of our time, that men are so ready and quick with glee to bring under suspicion a teaching simply because it may not be commonly heard, or because it is set forth with words that are not familiar, or because it is set forth by a man whom one otherwise holds in suspicion; or else men handle it in some other unpleasant manner—even if that teaching is commensurate with the holy scripture and Christian doctrine, it is brought under suspicion of error, immediately discredited publicly, even without sufficient proof; but generally a teaching in which one finds even the smallest bit of an ancient heresy or a new one, is immediately burdened with the name of the heresy, even when that doctrine has some agreement with the words which a Christian teacher has used." [Philipp Jakob Spener (1635–1705) is considered to be the "Father of Pietism." Ritschl dealt at length with Spener's work and thought in his *Geschichte des Pietismus,* II.]

76. Philipp Jakob Spener, *Theologische Bedenken,* I:420.

77. Ibid., III:535.

78. [George Conrad Dilfeld, deacon in Nordhausen, rejected Spener's insistence that theology could not be undertaken by reason alone, solely as an academic discipline.]

INSTRUCTION IN THE

CHRISTIAN RELIGION

INSTRUCTION IN THE CHRISTIAN RELIGION

This work is a summary of Christian doctrine that Ritschl originally prepared for use in the upper grades of German secondary schools. His activity on the provincial examining committee, which supervised graduation requirements, convinced him that religious instruction needed improvement. The book never succeeded as a school text except where Ritschl's students used it and supplemented it by their own explanations, thereby rendering it less difficult to understand. Some distinguished theologians began their careers teaching school, using this book, including Wilhelm Herrmann, Adolf von Harnack, and Theodore Link. Since Ritschl incorporated their suggestions into later editions, we might say that his text had exceptional field-testing! Ritschl saw, however, that the future of the book lay with theological students, and he rewrote later editions with that in mind. It did succeed in gaining him many followers among theological and philosophical students in his day, since it is the only complete survey of his doctrinal system in print.

The title of this book in German is the same as that which translates Calvin's *Institutes of the Christian Religion*. Ritschl chose the title deliberately, as he wrote in 1875, when the work first was published,[1]

> It is not food for babies, but on the contrary very strongly concentrated nourishment. . . . I hope that it will be worthy of the attention of theologians also. For this reason I choose the title, so as to indicate that I wish to pick up from Calvin and (implicitly, of course) also from Melanchthon's *Loci* and Lombard's *Sentences*. Don't I have high-flying aspirations?

Thus, it should be titled in English so as to carry the connotations Ritschl intended. However, inasmuch as the first translation by Alice Swing in 1901 has gained wide usage, her error is continued here.[2]

The first edition from Adolph Marcus in Bonn is dated 1875, with revised editions in 1881 and 1886. Unaltered printings of the third edition appeared in 1890 and 1895. Cajus Fabricius issued an excellent critical edition in 1924 which includes all the variant readings of the three editions, and a new printing of the first edition has recently appeared in German. The translation which follows, from the third edition, is a revision of Swing's with important variations from the first edition in footnotes.

1. Otto Ritschl, II:273.
2. In Albert Swing, *The Theology of Albrecht Ritschl* (New York: Longmans, Green and Co., 1901).

Instruction in the

Christian Religion

INTRODUCTION

1. Since the Christian religion has its origin in a special revelation, and exists in a special community of believers and worshipers, its peculiar conceptions of God must always be interpreted in connection (a) with the recognition of the one who bears this revelation and (b) with the right appreciation of the Christian community, if the total substance of Christianity is to be understood correctly. A system of doctrine which ignores either of these two elements will prove defective.

2. Christianity claims to be the perfect religion, in contrast to the other kinds and levels of religion; it furnishes man with that which is striven after, but only dimly and imperfectly realized in other religions. The perfect religion is the one within which the perfect knowledge of God is possible. Christianity claims to have this perfect knowledge of God because its community derives itself from Jesus Christ who, as the Son of God, ascribes to himself perfect knowledge of his Father[1] and because it derives its knowledge of God from the same Spirit in whom God knows himself.[2] These conditions of the existence of the Christian religion are referred to when we are baptized in the name of the Father and the Son and the Holy Spirit.[3]

3. Any understanding of Christianity can do justice to its claim to perfection (par. 2) only when undertaken from the point of view

of the Christian community itself. But because this point of view has often been shifted in the course of history, and because the intellectual horizon of the community has been clouded by outside influences, it stands as the fundamental principle of the protestant church that Christian doctrine is to be obtained from the Bible *alone*.[4] This principle refers explicitly to the original documents of Christianity gathered together into the New Testament, for the understanding of which the original documents of the Hebrew religion gathered together in the Old Testament serve as an indispensable aid. These books are the foundation of a competent understanding of the Christian religion from the point of view of the community, because the gospels set forth in the work of its founder the immediate cause and final end of the community's religion, whereas the epistles make known the original state of its common faith. The epistles do this, moreover, in a form not yet affected by the influences which as early as the second century stamped Christianity as catholic.

4. The instruction in the Christian religion must be so divided that the conditions referred to in paragraph 1 are adhered to. Moreover, that portion of doctrine which pertains to the life of the individual Christian will be governed by the communal conditions of the religion and its ethical development as set forth directly in the preceding paragraphs. The instruction in the Christian religion may be divided into the following doctrines:

1. Concerning the kingdom of God.
2. Concerning reconciliation through Christ.
3. Concerning the Christian life.
4. Concerning public worship.

I. THE DOCTRINE OF THE KINGDOM OF GOD

5.[5] The kingdom of God is the divinely ordained highest good[6] of the community[7] founded through God's revelation in Christ; but it is the highest good only in the sense that it forms at the same time the ethical ideal for whose attainment[8] the members of the community bind themselves to each other through a definite type of reciprocal action.[9] This meaning of the concept "kingdom of God" becomes clear through the imperative which is simultaneously expressed in it.

6. The righteous conduct through which the members of Christ's community share in effecting the kingdom of God finds its universal

law and its personal motive in love to God and to one's neighbor.[10] This love receives its impulse from the love of God revealed in Jesus Christ (pars. 13, 22). The broadening of the concept of neighbor to include men as men, i.e., as ethical persons, opposes the kingdom of God to the narrower ethical communities (par. 8) which are limited by men's natural endowment [Ausstattung] and by the natural restrictions on their common activities.[11] The law of love appears in contrast to the arrangement of human society based merely upon private right,[12] and it goes beyond the principle of personal regard for others set forth in the Mosaic decalogue.[13]

7. The Christian concept of God's kingly authority—to which the kingdom of God corresponds as the union of subjects bound together by righteous conduct—arose out of similarly expressed thoughts in the religion of Israel, thoughts which in turn indicate its original purpose.[14] These thoughts are, in their historical development, elevated by the prophets to the expectation that through God's supernatural judgment his dominion will be realized in the righteousness of a morally purified Jewish people and will be recognized even by the heathen.[15] This idea is to be distinguished from the heathen designation of their gods as kings, partly because of the background of the free creation of the world by God, and partly because of the humane content of the corresponding law (par. 6, n. 13); for these reasons it engenders the expectation of the religious and moral unification of the nations. The Christian meaning of this thought goes beyond its Old Testament form, in that the ethical intention of the dominion of God is freed from adulteration by the political and ceremonial conditions under which the Old Testament idea and the Jewish hope labored.[16]

8. The kingdom of God which thus (pars. 5–7) presents the spiritual and ethical task of mankind as it is gathered in the Christian community is *supernatural*, insofar as in it the ethical forms of society are surpassed (such as marriage, family, vocation, private and public justice, or the state), which are conditioned by the natural endowment of man (differences in sex, birth, class, nationality) and therefore also offer occasions for self-seeking. The kingdom of God is *supramundane*, even as it now exists in the world as the present product of action motivated by love, insofar as we understand as "mundane" the nexus of all natural, naturally conditioned and organ-

ized existence. And the kingdom of God is at the same time the highest good of those who are united in it, to the degree that it offers the solution to the question propounded or implied in all religions: How can man, recognizing himself as a part of the world and at the same time capable of a spiritual personality, attain to that dominion over the world, as opposed to limitation by it, which this capability gives him the right to claim? The supernatural and supramundane kingdom of God continues to exist as the highest good of its members even when the present mundane conditions of spiritual life are changed (par. 76).

9. Although actions prompted by love and charitable human organizations are empirically perceptible as such, the motive of love which inspires them is in no case completely open to the observation of others. Therefore, the presence of the kingdom of God within the Christian community is always invisible and a matter of religious faith.[17] Especially must it be noted that the real continuance of the kingdom of God is not identical with the continuance of the Christian community, as the latter is visible as the church in public worship.[18]

10. The equality of all men as such, regardless of differences of nation or rank (par. 6, n. 11), and the duty of universal brotherly love are recognized even in classical paganism. Greek poets recognize the equality of slave and freeman.[19] Stoic philosophers witness to the brotherhood of all men, and from this conception of human nature derive the virtues which are to lead to the establishment of the most comprehensive human fellowship[20] and all of this apart from any thought of God. Nevertheless, it is a fact that the transformation of human society in accordance with these views was a development of Christianity, not Stoicism. Two reasons account for this: *First*, a diametrically opposite conclusion from that of the Stoics may as easily be drawn from their conception of the nature of man, depending upon the empirical view which informs this conception. *Second*, a knowledge of universal ethical precepts, as such, is never sufficient to call forth and organize the activity that is appropriate to those precepts. This activity follows only when a special, indeed a religious, motive or ground of obligation is linked with knowledge of the universal precept. Accordingly, the principles common to some degree to both Stoicism and Christianity became fruitful only

upon the soil of the latter where they were taken up into the under-lying principle of obligation of that particular religious community. The highest criterion for those obligations is the thought of a supra-mundane, supernatural God.[21] Accordingly, the exercise of one's humanness is all the more reliably connected with the thought of a supernatural God rather than a fluctuating concept of human nature when the union of men, *qua* men, at which it aims, bears in itself the stamp of the supernatural and supramundane (par. 8).

11. The complete name of God which corresponds to the Chris-tian revelation is "The God and Father of our Lord Jesus Christ."[22] This name includes the fact, already recognized to some extent in the religions of all civilized nations [*Culturreligionen*], that God is a spiritual person. It includes also the characteristics brought out first in the religion of the Old Testament, that God is the only being of his kind, [23] that he is not encumbered with nature and thus did not come into existence with the world like the many heathen divinities; that rather, he is the creator of the universe who, as the will that determines himself and all things for himself,[24] in particular designs a community of men for religious communion with himself and ethical communion with one another.[25]

12.[26] Indirectly included in the complete Christian name of God (par. 1), "The God and Father of our Lord Jesus Christ," is also that he is the Father of all, of whatever nationality, who are united in the community of the Lord Jesus Christ. Therefore in the abbrevi-ated name, "God our Father,"[27] the thought is expressed that the one God directs his special purpose to this community, whose highest good and common imperative is the kingdom of God (par. 5). Now, however, the complete name of God means that he has assumed this special relationship to this particular community only because he is already and first of all the Father of Jesus Christ, who is recognized as Lord by his community. In this capacity, however, Christ stands nearer to God, nearer than any other, because he shares in God's attributes of being the end of creation[28] and recognizes himself as set apart from the world in his position of sonship to God the Father.[29] The key to the relationship between God the Father and the Son of God is found in the declaration that God is love.[30]

13. In the complete name of God the fact that God is the Father of human beings is connected with Jesus Christ insofar as he is recog-

nized as the Lord of a particular fellowship (par. 12). Through
Christ's mediation this community of human beings is also designated as the object of divine love.[31] Such a relation would be inconceivable if God's purpose were merely the maintenance of the natural
existence of the human race. In this case men would not be of like
nature with God (par. 12, n. 30). The concept of God as love corresponds to that idea of mankind which sees man destined for the
kingdom of God and for the activity directed toward this kingdom,
i.e., the mutual union of man through action springing from love
(par. 6).[32] This destiny, however, is realized by men only in their
union with the community of their lord Jesus Christ.

14. The correlation between the concept of God as love and the
kingdom of God as the final purpose of the world is confirmed by
the statement that God's decision to establish the community of the
kingdom of God was decreed before the foundation of the world.[33]
The eternity of God which this implies is not sufficiently contained
in the affirmation that his existence reaches out beyond that of the
world without beginning or end and that God therefore has a measure of time different from that of man.[34] Rather, we recognize God's
eternity in the fact that amid all the changes of things, which also
indicate variation in his working, he himself remains the same and
maintains the same purpose and plan by which he creates and directs
the world.[35]

15. The religious acknowledgment of the omnipotence and omnipresence of God, implied in the creation and preservation of the
world by God's will,[36] does not undertake to explain the continuance
of natural things in whole or in part,[37] but rather always seeks to
emphasize that God's care and gracious presence are certain for the
pious man, because the world-creating and world-preserving will of
God has the well-being of man as its purpose. Therefore, the thought
of the omnipotence of God finds its consistent fulfillment in the
thought of his wisdom, omniscience, and disposition to meet the
needs of men.[38]

16. The first perception to arise out of the thought of the omnipotence of God is the insignificance of man. However, inasmuch as
the same thought is also the foundation of our impression of God's
constant readiness to help (goodness, grace, pity),[39] omnipotence
receives the peculiar stamp of *righteousness* in the particular revela-

tion of the old and new covenants. By "righteousness" the Old Testament signifies the consistency of God's providence [*Leitung zum Heil*], validated on the one hand in the existence of pious and upright adherents to the old covenant,[40] and undertaken on the other hand for the community whose salvation would bring God's government to completion.[41] Insofar as the righteousness of God achieves his dominion in accordance with its dominant purpose of salvation, in spite of all the difficulties which proceed from the Israelites themselves, it is *faithfulness*.[42] Thus in the New Testament also the righteousness of God is recognized as the criterion of the special actions by which the community of Christ is brought into existence and led on to perfection;[43] such righteousness cannot therefore be distinguished from the grace of God.

17. The religious view of the world is based on the fact that all natural occurrences stand at God's disposal when he wishes to help men (par. 15). Accordingly, remarkable natural occurrences with which the experience of the special help of God is connected,[44] are regarded as miracles, and thus as special tokens[45] of his gracious readiness to help believers. Therefore, the conception of miracles stands in a necessary correlation to a special belief in the providence of God and is quite impossible apart from such a relationship.[46]

18. God administers the government of the world—and adjusting of the relation between man and the world—by means of retribution. This legal conception is employed in Christianity, as in all religions, because several of its characteristics correspond to the relations which are recognized in every religious view of the world. For law as well as religion has to do with regulating *the position* of the individual *vis-à-vis the world* in accordance with his social or moral worth, and has to do further with the fact that this position is assigned or recognized by an external will (of society, or the state, or God). Thus the concept of divine reward and punishment is also employed in Christianity.[47] The analogy with law extends also to the fact that as the exercise of the right of punishment in the state is only a means of upholding the public well-being, so also the divine punishments which are visited upon godless and persistently rebellious men are always subordinate to the purpose of perfecting the salvation of the righteous and maintaining their cause in the world. But in his purpose these dispensations of God are never a matter of equivalents.

On the contrary, there is in this divine administration of justice, *first of all*, no admission of human right over against God,[48] *secondly*, no equality between reward and worthiness on the one hand, and punishment and unworthiness on the other,[49] and, *thirdly*, no immediate congruence between misfortune and guilt or prosperity and goodness in individual cases, as might have been expected from the divine power. Any such congruence is referred rather to the future, particularly to the final judgment and the future life.[50] Therefore, the familiar conclusion drawn by the pre-Christian manner of judgment, i.e., that great misfortune was evidence of great guilt, is especially invalidated,[51] and the probability is introduced that a high degree of worldly misfortune may exist precisely in connection with religious and moral worthiness.[52] Finally, a point of view is introduced that substitutes an organic relation of cause and result[53] for the mechanical relation between reward (punishment) and worthiness (unworthiness) which is recognized in human law. That such a principle as this is operative in all cases can, in truth, be discerned only at the end of time. In the course of history clear examples of this principle are surrounded and obscured by manifold instances of exactly opposite nature. But the Christian faith does not allow itself to be confused as to the consistent direction of the world by God through the apparently purposeless complications of the present and the suffering of the righteous in consequence of the guilt of the unrighteous,[54] because the regular experience of an exact and immediate connection between happiness and worthiness would endanger the freedom and dignity of the moral disposition.

19. The imperative of the moral association of all men as men could become effective as a practical principle only insofar as it grew out of the religious motive of the specifically Christian community (par. 10). Moreover, since that imperative raises itself above all naturally conditioned moral motives, its authority in the Christian community finds its necessary criterion in the idea of a supernatural God developed in paragraphs 11–18. Moreover, the peculiar fact of such a community, which sets itself to the realization of this universal task as the thrust of the kingdom of God, is not a natural "given" but is comprehensible in its distinctive nature only as the work of Christ's own establishment (par. 13). Therefore, in order for us to understand and rightly participate in the existence of this

community, it is necessary to acknowledge and understand the permanent relation which exists between the community of the kingdom of God and its founder Jesus Christ.[55]

20. The historical connection of Christianity with the religion of the Old Testament (par. 7) makes it natural that Jesus should in general represent himself as a prophet sent by God who was ordained in God's decree concerning the world and mankind.[56] However, he sets himself above all the preceding prophets of the Old Testament by making himself known as the Son of God and the promised king of David's race (Christ the anointed),[57] who need not first prepare the way for the kingdom of God but effects *the* work of God,[58] i.e., himself exercises immediate divine rulership over the new community of the sons of God, and establishes it for the future (par. 5, n. 7). The prophetic vocation of Jesus is not annulled by his claim to messianic dignity, but only modified by it, since he exercises his right as lord only through his morally effective teaching and by his readiness to engage in the action of servant—not by the compulsion of legal judgment.[59]

21. In the moral world all personal authority is conditioned by the nature of one's vocation and by the connection between one's fitness for his particular vocation and his faithful exercise of it. Accordingly, the permanent significance of Jesus Christ for his community is based, *first*, on the fact that he was the only one qualified for his special vocation—bringing in the kingdom of God;[60] that he devoted himself to the exercise of this highest conceivable vocation in the preaching of the truth and in loving action without break or deviation;[61] and that, in particular, as a proof of his steadfastness[62] he freely accepted in willing patience[63] the wrongs brought upon him by the opposition of the leaders of the nation of Israel and the fickleness of the people, all of which were so many temptations to draw back from his vocation.

22. *Second*, the imperative of Jesus Christ's vocation, or the final purpose of his life, namely, the kingdom of God, is the very purpose of God in the world, as Jesus himself recognized.[64] The solidarity between Christ and God, which Jesus accordingly claims for himself,[65] has reference to the whole range of his activity in his vocation and consists therefore in the reciprocal relation between God's love and Jesus' vocational obedience.[66] Since he is the first to actualize in

his own personal life the final purpose of the kingdom of God, Jesus is therefore unique, for should any other fulfill the same task as perfectly as he, he would be unlike him because of his dependence upon Jesus. Therefore, as the prototype of the humanity to be united into the kingdom of God, he is the original object of God's love (par. 12), so that the love of God for the members of his kingdom is also mediated only through him (par. 13). Therefore, when this person is valued at his whole worth, this person who was active in his peculiar vocation, whose constant motive is recognizable as unselfish love to man, then we see in Jesus the complete revelation of God as love, grace and faithfulness.[67]

23. In every religion, not only is some sort of communion with God (or the gods) sought after and attained, but there is also a search at the same time for such a position of the individual vis-à-vis the world as will correspond with the idea of God which guides that religion. Hence, *third*, Jesus Christ's prerogative, that the rulership of the world is delivered over to him,[68] corresponds to the solidarity of Jesus with the supramundane God in the realization of the supramundane (par. 8) kingdom of God, which as the final purpose of God is also the final purpose of the world. The significance of this attribute is not secured if we suppose that Jesus did not exercise it, but allowed it to remain inactive in his public historical life. Moreover, he did not merely exercise it indirectly, as if by his deeds and his words and his patience in suffering he prepared the way for the kingdom of God in his community, so that his dominion over the world would be established only in the world-historical progress of that community. Rather, he exercised this dominion directly, not only in the independence of his action from the standard of religion peculiar to his people,[69] but also in his very readiness to suffer everything even unto death for the sake of his vocation.[70] For through this suffering he transformed the world's opposition to his life purpose into a means of his glorification, i.e., into the certainty of overcoming the world by the very fact of this momentary subjection to its power and assuring the supramundane continuance of his life.[71] Accordingly, his resurrection through the power of God is the consistent fulfillment, corresponding to the worth of his person, of the revelation effected through him which is final in respect to both the actual will of God and the destiny of man.

24. In Christ's vocational activity, directed to the divine purpose of the kingdom of God, the same acts of love and patience are both manifestations of the grace and faithfulness which are essential to God himself and proofs of his dominion over the world.[72] These relations, which are necessary to the full appreciation of Jesus and are evident in his life, are referred to in the confession of the Godhood of Christ which the Christian community has made from the beginning. That is to say, this attribute of Godhood cannot be maintained unless the same activities in which Jesus Christ proves himself man are thought of as being simultaneously and in the same way also distinctive predicates of God and the peculiar means of his revelation through Christ. If the grace and faithfulness and dominion over the world, which are evident both in Christ's active life and in his patience in suffering, are also the essential attributes of God and decisive for the Christian religion, then the right appreciation of the completeness of the revelation of God through Christ is assured by the predicate of his Godhood, in accordance with which Christians are to trust in him and to worship him even as they do God the Father.[73]

25. The estimate of Christ set forth in paragraphs 20–24 is intentionally directed with the greatest possible exactness to the historically certified characteristics of his active life, but at the same time it is undertaken from the standpoint of the community of the kingdom of God founded by him. These two criteria, historical and religious, for the understanding of his person should coincide[74] inasmuch as Christ's purpose was directed at founding the community in which he was to be acknowledged in religious faith as the Son of God. And if this purpose is in any measure historically realized, it follows that the perfect historical estimate of Christ is possible only for his religious community and that this estimate will be religiously correct in proportion as his community remains faithful to its historically unquestionable task. Accordingly, it is essential to the continuance of the Christian community as such, that it should keep alive within itself the memory of the finished life-work of Christ[75] and that accordingly the personal impulses of its founder should be ceaselessly operative in like efforts on the part of the members of his community.[76] In the fulfillment of these conditions we see the visible side of the mystery of Christ's exaltation to the right hand of God,

which is acknowledged by his community[77] as a guarantee that the purpose of his life was not frustrated but rather fully accomplished in his death.[78]

II. THE DOCTRINE OF RECONCILIATION
THROUGH CHRIST

26. In the Christian community the concept of the perfect common good included in the notion of the kingdom of God and the concept of personal goodness included in our understanding of God and in our view of Jesus Christ lay the foundation for a corresponding concept of sin and evil. Everyone judges himself by this concept of sin and evil to the extent that he stands in reciprocal relation to the world, i.e., to that structure of human society which in all conceivable degrees and variation is in contradiction to the good as recognized in Christianity.[79]

27. The imperative of the kingdom of God is assigned to the members of the Christian community, since their capacity for good in general is to be presupposed according to the revelation of God's love in Christ and its special effect upon them (par. 13). But it must also be remembered that we conceive the kingdom of God, insofar as the Christian community is active in its realization (par. 5, n. 9), to be in the process of becoming; it therefore is mingled at all points with the opposing currents of evil springing up on every side from the merely natural impulse of human will. Thus, while everyone born of Christian parents is born into the community of Christ, he is, at the same time, put into connection with evil, against which his natural will as such does not contend.[80] Sins are evil volitions, but they are also corresponding intentions, habitual inclinations and dispositions, not only insofar as these thwart the intended union of men into the kingdom of God or offend against the moral law of Christ (par. 6, n. 10) or run counter to the glory of God (par. 11, n. 24),[81] but in addition, insofar as they manifest in varying degrees a lack of reverence and trust in God.[82]

28. The possibility and probability of sinning, and this only, can be derived from the fact that the human will, which should decide for the recognized good, is a constantly growing power whose efficacy is not accompanied from the outset by a complete knowledge of the good. A universal necessity of sinning can be derived neither from

the natural endowment of man nor, least of all, from a discernible purpose of God.[83] The fact of universal sin on the part of man, in accordance with experience, is established by the impulse to the unrestrained exercise of freedom, with which everyone comes into the world and meets the manifold attractions to self-seeking which arise out of the sin of society. Therefore, it happens that some degree of self-seeking takes form in every person, even before a clear comprehension of the state of society's self-consciousness is awakened in him.

29. Sins are, in particular, actions or other volitions which come into conflict with increasingly severe social and legal ordinances, as is the case with rudeness, immorality, careless or intentional wrong, and crime. For at the same time, they oppose the highest law of good. Even actions and dispositions, which follow a justifiable end in a narrower sphere (par. 57, n. 162), are sins when they follow it in such a way as to come into conflict with higher common ends. On the other hand, we also recognize various degrees of sin in comparisons between a single action and a propensity to or a habit of sinning, between a carelessly and a willfully sinful act, between prudent self-seeking, unbridled passion, vice, insolence, and malice. Although all these forms of sin are alike in their opposition to the good, yet they are different in the degree in which they are detrimental to it and in the possibility still existing of improvement and conversion.[84]

30. The cooperation of many individuals in these forms of sin leads to a reinforcement of the same in common customs and principles, in standing immoralities, and even in evil institutions. So there develops an almost irresistible power of temptation[85] for those who with characters yet undeveloped are so much exposed to evil example that they do not see through the network of enticements to evil. Accordingly, the kingdom of sin, or the (immoral, human) world[86] is reinforced in every new generation. Corporate sin [die gemeinsame Sünde], this opposite of the kingdom of God, rests upon all as a power[87] which at the very least limits the freedom of the individual with respect to the good.[88] The limitation of the freedom of the individual for the good, by his own sin and by entanglement with the common condition of the world, is, strictly speaking, an absence of the freedom to choose the good [Unfreiheit zum Guten].

Apart from the kingdom of God, however, this is the common condition of all men, because the form even of the partial good is assured only through the existence of the whole.

31. It is true that the full extent of the existence and guilt of sin appears only from a comparison of sin with the imperative of the kingdom of God (par. 26). Yet its character—contrary as it is to the destiny of man, to the freedom of the will, and to the commands of God—is made evident in all the preceding levels of moral development through a self-condemnation which, arising everywhere as an act of the individual, in some measure grows into a common conviction. At the heart of all individual as well as corporate condemnation of evil is the feeling of guilt as an expression of the individual accountability included in the freedom of the will. This sense of guilt is a witness to the fact that even the single sinful act does not by any means come to an end with the act, but continues to work as a disordering or perversion of moral freedom; it further testifies to the fact that the consciousness of an opposite destiny, so necessary to freedom, maintains itself in spite of the sinful action and desire. The feeling of guilt, in the form of this unavoidable judgment of condemnation, springs from the conscience,[89] whose presence in every man is to be counted upon as long as he has a measure of free will in connection with his sin. To be sure, the feeling of guilt, as such, does not have the power to undo the sin or to limit the continuance or increase of the sinful propensity. Rather, in many cases this feeling of guilt becomes the occasion for a stubborn maintenance of the sinful propensity or an increased rejection of God or, at least, an aversion to his authority. In yet worse cases, through the growth of this sinful propensity, the conscience itself is weakened and the feeling of guilt is practically lost, even in great sin. In spite of this, it is not consistent with our regard for human worth to admit, even in the cases of those apparently most hardened, the complete absence of this manifestation and thus the impossibility of repentance.

32. By evils, we mean natural events which, proceeding partly from the course of nature and partly from the operation of man, limit the exercise of our freedom for the attainment of our purposes. In part evils are, directly or indirectly, the result of sinful actions. The pre-Christian world held to a view which regarded great common misfortune as divine punishment and therefore as necessarily

the result of unusual transgression against the gods; to this was added the corresponding principle that all evils without exception are only the consequences of one's own sins and God's punishments. This pre-Christian perspective is in part out of harmony with experience and in part contrary to the view of the world set forth in Christ.[90] Thus it is that, in general, the estimate of evil by different men varies according to their strength of will or their habit and is therefore subjectively conditioned. On the other hand, Christianity teaches us to recognize that through our very devotion to our faith we necessarily draw suffering upon ourselves as the result of our coming into collision with present historical forces (par. 18, n. 52). The Christian view of the world differs therefore from the heathen and Jewish views in that tenderness of feeling which prevents us from reckoning a man's personal sufferings as divine punishments.[91] It follows, finally, that the Christian regards death, even though it may have entered the world as a universal decree in consequence of the first sin of man,[92] neither as a punishment of his personal sin nor as at all the specific hindrance to his communion with God or to his salvation, and therefore not as the greatest evil.[93]

33. Strictly speaking, only the individual person himself can determine that the misfortunes which come upon him are divine punishments for sin, when he thus reckons them to himself because of a feeling of guilt. This is true as much when through redemption one has attained to trust in God (par. 51) as it is in the case of defiance toward God. Still worse, to be sure, is the condition of a sinner who regards deserved misfortunes as injustice, or connects no thought of a divine government of the world with his experience. So far the analogy holds between the punishments inflicted by God and those decreed by human law. In both cases the curtailment of rights which follows upon the illicit extension of those rights is evident in connection with the occasion of misfortunes. But punishment in the religious relation to God, apart from external misfortunes, is the lessening or dissolution of the designed or desired communion with God. Accordingly, the continuance of unforgiven guilt, whether felt more or less strongly or even not at all, is to be regarded as divine punishment in the fullest sense, as the real condemnation, insofar as it is connected with that lack of trust in God which gives expression to separation from God (par. 27, n. 82).

34. As a member of the Christian community one is called to the kingdom of God as man's highest good and his highest common duty (par. 5), because it is the final purpose of God himself (par. 13). At the same time, however, by the very recognition of this destiny there comes an increase of the feeling of guilt and separation from God which arises from our own sin and our solidarity with the sin common to all men. Thus Christianity seems to require of us a self-contradictory judgment of ourselves, but at the same time it does away with this contradiction in that it also brings the certainty of a God-given *redemption*.

35. Redemption in Christianity has both a thoroughly internal and a universal religious significance. From the first rubric, it follows that we are not, as in the Old Testament, to include under redemption the removal of social evil, especially political dependence upon foreign nations, to say nothing of the establishment of economic prosperity.[94] The second rubric implies that redemption does not pertain directly to the setting aside of the condition of sin which dominates the individual.[95] For while this condition is common to all, it is also distinctive in each individual and, therefore, can be contended against and set aside only by means of a particular opposition in the form of the resolution of the will, after one has experienced for himself religious redemption. In Christianity, such redemption denotes the forgiveness of sins or pardon through which the guilt of sin which separates man from God is removed, provided that neither indifference to nor defiance of God is joined with the feeling of guilt.[96]

36. The forgiveness of sins or justification [*Gerechtsprechung (Rechtfertigung)*], which guarantees the existence of the Christian community, is, as a divine purpose of grace, part of a free judgment. That is to say (without taking up at present the conditions to be considered in pars. 39–44), sinners are given by God the right to enter into communion with him and into cooperation with his own final purpose, viz., the kingdom of God, without their guilt and their feeling of guilt acting as a barrier thereto.[97] The freedom and independence of this divine judgment consist in this, that on man's part, situated as he is, no moral work (merit) is conceivable which might call for this positive judgment of God or actually establish it. Rather, this judgment needs only religious faith[98] or confidence in the

free grace or righteousness of God (par. 16, n. 43) in order to become actual and effective.

37. The more specific conceptions of reconciliation with God and adoption as his children coincide with the forgiveness of sins, pardon, and justification. These specificities merely add something individual. In reconciliation, for example, the forgiveness of sins appears no longer merely as the purpose of God but also as the result of that purpose. According to the conception of reconciliation with God, the individual has in faith and trust appropriated to himself the final purpose of God and given up his opposition (enmity) to God.[99] In adoption (acceptance as children of God) the gracious purpose of the judgment of forgiveness or justification is put into effect, so that God confronts the believer as a father and gives him the right to the full confidence of a child.[100] But these effects of divine redemption find practical application only on the condition that the believer at the same time takes an active part in the recognized purpose of God's kingdom and has given up the pursuit of selfish ends and inclinations, whether intentional or habitual.[101]

38. The forgiveness of sins, or reconciliation, as the common fundamental condition of the Christian community, within which the individual appropriates this gift of God,[102] is as essential to the peculiar character of that community as is the fact that it is called to realize the kingdom of God or the fact that the impulse to this realization is contained in its calling. It is a regression to the point of view of the Old Testament religion, or a falling back into the catholic conception of the matter, to preach forgiveness of sins merely to individuals as such, in relation to their personal feeling of guilt and their need as thus measured, or to preach it as a good which is always yet to be attained.[103]

39. Forgiveness of sins cannot be inferred as necessary from any universally established conception of God.[104] Rather, as the positive fundamental condition of the Christian community, it is to be gained from the positive Christian conception of God. Therefore its validity (par. 38) is linked to the peculiar work of Christ (par. 19).

40. Redemption or forgiveness of sins is not assured to the Christian community through Christ simply because he made, in his role as prophet and thus revealer of God, a universal promise to that effect (par. 20). On the contrary, that is just what he did not do.[105]

Rather, he himself beforehand and after him the earliest Christian witnesses linked such a result to the fact of his death. And this takes place insofar as his death is capable of comparison with the Old Testament sacrifices[106] which, in accordance with the grace of God, were offered for the whole people of Israel, partly to indicate their own entrance into the covenant with God and partly to serve in yearly repetition for the forgiveness of sins, i.e., to maintain the integrity of the covenant.[107]

41. The death of Christ has the value of the covenant-offering and the universal sin-offering, not because his enemies put him to death but because he obediently yielded himself to this fate as being, in the providence of God, a sure result of his distinctive vocation.[108] This significance of Christ's death is also expressed in the relationship between the images of the priest and the sacrifice, since in bringing his life-work to completion he conformed to both of these images.[109] Therefore his death stands as a sacrifice offered for the purpose of bringing forgiveness to his community or consummating their new covenant with God only insofar as we connect him with the very offering of the sacrifice or with the priestly self-awareness which dominates all of his vocational activity.[110]

42. The obedience of Christ to his vocation can be interpreted as a gift of God or as a sacrifice and priestly offering, because his righteous life, his patience and his preachments of truth were the result not only of his divine charge but also of his free consecration of himself to God. For by this vocational obedience he maintained the special fellowship of reciprocal love between God and himself.[111] Now he rendered his vocational obedience not only for its own sake, but at the same time necessarily for the purpose of bringing mankind into the same relation toward God which he occupied, as their father.[112] For this very purpose, furthermore, he also accepted with patience and resignation to God's will increased sufferings and death as a proof of his fellowship with God. And, finally, in this way he performed everything that was necessary to prove the genuineness of his fellowship with God and the possibility of a similar fellowship for all. In these respects, therefore, he represented the community before God as its royal priest for the purpose of establishing it completely.[113]

43. Now if we compare the fact of the existing community of

Christ to which we ourselves belong with his purpose in its foundation and with the priestly significance of his life and suffering unto
death, there appears clearly in his death, i.e., in the completion of his
life from the point of view of sacrifice, an analogy between it and
the Old Testament types. For the universal meaning of the symbolic
actions performed by the ministering priest, that the sacrifice might
be accepted by God, is rightly expressed by Peter when he says, in
speaking of Christ, that believers are thereby led to God,[114] are
brought near to him in the sacrifice.[115] In the case of the community
to be founded by Christ, this bringing near of men takes place because
they are originally separated from God by their sins and feeling of
guilt. Therefore, the sacrificial act of Christ's priestly completion of
his life-work serves to equip the new community with the divine
forgiveness of sins, because as their intentional representative he
transforms this separation of man from God into fellowship with
him as their father.

44.[116] Christ's victory over the world through patience in the
suffering made necessary by his vocation is not only a mark of his
Godhood in his office of revealer (pars. 23, 24) but is also the mark
of the completeness of his work as priestly representative of the
community which he is bringing to God. The same scope of Christ's
vocational obedience which filled his life and came to fulfillment in
his death is conceived under the two contrasting viewpoints of the
office of royal prophet and the royal priesthood, the representing of
God to men and of men (in the community) before God. Of these
two sides of his vocation (or offices), the latter is, it is true, subordinate to the former. But in this double value of his life Christ is the
mediator of the highest conceivable fellowship between God and
man.[117]

45.[118] The distinctiveness of the community founded by Christ is
not determined by his life in its aspect as representative and revealer
of God, that is, as God himself,[119] for in this relation Christ stands
over against the community. But the character of the community
which is itself reconciled to God, as is every individual within it who
appropriates justification through faith in Christ,[120] corresponds
rather to the position that Christ took as representative of the community in relation to God and the world. Since his dignity as Son of
God is also his because he sacrifices his life for the sake of the com-

munity,[121] so the adoption as children belongs to the members of his community as a result of the reconciliation with God (par. 37, n. 100). Because his patience in suffering and death establishes his dominion over the world for the sake of his believers, so faith in Christ includes in itself spiritual dominion over the world,[122] i.e., eternal life or Christian freedom.[123]

III. THE DOCTRINE OF THE CHRISTIAN LIFE

46. The individual believer within the Christian community does not appropriate to himself the call to the kingdom of God and reconciliation or acceptance as a child of God without simultaneously experiencing these effects of grace as impulses for corresponding personal activity.[124] Therefore, conversely, in the religious estimate of our total life-work which corresponds to these impulses, we recognize everything good as the effect of divine grace in us.[125] This agreement between these impulses and the purpose of God, and their similarity in different individuals, is grounded in and assured by the Holy Spirit in the community.[126] This is to say that the impulse to right conduct, i.e., to fulfilling the imperative belonging to the kingdom of God, and the impulse to give practical proof of our sonship with God have as their criterion the knowledge of God as our Father which is given to us in Christianity. However, the Christian knowledge of God, springing as it does from definitive revelation, is congruent with God's knowledge of himself. Hence, seen from the divine point of view, the development of the Christian community (resulting from the exercise of love in accordance with this knowledge of God) is a part of the divine self-revelation (par. 13, n. 32). From these considerations, it appears that the common spirit through which the members of the community receive their like knowledge of God and their like impulses toward the kingdom of God and toward sonship with God, is God's Holy Spirit.[127]

47. Practical proof of sonship with God in spiritual freedom and dominion over the world and labor for the kingdom of God fill out the Christian life which is a new creation of God, when compared with the sinful state which is presupposed in man.[128] It is as certain that these two activities stand in reciprocity with one another (par. 37, n. 101) as that the ends and motives in both cases exist on the same supramundane level. The reciprocal relation of these activities,

the first religious and the second ethical, is evident in the fact that the religious imperative of dominion over the world demands the same effort of the will as the ethical imperative of the kingdom of God, even as the latter includes in itself religious elevation above the world. The unity of this twofold destiny of life is evident in the joy or blessedness which springs from them both.[129] This is the feeling of religious-ethical perfection.[130] Insofar as blessedness is expected in the Christian life, the possibility is also therein admitted of perfection, which is set before us as an imperative in those two dimensions of our striving—for God's kingdom and its righteousness and for the exercise of freedom over the world.

48. Of course it is true that the series of dutiful actions, which we would represent to ourselves as the embodiment of the ethical task of our lives, always remains imperfect, partly because in our conceptualizing such a series can be carried out into infinity and partly because in any single moment our responsibilities may seem staggeringly heavy. In reality, it is not the fact of the actual continuance of sin,[131] but this external and quantitative conception of the imperative of the Christian life which is the ground of the traditional assertion that defect in good works is unavoidable and the possibility of Christian perfection is therefore out of the question. Nevertheless, in spite of the unavoidably defective quality of human conduct, we must uphold man's destiny as one who may attain personal perfection, since this destiny is correlative with the qualitative judgment that the religious-ethical life is a whole in its own right [*ein Ganzes in seiner Art*]. Now the concept of the whole signifies that the component parts of an organic existence are in a special way united by a common end. In accordance with this conception, Christian perfection consists in the process which fosters a person's ethical life-work[132] and in the development of ethical and religious character.[133] Included in this is the fact that one directs his action toward the end of the kingdom of God in a particular ethical vocation[134] and authenticates his sonship with God and his dominion over the world in the particular conditions of life into which he is placed.[135]

49. The struggle against and suppression of selfish impulses and habits are included in sanctification or the formation of Christian character.[136] The task here is not rooting out any impulse or affection, but ennobling and purifying it by the opposing force of moral prin-

ciples (par. 72). This task cannot and should not be accomplished
by special scrupulousness or special ascetic practices before the beginning of right action or the attainment of positive virtues. The similar
attempt of monasticism to avoid certain temptations to sin by isolation from the fundamental institutions of human society is also a
mistake. For evil inclinations and habits are rendered ineffective
only by the development of contrasting good inclinations and habits;
while virtues are produced only by the reaction of dutiful or righteous
action upon the will itself.[137] Therefore, the Christian imperative of
perfection and the consciousness of continual sinfulness are balanced
in the command to strive for the common good with the idea that as a
member of the Christian community one is no longer alive to sin.[138]
This is also the intended purpose of all honest and effectual repentance, to which, in the process of sanctification, one is all the more
inclined as he becomes more sensitive to the effect of sin upon himself.[139] Such repentance, however, is not attained when one dulls
his perception or observation of his own particular sins by mirroring
them in the uncertain reflection of the immeasurable general sin of a
society. It is in the constant readiness for real repentance that the
change of heart prescribed by Jesus stamps the whole life.[140]

50. The Christian perfection which corresponds to the personal
example of Christ himself[141] is shaped by the religious functions of
sonship with God and dominion over the world (i.e., faith in the
fatherly providence of God, humility, patience, and prayer) and by
the ethical functions of dutiful action in one's particular vocation
and the development of ethical virtues.[142] In this coherence of the
spiritual life the individual person possesses the significance of a
whole which exceeds the significance of the entire world which is
viewed as the order of a divided and naturally conditioned existence.[143] Included in this is autonomy from every particular authority.[144] This consequence of the Christian religion is the goal of that
impulse which is found in all religions (par. 8), namely, to make
certain through the appropriation of the divine life or the evident
divine purpose the significance of our spiritual life in the midst of the
limitations which grow out of its involvement in nature or the
world.

51. Faith in the fatherly providence of God is the Christian
world view in an abbreviated form.[145] In this faith, although we

neither know the future nor perfectly comprehend the past, yet we judge our momentary relation to the world on the basis of our knowledge of the love of God and on the basis of what we derive from this knowledge, namely, that every child of God possesses a significance greater than the world which God directs in accordance with his final purpose, i.e., our salvation.[146] From this faith there springs that confidence which in all its gradations is equally far removed from the gnawing anxiety which might arise from our relation to the superior power of nature, as it is from dull indifference or bold recklessness or from stoic imperturbability, since none of these are an expression of ongoing spiritual freedom. More specifically, faith in providence furnishes a standard by which the first impression of evils as limitations of freedom or as divine punishments is transformed into an interpretation of them as blessings, i.e., as means of education or testing.[147] In this assessment of evil occurrences he who trusts in providence gives evidence of his dominion over the world, as well as his redemption from the guilt and power of sin and his reconciliation with God. In an equally clear manner, faith in providence illumines the experiences of prosperity or happiness as gifts of God which call for our thankfulness to him and the purification or moderation of our self-reliance.[148]

52. Humility is that quality of feeling which springs from the knowledge of God's fatherly guidance and either accompanies this knowledge or, as a constant readiness to concur with all the dispensations of God, takes the place of the conscious exercise of trust in his providence. As a distinctively religious virtue, it is again that power of self-consciousness which leads us to assess both unpleasant and agreeable experiences as dispensations of God, and in such a way, therefore, that we are neither crushed nor unduly exalted by them.[149] The humility of the Christian does not spring from a constant consciousness of his sin, but neither is it indifferent to it. Rather, it involves a more lively sense of God's grace in view of sin and accordingly a hesitation to regard our religious and moral convictions, however well intended, as God's cause or to defend them as such. The religious man is unconscious of his own humility,[150] and still less is that humility an object of observation and exhaustive judgment on the part of others, since it does not manifest itself directly in any moral quality or mode of action.[151] Least of all does

it find its necessary manifestation in ceremonially proper ascetic actions, although from the first, thanks to a dualistic view of the world, a low estimation of the natural conditions of human life has been accepted as an especially clear proof of humility toward God.[152]

53. Patience under the hampering limitations of the world,[153] which arises from the judgment of faith in providence through the feeling of humble submission to God's fatherly guidance, accepts deserved evils as divine punishments and also as a means of education, undeserved evils as tests, or, perhaps at the same time, as the honor of martyrdom. Patience is fundamentally always a determination of the will; but it may take the form of a quality of feeling and thus unite itself closely with humility, when the original determination of the will proves adequate for countering the concrete limitations which the world continually sets before it. Since, however, the Christian world view holds that the difference between the significance of evil and prosperity is a relative one, patience as a religious virtue has room for exercise not only in experiences which appear at first as direct limitations, but also proves itself of value in connection with humility as a moderation of self-reliance in the context of experiences of prosperity, which can spoil men and make them dependent on the world.

54. Prayer, whether as thanksgiving or as petition, is the conscious and intentional exercise both of faith in God's providence[154] and of humility. It is also, as thanksgiving, the proof of patience and, as petition, the means of gaining or of strengthening patience. In these respects prayer is the proof of his reconciliation which the individual gives before God and to himself as well as being the means by which he establishes himself in the same. As the common offering of the community, it has still other characteristics (par. 79).

55. The answer to the prayer for specific blessings which we direct toward God in the midst of life's difficulties, although it seems to be assured without any limit,[155] is nevertheless limited by the reservation that the petition must accord with God's providence over us,[156] and that the one who prays must be engaged in the fulfillment of the divine commands.[157] Finally, the significance of the petitions addressed to God is made independent of the test of their direct and complete fulfillment by the fact that to know that God hears us is also to know that we have the blessings which we requested.[158]

56. The ethical imperative of the kingdom of God (par. 47) is performed as the most universal imperative of the Christian community, but only when the ultimate motive for all conduct is love for one's neighbor. We carry out this action in naturally conditioned moral communities which are narrower in scope (marriage, family, civic and social life, the nation), and we do so according to the specific principles that govern each. For the universal is always realized only in the particular. If the opposite were true, and one wished to fulfill the Christian imperative outside the natural orders of life, he would give a false particularity to that which should be universally valid and create something bizarre.[159]

57. Conduct in the narrower and naturally conditioned communities is subordinated to the most universal end of the kingdom of God and brought into direct relation to the same, when the regular activity incumbent upon each one in these communities is exercised in the form of an ethical vocation (par. 50, n. 142) for the common good.[160] The intention to serve the common good, with which the work of every vocation in society should be undertaken, does not exclude personal interest in its success or the acquiring of property; this latter becomes a motive to selfishness, however, unless it is balanced, in this ethical conception of vocation, by the communal ends. Accordingly, fidelity to one's vocation is at the same time following the example of Christ.[161] Moreover, this assessment, which sees ethical vocations as constitutive elements in the kingdom of God, overcomes the temptations to selfishness which adhere as such to the particular circumstances of each area of life[162] and disproves the catholic assumption that one lives a spiritual life only in separation from worldly vocations.[163]

58. The significance of marriage as the union of two persons of different sexes into one (monogamy), which is set forth in the Old Testament and recognized by Christ as God's original ordering,[164] not only implies that in marriage husband and wife are of equal honor [Wert], and that their union is indissoluble during earthly life,[165] but also proves itself in the fact that in this relation the self-sacrificing power of love for one's neighbor can and should test itself in the most intense and blessed manner.[166] Nevertheless, when love is demanded of the husband and obedience of the wife,[167] it is because of that difference in the spiritual nature of the two sexes which leads

the wife to subject herself to her husband as the representative of their mutual union.

59. Since the realization of love for one's neighbor, which is intensified in marriage, is further continued in the care and training of children by their parents, the relation of these children to Christianity is already assured by their birth from Christian parents.[168] The children, in turn, during their upbringing realize their Christian destiny in that obedience to parents which in general is fitting.[169] Moreover, as brothers and sisters, the children of a household are admonished both to develop a consciousness of mutual rights and to form especially close friendships with one another. In these two respects their relation serves them as a school for their necessary participation in the public community of rights and in common ethical interaction. And the real effectiveness of the latter depends precisely upon the broadening and solidifying of the ethical individuality of each one through the winning of friends.

60. Law [das Recht] is the ordering of mutual or concerted actions which have reference either to personal ends (civil law) or to such common ends (public law—constitutional and criminal) as are of narrower scope than the ethical end of the kingdom of God. Inasmuch as judicial law directly controls only actions, actions which are in accordance with the law are not necessarily nor always the expression of a corresponding disposition; rather, judicial law is always accompanied by a compulsion to enforce right-doing among those who are otherwise disposed. But since law, when completely understood, is conceived of as the means by which ethical freedom attains its ends and therefore as an ethical product, the right ethical disposition includes necessarily a disposition to uphold the law, and in the community of laws we customarily presuppose such a disposition on the part of every individual.[170]

61. Therefore, the legal constitution of a people or a state is in itself indifferent to Christianity, regarded either as worship or as the practice of the kingdom of God;[171] yet the state is acknowledged as God's ordering, and obedience to judicial authority is prescribed as a religious duty.[172] This is because the community of laws, being a necessary means for securing ethical freedom, is also the indispensable condition for the Christian, if he is to fulfill the imperative of the kingdom of God in all the spheres of ethical interaction.[173]

62. Accordingly, while active participation in the state, insofar as it springs from patriotism and a general sense of justice, is not an activity which belongs directly to the kingdom of God, yet (as we may conclude from par. 61) it is not only compatible with the Christian life but the two activities have a necessary reciprocal relation to one another.[174] On the one hand, the Christian will find it incumbent upon him to promote the legal authority of the state for the very purpose of gaining room for striving after the kingdom of God. On the other hand, the pedagogy by which a Christian people is brought to its humanity, a pedagogy demanded by the welfare of the state, is founded upon an effort to realize the kingdom of God and must be regulated by an insight into the morality suitable for it, an insight which a statesman in a Christian nation can ill afford to be without. To the degree that this disposition pervades the different nations, it strengthens regard for their mutual rights. But as long as statecraft has to defend the rights of a people or a state against hostility from others, although it is never justified in the use of criminal means to this end, yet it is not bound by the same rules which hold for the legal and ethical action of the individual Christian in his relation to the state and in intercourse with other men.

63. Virtue and duty are concepts which, in that form, are derived from philosophical ethics. Both concepts must be used in Christian ethics, however, because their content is included in the right apprehension of the Christian life. Ethical virtues and actions regulated by the concept of duty are the products of a will directed toward the purpose that is ultimately good. The difference between the two is that actions in accordance with duty go forth from the will, while virtues are acquired in the will itself; the former relate to intercourse or association with others and the latter belong to the individual as such. When, nevertheless, we judge actions to be virtuous, we have in mind not their relation to interaction with others, but rather their relation to the distinctive personal force of the doer himself. On the other hand, when it is declared a duty to become virtuous, this concept of duty, against its own nature, departs from the usual concept of duty, and that departure is likely to cause confusion. In other words, such an expression is in part an unnecessary circumlocution with regard to personal rights, e.g., that of self-preservation or the choice and maintenance of the ethical vocation,

and in part an expression, permissable in pedagogics, of the necessity for the immature to acquire virtues.

64. In reality, dutiful actions and the acquisition of virtues are separate from each other in neither time nor space. On the one hand, the very means by which virtues are acquired is constant dutiful action (par. 49, n. 137); on the other hand, virtues are already being employed in the formation and implementation of the right concepts of duty.[175] And as they are exercised they are confirmed or rather acquired in ever higher degrees. This is not the description of a self-contradictory and hence falsely conceived and impossible process. The ethical will is a force whose effect upon others and whose effect upon itself stand in an inseparable reciprocal relationship to one another. For the ethical development of the individual will is utterly inconceivable apart from social interaction with other persons.

65. The virtues are derived from the various relations in which the will that is directed toward the highest purpose is to be recognized as a whole. To the extent that the will subjects the impulses of the individual disposition to that purpose which is ultimately good, it gains *self-control*. To the extent that it establishes firmly for itself the condition upon which the ethical vocation depends (par. 57), whether this results in the limiting or in the strengthening of that vocation, it gains *conscientiousness*. To the extent that it orders its planned activity in consistency with its intentions, purposes and resolves, it gains *wisdom, discretion, decisiveness* and *constancy*. To the extent that it directs the good disposition through the motive of love toward the individual persons with whom one is in moral association, the will gains *kindliness, thankfulness,* and *justice*.[176]

66. The *first* group of virtues—self-control and conscientiousness[177]—makes for autonomy and honorableness of character. In the opposite vices, sensuality, intemperance, immoderate ambition, imperious dogmatism, unscrupulousness, untrustworthiness—the will is lacking in the capability of determining itself in a consistent manner. Honor is the moral autonomy of a man insofar as it is recognized by other autonomous men. Thus the man without virtue has no moral honor. Moreover, no one gains honor by winning for himself the regard of his companions through yielding to the prejudices or immoralities of a special group. Finally, honor must not be confused

with that negative regard which is to be accorded to the dignity of the human being *qua* human being, which is accorded even those who are without virtue.

67. The *second* group of virtues—wisdom, discretion, decisiveness, and constancy[178]—makes for clarity and energy of character. For the good end at which one aims is without effect upon one's character if he is wavering in his purpose, reckless in his principles, indecisive in particulars and changeable as to the whole. In the accomplishment of conduct which is systematic and also expedient for the moment, prudence alternates with discretion,[179] the latter estimating the intended measures according to one's resources, the former according to the resistance to be expected from others.

68. The *third* group of virtues—kindliness,[180] thankfulness, and justice—makes for a good disposition or amiability of character. It is at the very least a lack of virtue when, out of a thoroughly good intention, the moral ends of society are treated in a purely, or largely, impersonal manner, hence with a harshness and lack of consideration for the very persons to whom one nevertheless wishes to show love. The full scope of love proves itself rather when, in kindliness, we gain facility in adjusting our manner of action to the claim which others have upon our love; when in thankfulness we gain the readiness to depend upon the kindliness of others; when in justice we gain the disposition so to bear the lack of kindliness and of thankfulness in others as not to allow ourselves to be led by our perception of that fault into harshness toward them. Thus justice will not exercise the necessary severity toward others without tempering it with a perceptible measure of kindness.[181]

69. The moral law is expressed with such generality in Christ's precept of love to one's neighbor (par. 6) that all morally necessary and desirable actions fall within the scope of this rule. But it has direct reference to the disposition alone, and leaves undetermined all the other conditions under which the necessity for individual benevolent action is to be recognized. To these conditions belong not only the determination of the ways in which love is to be exercised (par. 72), but also the judgment whether in any particular instance we have to deal with a neighbor in the full sense, or with one who is undeveloped in character and in need of education, or with an enemy (par. 6, n. 11). And, finally, it must be determined

whether in a particular instance one ought, at all cost, to act from the disposition of love or should refuse to act. A firm decision concerning these conditions must be included, however, if one is to be able to assure himself that a particular action, or its omision, in any given instance accords with the moral law.[182] But these conditions are so innumerable that they could never be dealt with exhaustively in any systematic, statutory exposition of the moral law.[183] For a judicial law can be laid down as statutory and exhaustive in its definite commands and prohibitions only because the actions which are neither commanded nor forbidden are permitted, i.e., remain legally undetermined. The moral law on the contrary reckons upon a measure of virtuous autonomy in the individual, according to which he has to determine his moral duty in each instance (par. 64, n. 175), namely, whether he is obliged by the universal moral law now to act in accordance with it, or under the circumstances not to act at all. Under these conditions the moral law, perfectly understood, becomes the law of liberty.[184]

70. Therefore, moral duty is the judgment of the virtuous man that in a particular instance, determined by an estimate of the personal and objective circumstances, the moral law requires him to act from the disposition of love. The element of freedom, inseparable as it is from this judgment of the necessity of a loving act, entails that in the same instance one individual may be under obligation to act and another not to act. But the disparity allowed by the conception of duty does not imply lawlessness. For since it is in his own particular ethical vocation (par. 57) that each one is to work at the common task of the kingdom of God and fulfill the universal moral law, most of the moral duties are thereby determined in advance. Thus the duties of one's vocation are the ordinary duties of love.[185] And the disparity in the duty of different individuals in the same instance is explicable from the difference in their ethical vocations. In addition, those actions not provided for by one's particular ethical vocation are also recognized as necessary or obligatory when found to be analogous to those of one's own calling. In these instances a person forms the judgment that through particular circumstances he is called to the exercise of an extraordinary duty of love.

71. Yet the network of ordinary (belonging to one's vocation)

and extraordinary duties of love does not extend so far as to cover all the voluntary expressions of good character. It is a question, therefore, whether all that action which one assumes is morally allowable, and which one is thus accustomed to withdraw from the direct application of the conception of duty, is (1) to be regarded as altogether morally indeterminable, or (2) still to be subsumed under the severity of the concept of duty, or (3) perhaps to be regulated morally in some other way. The *first* case is improbable, because the coherence of the good character would not admit to the morally indifferent nature of such a large range of its activities. The pedantic rigorism of the *second* case is not to be recommended for the very reason that we must be able to assure ourselves of our moral freedom as such, when it encounters legal necessity in the concept of duty. For instance, we must be able to preserve our freedom by not following any prior duty in the choice of our particular vocation; by being under no obligation to marry any particular person or to marry at all; by not being obligated in all cases to defend our vocation against hostile attacks. In these respects one exercises, rather, only rights which may be ignored or exercised in a choice that is not amenable to any concept of duty. However, the way in which this exercise is ethically measurable will become clear when the other realm of what is morally allowable is taken into consideration. This realm is, namely, that of recreation, partly as rest from exertion of work and as sensuous and intellectual enjoyment, i.e., as luxury over and above the indispensable needs of life,[186] partly as social entertainment and amusement, and partly as a combination of both. Rest from moral activity and for enjoyment is occasioned by the dependence of our spiritual life upon bodily conditions. Social amusement in bodily and mental exercise is occasioned by the nature of our spirit, which seeks the individual artistic self-expression that exists along with the necessity for moral association. Thus it corresponds more to the dignity of man to seek his recreation from useful work by entering into all possible artistic activity than in sitting still by himself. The nature of recreation is therefore essentially such as not to be directly subordinate to the moral concept of duty. Only when health is impaired is one led to recreation from a sense of duty to oneself or to one's usefulness in his vocation. Nevertheless, recreation is limited indirectly and negatively by duty.

The kind and duration of recreation is to be so regulated that one will not be less fitted for the fulfillment of his vocation after the recreation than before. Whenever this is the case, recreation is contrary to duty and morally prohibited. Hence, since the regulation of recreation by the concept of duty does not extend further, the *third* case holds good, because all recreation, especially social recreation, must work to maintain virtue. In all recreation conscientiousness, self-control, discretion, kindliness, thankfulness and justice are to be maintained, and all amusement and all entertainment are prohibited which interfere with the exercise of these virtues. Thus it follows that in this realm the same thing is permissible for one and not for another, to the degree that these virtues are exercised therein or not. Finally, it is evident that even in the exercise of personal rights as discussed above, virtue must also make its contribution as the moral standard.

72. The duties of love, which are to be derived from the general disposition toward love, may be divided according to the varieties of the application of this kindliness; and hence specific principles follow which facilitate the decision concerning particular duties. Kindliness authenticates itself either in the positive loving *regard* for other persons, or in the *support* of their justifiable ends, or in *forbearance* with the defects in their virtue. In the first instance, the principles of *modesty* and *sincerity* result; in the second the principles of *rectitude, readiness to serve, benevolence, truthfulness*; in the third the principles of *compatibility* and *willingness to forgive.*

73. Loving regard for others includes the negative regard for the dignity of the human being as such and care for the possessions (of whatever sort) of others as such, these being antecedent conditions of love, maintained even by the order of public justice.[187] For in and of itself this negative regard can be exercised in connection with complete indifference toward others, and leads therefore to no moral fellowship. But the principles of modesty and sincerity do imply such a regard for another, since by action and speech we do enter into moral fellowship with him. Modesty is that limiting of the sense of self to which we are obliged because we acknowledge in the person that the fellowship into which we are entering is of value.[188] Sincerity is the expression of the constant spirit of solidarity with others [*Gemeinsinn*] (to which we are also obliged) which

recognizes the value of the other for the purpose of the fellowship we are entering into.[189]

74. The loving support of the justifiable purposes of others includes righteous behavior in all our relations to them which are governed by contract. For since the administration of justice is the means of assuring the exercise of moral freedom, the disposition to uphold justice is included in the disposition to love (par. 60) and orders our legal duties to others by the principle of rectitude.[190] Rectitude has reference, it is true, to those relations with others which depend upon mutual advantage while, on the contrary, the trait of unselfishness (that is, the surrender of our own advantage in the assistance of others) is necessarily involved in readiness to serve, benevolence and truthfulness. Yet the distance between the principle of rectitude and these other principles is lessened by the fact that the principle of rectitude includes equity in dealing with those who are under legal obligation to us and can lay claim only to our rectitude. Of course, equity is no measure of our duties of love, but it expresses the recognition that our relations to others, while ordered momentarily only by contract, are not exhausted by legal justice. Rather, he who is presently under legal obligation to us possesses at the same time human dignity and moral freedom, and he can at any moment give us occasion to exercise the duties of love. The real duties of love first arise, however, when no question of mutual right is involved and thus when unselfishness is possible. This is the case when the justifiable ends of others are supported in helpfulness by giving personal assistance—in benevolence by the sharing of property, in truthfulness by the sharing of knowledge.[191]

75. Benevolent forbearance in the face of a lack of virtue in others expresses itself basically in compatibility during existing intercourse, and in the willingness to forgive when this intercourse has been interrupted by strife. Both are distinct from a weak indulgence toward wrong, in that they are connected with sincerity.[192] Moreover, right action in accordance with these and the preceding principles (with the exception of rectitude) is limited by the consideration whether the kind and degree of formation of moral character in others allow moral fellowship with them at all, or to what extent.[193] The exercise of rectitude is imperative, however, under all circumstances.

76. Perfection, which, on the foundation of the grace of God and in conformity to the redemption through Christ, consists in the exercise of religious and moral virtues and in the performance of the duties of love regulated by our ethical vocation (par. 50), is necessarily accompanied by a feeling of blessedness (par. 47).[194] But insofar as individuals have succeeded in attaining this height of Christian character-formation and in maintaining it in the conflict with their own sin and in patience under external limitations, they will, as a result of their intensified sensitivity of feeling, be the very ones to judge themselves full of defects and imperfection. Therefore, these will be the very ones to refuse to organize a group of the perfect, so as somehow to form a narrower circle of the same within the community of worship.[195] But the Christian faith, which is certain of eternal life through the reconciliation in Christ (par. 45) and maintains this blessing in the exercise of righteousness as well as in sanctification, orients itself upon the hope that the consummation of the kingdom of God as the highest good will be realized upon conditions which extend beyond this world of experience (par. 8).

77.[196] Christ and the apostles looked forward to the coming of this end and these conditions in the near future. Following the Old Testament prophets, they counted on the divine judgment of the world as a perceptible event upon this earth, through which the way was to be prepared for the dominion of Christ over the kingdom of God on earth.[197] This epoch was to be introduced (and at the same time differentiated from the previous epoch) by the resuscitation of the believers who had died and by the visible reappearance of Christ himself.[198] This form of future expectation has not maintained itself in the church, though it is still held in sectarian circles. The hope cherished in the church gives up the expectation that this earth will be the scene of Christ's dominion, while it holds fast the practical truths of the divine judgment and the separation of the blessed and the lost, as well as the final attainment of the highest good in the case of the former.[199] Since a consistent eschatological theory cannot be gained from the data of the New Testament, the hints of the New Testament as to the condition of the blessed and the lost lie beyond the possibility of a clear presentation.[200] The important thing, however, is not the satisfying of curiosity but the assurance that no one is blessed except in union with all the blessed in the kingdom of God.

IV. THE DOCTRINE OF PUBLIC WORSHIP

78. Prayer is not simply an act or a need of the individual believer (par. 54), but it is intended as well for a public exercise.[201] Prayer is the most spiritual form of divine worship. Therefore, in the perfect religion of Christianity, it has replaced all the material offerings and sacrifices used in the worship of God in other religions.[202]

79. In the generic concept of prayer, petition and thanksgiving are not equally important parts. Otherwise, the error would be encouraged that self-seeking petition may serve as justifiable worship of God, and that one has to return thanks to God only when his petitions are granted. Prayer is represented, rather, as a whole and under all circumstances as thanksgiving, acclamation, praise, recognition and worship of God.[203] The "confession of his name" is thus the recognition of God as our Father, inasmuch as he has revealed himself as such to us through his Son,[204] and proven himself such in the direction of our destiny (par. 54, n. 154). Petition is a variation of the prayer of thanksgiving. For the humble and unselfish recognition of God, or thanksgiving, governs in all cases the petitions which issue from the needs of the one who prays.[205] This also indicates the limits within which we may be confident that our petitions will be granted (par. 55). In particular, petition cannot be public except in the certainty that what is desired will serve not only our need but also God's glory. There is thus the assurance that such petitions will be granted as are offered in the name of Jesus Christ,[206] i.e., aimed at the bestowal of the blessings which are directly related to the purpose of the revelation through Christ. The right and the duty of mutual intercessory prayer is thus preeminently established.

80. The prayer which Christ taught his disciples at their request[207] offers a characteristic confirmation of Paul's direction that every prayer be accompanied with thanksgiving, and it offers the key to the sense in which the confession of God's name is to be understood as a sacrifice of praise. For, in the first place, all the individual petitions of this prayer are clearly subordinate to the invoking of God as our Father, and are embraced in this confession of his name. Further, every petition includes in itself the recognition that God assures to the praying community the blessings to which the petitions relate in varying degrees. The desire that God's name be hallowed presupposes that God has made his being and his power

known to man[208] and therefore that the hallowing of his name, or
the recognition of him,[209] is in the same measure possible. On the
lips of his disciples, the petition that God's dominion may come
presupposes that in the full sense this dominion has already been set
in motion by Christ precisely in their own circle (par. 5, n. 7). The
prayer for daily bread presupposes the assurance that God cares for
the maintenance of the one who prays;[210] and for him, however, who
has won the bread he needs by his own toil the petition bears the
character of a thanksgiving for divine blessings he has enjoyed. The
petition for the forgiveness of sins in no sense gives expression to a
just claim on God's favor because it is conditioned upon our forgiveness of others. This condition signifies rather that we are engaged
in the exercise of ethical duty characteristic of that community
(par. 6, n. 11) which is bound together through the forgiveness of
sins, or reconciliation with God (par. 38). The petition for the continued or ever-to-be-renewed application of this gift of forgiveness
presupposes therefore the recognition that it is a universal datum in
the life of this community. Finally, the petition that we may be
spared the temptation that grows out of the particular relationships
to the world into which we have been placed or preserved from the
evil likely to arise out of those relationships is inconceivable apart
from a recognition of God's direction of the world and his loving
purpose to direct it for the good of his children.

81. Since Christians call themselves *ekklesia,* church, their uniform and common prayer is considered the essential mark of their
unity. For even though this community is at the same time called
to the ethical task of carrying out the kingdom of God, yet this
activity does not assume a direct, empirically measurable manifestation (par. 9, n. 18). But common prayer, as the manifestation of the
religious worship of God, is not only in itself the church's purpose,
but serves also to mediate the believers' sense of solidarity in the
task of God's kingdom. Apart from this, therefore, the confession of
God's name (as our Father) in common prayer is the mark which
corresponds to the church's nature as the religious community of
Christ. In its exercise all Christians are priests.[211] In addition, the
confession before men of Jesus as the Christ or as our Lord is the
characteristic of this community which corresponds to its placement
in world history.[212]

82. As every religion relates itself in some way to divine revelation, no religious community maintains its peculiar character without resting upon a repeated series of similar revelations, or upon the original revelation as it is held in remembrance and reproduced in speech. It is particularly indispensable for the existence and authentic maintenance of the Christian religious community, that its activity of prayer be regulated by a common and publicly controlling remembrance of its founder and the revelation of God presented through him (pars. 19, 25). Therefore the word of God or the gospel is also the mark of the Christian religious community or church. By "gospel" we mean the revealed divine will of grace which has as its end the kingdom of God and therefore includes the right interpretation of Christ—that he makes actual the grace and faithfulness of God (par. 22) and, as the one who reconciles sinners with God, founds and represents the community of the kingdom of God (par. 42). The entire content of this knowledge is called the word of God, since it is set forth in the form of the will of God and his purpose that we be destined for the kingdom of God (par. 5), and for freedom over the world (par. 45). So constituted, the word of God is effective not only for gaining knowledge, but also for the corresponding stirring of the feelings and the will; it is therefore effective for personal conviction and effective as the motive and criterion of that worship of God which forms the essential active characteristic of the Christian community (par. 81). Given such content and effectiveness, the word of God, even as spoken by man, has its significance as God's word.[213]

83. The two acts of baptism and the Lord's Supper, which Christ instituted and whose observance is maintained by the piety of the Christian community, are in their uniform repetition also marks of the unity of the Christian church.[214] In their visible form, they are cultic acts of the community and are inconceivable apart from that community. Accordingly, they are of the same nature as common prayer and, like it, are acts of confession on the part of the community.[215] But inasmuch as the Lord's Supper refers to the event of Christ's sacrificial death, which includes the founding of the community (par. 42), this cultic act of the community at the same time assures the continuance of the forgiving grace of God by virtue of which Christ founded the community. This is also true of baptism

insofar as it has reference to the revelation of the Father through the Son and through the Holy Spirit bestowed upon the community (pars. 54, 55). Their validity as sacraments or means of grace rests upon these considerations.

84. The catholic concept of the church makes the significance of the common Christian faith and liturgy dependent upon acknowledgment of the specific canons of the catholic church. Now a right appreciation of the community or church of Christ belongs of necessity to the religious view of Christianity as a whole. This not only involves a right appreciation of the community in its relation to the kingdom of God as its highest good and common task (par. 5), but also in its existence as a community of faith and worship that is directed by God's word (par. 82) and, as such, itself maintains the efficacy of the revelation of God in Christ. Therefore it is necessary, even in the protestant view, to believe in the church under these marks when one is a participant in its worship of God. But in the protestant sense one believes thus in the church without reference to the authorized forms in which it exists.[216] For, although the religious elements of the church could not have become historically effective without the mediation of authorized forms, yet the perspective of the community of religious faith and prayer, in which the Christian church universal really consists (par. 86, n. 222), is thoroughly indifferent to the canons which vary from one segment of the church to another.

85. Understood according to its nature and true destiny under the marks already discussed (pars. 81–83) as the fellowship of believers in one and the same divine worship, the Christian church as such entered into the public sphere of history on Pentecost.[217] But it did not attain to permanence without developing within itself functions other than those which are primarily essential to it. For example, the ordering of fellowship in the liturgy and its propagation in succeeding generations necessarily led to the creation of an official class whose privileges over the community had to correspond to the legal as well as to the moral obedience due them.[218] But this organization of the Christian community attained a larger scope than the immediate exigency demanded, because the Christian church found itself originally placed over against a society whose moral ordinances were determined either by pagan or Jewish religion and

whose legal ordinances left no place for the Christian community as a religious body. The latter was thus forced by historical circum-stances, not only to develop its customs in contrast to the surround-ing society, but also to protect them by legal ordinances and to entrust the management of these structures to the officers of the liturgy. As early as the apostolic age the Christian church began, by means of free-will offerings and regular alms, to attain economic independence, to decide questions of private justice among its mem-bers, and to develop a new marriage code;[219] it continued this development by exercising the punitive law of excommunication (the ban) against unworthy members and recognizing the bishops as divinely appointed organs of those judicial forms. In these func-tions the Christian church—holding itself distinct from the Roman Empire—itself became a state without national foundations. After three centuries it was recognized as such a state in the Roman Empire, and the Roman Catholic church emphasizes now more strongly than ever its claim to the divine establishment of this her organization. On the other hand, according to the protestant view, all the attributes of a state are excluded from the concept of the church. Yet inasmuch as the liturgical fellowship as such is in need of lawful ordering, this ordering is limited essentially to the mainte-nance of the preaching office.[220]

86. The unity of the liturgical community of Christ is such an essential part of the world view which belongs to the Christian religion[221] that the splitting of the church into a multitude of divisions and sects, and the ceaseless continuance of controversy among them, forms a great hindrance to the convincing power of this religion. Still, in the *first place,* this very fact is a proof of the significance of Christianity as the religion of humanity. For the divisions and con-troversies of the church are occasioned by the fact that all possible religious, moral, and intellectual tendencies of pre-Christian human-ity are to be brought into union with Christianity. This phenomenon, therefore, which is impossible in any folk religion, which does not appear in Buddhism and only to a very limited extent in Moham-medanism, is a proof that Christianity attracts to itself all the forma-tive elements of the human spirit, even at the risk of its own deformation. Besides this occasion of divisions, in the *second place,* the unity of Christian liturgy as a matter of fact may be recognized

in all divisions and sects in that they without exception make official use of the Lord's Prayer[222] and thereby maintain the *intention* of a pure understanding of God's word. Nevertheless, divisions arise because variations, partly in the different cultic forms, partly in the understanding of God's word, are regarded as necessary grounds of separation. For this reason, however, the Christianity which is embodied in the different churches varies not only as to kind, but also as to the level of its development. Therefore, whenever one is conscious of sharing a higher degree of Christian development in that branch of the church to which he necessarily belongs, a degree not possible in other branches, he is under moral obligation just there within his own church to fulfill the universal imperative of Christianity—religiously, liturgically, and ethically.

87. The liturgical community becomes at the same time a school, in that it expresses its understanding of the pure word of God or the religious world view of Christianity in universal statements of truth or dogmas.[223] Variation in dogma (doctrine, system of doctrine) is not the only possible source of church division. The eastern and western catholic churches were originally one in doctrine, but separated because of differences in cultus, church ethos and church order. On the other hand, the great division of the western church, even in cultus, is based on variations in doctrine. A protestant Christian interprets this to mean that as such he occupies a more mature level of Christian development than the catholic church offers (par. 45, n. 123). The positive interest of protestant Christians in the doctrinal system of their church, a system which is the natural consequence of this interest, is regulated by two conditions. *First,* the doctrinal system of the church must be normed by scripture (par. 3) and, where it is appropriate, corrected by scripture. *Secondly,* the doctrinal system always marks the church as a school. It brings confusion, therefore, when the doctrinal system is designated exclusively as the "confession of the church," without regard to that which is set forth in paragraphs 79–81. For the ecclesiastical doctrinal systems which stem from the reformation period can only be appropriated through a *fundamental* theological training, even though theological training generally cannot be expected of the members of the church as such. Membership in the protestant church is to be determined, rather, by what constitutes Christian perfection

according to protestant teaching (par. 50, n. 142). By this means, the distinction is also made clear between churchly protestant Christianity and the sects (including sectarian tendencies within the former) who in the protestant church tend to define Christian perfection in terms other than those set forth in the Augsburg Confession.

88. The properly limited and privileged preaching office (par. 85, n. 220) aims at morally directing the church toward the attainment of the destiny that is embodied in its liturgy. The principle of the German reformation that the religious-ethical authority of the preaching office is not a legal-political authority, nor to be confused with the same,[224] is maintained without difficulty, since a protestant parish is constituted as community [*Gemeinde*] by its property and the administration of the same, and as church by the maintenance of the office of the word and the administration of the sacraments. The official preaching of the divine word (par. 82) may, as occasion demands, take the form of rebuking certain specific persons for their errors and immoralities, and under certain circumstances the local parish may be obliged to deny individuals the privilege of participating in its worship. But even this exercise of a natural right of the community is properly understood only as a moral influence and the application of moral entreaty. The protestant church acquires a legal character in the proper sense of the term, bearing the characteristics of external compulsion, only when the many local parishes wish to become a unity and at the same time stand forth as a corporation privileged by the state. This calls for a legal organization with a gradation of offices, as well as the supervision of those holding office in the interest of the whole; however, the legal compulsion which is necessary for such purposes cannot be exercised by the church as such, but only by the state[225] which recognizes and protects the church as a public corporation. For, as the legal representatives of a Christian people, the authorities [*Organe*] of the state cannot be indifferent to the church. In Germany, at least, historical circumstances brought it about that in the sixteenth century the authorities in representing the territorial churches bestowed upon them their legal organization and assured its operation by special state-church officials. This for a time produced anew a general confusion of religious and legal authority, since under the influence of medieval per-

spectives the chief object of the state was considered to be the direct furthering of the Christian religion and its morality. On the other hand, within Calvinism, several forms of church constitution were developed which were independent of or indifferent to the state. Of these forms, however, the synodical constitution of the old French church could not have existed without forming a state within the state and in contrast to it. The independence movement in England and America abandoned the legal organization of the whole church, making the local parishes sovereign and recognizing only a moral bond between them. Finally, in Scotland, a synodical church constitution arose, partly in union with the state and partly independent of it, whereby, however, a church absolutely identical in cultus and faith is divided in polity.

The provincial government of the church in Germany is now a condition for the union of the different protestant provincial churches within themselves and with each other and ought not be judged and depreciated by the example of the conditions in America or Scotland. According to protestant doctrine, there is no exclusively ideal form of church government, and the course of protestant history in Germany justifies the assertion that the maintenance of the unity of the provincial churches has protected the protestant church against being split into sects and conquered again by Romanism. Nevertheless it is true that the legal foundation of the provincial government of the church should be guided in a way very different from previous methods. That provincial government can no longer be derived either from the so-called religious purpose of the state, nor from a fictitious transfer of the catholic episcopal office through the princes, nor from the scope of state sovereignty as such. Yet the legal government of the church by the princes as an independent addition to their sovereignty is still comprehensible, since the national state, for the sake of the spiritual well-being of the people, must maintain the protestant church as a whole, and since all public administration which involves compulsion falls within the sphere of the state. And such administration is necessary, because it would be no advantage to the protestant church itself were it to form a state within the state through legal autonomy, and because its autonomous religious calling would be injured if it should be forced into this course. And the governing of the protestant church by the provincial authorities preserves the fundamental distinction between religious and legal authority in the church. For, on the one hand, the provincial officials spare the pastors from extending their office to include the government and administration of the whole church and thus impairing their moral authority; on the other hand, the provincial authorities are to be trusted to maintain the peculiar character of the protestant church, both in worship and in doctrine, and to impose nothing upon it that offends against the gospel. At present it remains undecided how far it will be possible to strengthen the existing church government by establishing synods and, at the same time, preclude the danger of dissolving the provincial church.

89. Baptism (immersion) *in* the name of the Lord Jesus, or Jesus Christ, or in the name of the Father, Son, and Holy Spirit,[226] is in its visible form an act of the community, by which it pledges the individuals joining that community to the revelation of God to which it owes its existence. This pledging includes the purification and renewal of the spiritual life which is signified symbolically in the washing of the body and to be understood factually as acceptance into the circle of forgiveness or reconciliation.[227] The rite, however, is not to be understood merely as the confession of the individual who enters as a believer into the community, but as a sacrament, because it is an act of the community, since the continuance of the community depends upon the revelation of the Father through the Son and as such assures the distinctive blessing of this revelation to the one newly received. This significance of the act is clearly expressed in the baptism of infants.[228] Although this practice rests only on very old tradition, and not on the command of Christ or precedent of the earliest church, yet it finds its justification in connection with religious and moral education within the church. On the other hand, the principle of the baptist sects that only adults and such as can be recognized as sanctified and regenerated may be baptized rests on the mistaken supposition that one can attain to the formation of Christian character outside the community.

90. The Lord's Supper in its visible form is an act of the whole community (and of the individual insofar as he presents himself as a member of the community), by which it thankfully recognizes the significance of Christ's sacrifice of his life for the establishment of the community.[229] As Christ himself, however, set forth the sig-

nificance of his approaching death to the community of his disciples as the sacrifice of the new covenant (par. 38, n. 102), so the repetition of the Lord's Supper in the same form becomes analogous to the sacrificial meal of the Old Testament. And since, further, the community founded through the sacrificial death of Christ stands in the relation to God characterized by the forgiveness of sins or reconciliation, the act is not only an act of confession on the part of the community, but also a sacrament. This significance of the act to the individual participant follows from two considerations, one more important than the other. First, the community within which he partakes of the Lord's Supper assures to him the forgiveness of sins, the forgiveness which forms the foundation for the community's existence.[230] But at a deeper level, however, Christ himself assures this to the believer, insofar as the act is repeated through which, in advance, he appropriated the reconciling efficacy of his death for the community. Accordingly, the Lord's Supper has the practical significance of intensifying the sensitivity of moral feeling, of stimulating the life emerging from reconciliation that moves toward humility, trust and patience (par. 50), and finally of arousing the lively sense of fellowship in the community.

Christian churches of different confessions are divided as to how the body and blood of Christ, represented by the bread and wine, are combined in the act of the Lord's Supper with these elements. Catholic doctrine asserts the transformation of the natural elements of bread and wine into the body and blood of Christ while retaining the appearance of bread and wine; the Lutheran doctrine asserts the nonspatial coexistence of these substances within the space of the natural elements; and both teach the oral reception of the body and blood of Christ. The Calvinist doctrine teaches that the administration of the body and blood by Christ for spiritual participation coincides in time with the oral reception of the bread and wine. The controversy between these doctrines cannot be settled by an appeal either to the words of Christ at the institution of the Supper or to the later explanation of Paul. And especially is this true, since none of the confessional doctrines take into consideration the fact that the broken bread and poured wine make present the body and blood of Christ under the characteristics of his violent death. Finally, it is unquestionable that Christ established this sacrament in order that all might unite in it, and not in the expectation that they would be divided as to its meaning and content and so separated from one another in its celebration.

NOTES

1. Matt. 11:27.

2. 1 Cor. 2:10–12.

3. Matt. 28:19.

4. *AS* II, 2: "The word of God shall establish articles of faith and no one else, not even an angel." Also *Formula of Concord,* Epitome 1.

5. [In the first edition, 1875, this paragraph reads as follows: "The kingdom of God is the universal end of the community that was founded through God's revelation in Christ, and it is the corporate product of that community, since the members of that community bind themselves to each other through a definite type of reciprocal action."]

6. Rom. 14:16–18. The kingdom of God is the divinely ordained end of the preaching of Christ, extending the invitation to a change of heart and to faith (Mark 1:15), and forming the principle subject of prayer to God (Luke 11:2; Matt. 6:10). The value of the highest good is especially set forth in the parable of the wedding feast (Matt. 22:2–14; 8:11; Luke 14:16–24; 13:29). In John the promise of eternal life has the same significance.

7. Christ in his office of revealer actualizes the kingdom of God (Matt. 12:28); in order to assure its task for men, he calls the twelve disciples so that they may be with him (Mark 3:14; Luke 12:32), may learn the mysteries of the kingdom (Mark 4:11), and enter into the same fellowship with God which he himself maintained (John 17:19–23); in accordance with this purpose he distinguishes them (the sons of God) as a special religious community, distinct from the Israelite community of the servants of God (Matt 17:24–27).

8. The parables (Mark 4) which set forth the mysteries of the kingdom in figures of the growth of grain, etc., always signify by "fruit" a human product, springing out of an individual activity called forth by the divine "seed," i.e., by the impulse of the divine word of revelation. The parable of the laborers in the vineyard has the same meaning (Matt. 20).

9. Fruit is the figure for a good deed or for righteous conduct (Matt. 7:16, 20; 13:33; James 3:18; Phil. 1:11). The kingdom of God consists in the exercise of righteousness, in the peace produced by it among all its members, and in the joy of blessedness proceeding from the Holy Spirit (Matt. 6:33; Rom. 14:17, 18). As to peace, compare Mark 9:50; Rom. 12:18; 14:19; 2 Cor. 13:11; 1 Thess. 5:13; Heb. 12:14. As to joy and blessedness, compare Gal. 5:22; James 1:25; and Luther's Small Catechism, II, 2: "That I might live under him in his kingdom and serve him in everlasting righteousness, innocence, and blessedness."

10. The law which Christ points out in the two chief commandments of the Mosaic law (Mark 12:28–33) has reference to the conduct suitable to the

kingdom of God. Love to God has no sphere of activity outside of love to one's brother (1 John 4:19–21; 5:1–3).

11. One's neighbor is no longer one's relative or compatriot alone, but possibly also the benevolent citizen of a hostile people (Luke 10:29–37); thus love of one's enemy in its generally permissible manifestations is included in the Christian love which embraces all mankind (Matt. 5:43–48; Rom. 12:14, 20, 21). This special command does not mean that we shall support an enemy in what he is doing against us, but we shall have regard for his dignity as a human being. The ordinary duty, of course, is love of the brethren (1 Pet. 1:22; 3:8; 1 Thess. 4:9; Rom. 12:10; Heb. 13:1), to whom one is also bound to extend forgiveness (Luke 11:4; 17:3, 4); but since the Christian community is the special body in which the members of different peoples are bound together into a moral fellowship whose principle is brotherly love, the circle of the kingdom of God is in this latter command also extended to include all men (Gal. 3:28; 5:6; 1 Cor. 7:19; Col. 3:10–11).

12. The surrender of private rights which follows from the law of love is the rule in intercourse with the brethren (Matt. 5:23–24, 38–42; the evil doer referred to in 5:39 must also be understood to be a brother).

13. The Mosaic decalogue, except in the command to honor one's parents, prescribes negative regard for the personal rights of everyone, in the sense of not inflicting injury (Exod. 20:12–17). This negative care for the rights of others is always the presupposition of the positive regard which finds its completion in the love of others (Rom. 12:10); this love manifests itself in the positive demand for the good of all, therefore in the exercise of public spirit (Rom. 12:16–17; 15:7; Phil. 2:2–4; 2 Cor. 13:11; 1 Thess. 5:11; Heb. 10:24; 1 Pet. 3:8). Thus the "royal law of love" includes in itself the decalogue and has a broader reach than its prohibitions (James 2:8–9; Rom. 13:8–10).

14. The one and only God who created the world and therefore is the king of all nations (Jer. 10:10–16; Ps. 47; 97; 103:19–22) will especially lead his chosen people as their king, on condition that they by obedience keep his covenant (Exod. 19:5–6; Judg. 8:23; Isa. 33:22). As their ruler God administers justice among all peoples (Ps. 9:7–8; 1 Sam. 2:2–10; Isa. 3:13), but especially among the chosen people, partly as their leader in war, maintaining their cause against other peoples (Exod. 7:4; Ps. 7:6–13; 76:4–9; 99:1–5), and partly procuring justice for righteous individuals against their insolent oppressors (Ps. 35; 37; 50).

15. Isa. 2:2–4; Mic. 4:1–4; Jer. 3:14–18; 4:1–2; Isa. 42:1–6; 51:4–6; 56:6–8.

16. Mark 10:42–45; 12:13–17; 2:27–28 (Compare with Isa. 56:2–5); Matt. 17:24–27.

17. Luke 17:20–21; Heb. 11:1.

18. The name of the community of believers (church, *ekklesia*, Heb. *Kahal*), as a result of this harmony with Old Testament use of terms, refers directly to the visible liturgy (sacrifice, prayer) (par. 81). But this religious community must at the same time unite itself to the kingdom of God by the mutual exercise of love. By virtue of the different nature of these two activities and the different conditions under which they arise, it follows that they are never exercised to an equal extent during the historical existence of the

community. The community of believers must fulfill its mission in these two relations in such a way that the two lines of their activity shall stand in reciprocal relation to one another, but it is a mistake so to identify the two as to use the same name interchangeably for them both. For the actions by which the community becomes a church are not those by which it unites itself to the kingdom of God, and vice versa. And it is particularly misleading to claim, as the Roman Catholic church does for itself, designation as the kingdom of God because of a certain juridical form [rechtliche Verfassung].

19. Menander: "The slave becomes base, when he learns merely to bend himself to every service; give freedom of word to the slave and he will surely become the best of the good" (Ex incertis comoediis, 254). "Serve in a free spirit and you are not a slave" (Ibid., 255). Philemon: "Even he who is a slave, madam, is still none the less human, since he is truly a human being" (Ibid., 29). "Though one be a slave, he is yet of the same flesh; for nature never created a slave, it is only fortune that has thrust the body into servitude" (Ibid., 84).

20. Antiochus of Askalon, in Cicero's De finibus bonorum et malorum, V. 23:65 [trans. H. Rackham, Loeb Classical Library (New York: Macmillan, 1914), pp. 467–69]: "But in the whole moral sphere of which we are speaking there is nothing more glorious nor of wider range than the solidarity of mankind, that species of alliance and partnership of interests and that actual affection which exists between man and man, which, coming into existence immediately upon our birth, owing to the fact that children are loved by their parents and the family as a whole, is bound together by the ties of marriage and parenthood, gradually spreads its influence beyond the home, first by blood relationships, then by connections through marriage, later by friendships, afterwards by the bonds of neighborhood, then to fellow citizens and political allies and friends, and lastly by embracing the whole of the human race. This sentiment, assigning each his own and maintaining with generosity and equity that human solidarity and alliance of which I speak, is termed justice." Compare the collection in Schmidt, Die bürgerliche Gesellschaft in der altrömischen Welt, 306. Seneca expresses himself similarly.

21. Concerning a standard of this relation which comes closer to us, cf. par. 19.

22. 2 Cor. 1:3; 11:31; Rom. 15:6; Col. 1:3; Eph. 1:3; 1 Pet. 1:3.

23. 1 Sam. 2:2; Isa. 45:18, 21–22; Exod. 20:2–3. The Old Testament conception of the gods of the heathen is accordingly either that they are nothing or vanity (Lev. 19:4; 2 Kings 17:15; Jer. 2:5; 8:19) or, insofar as their existence is granted, that they are subordinate organs of the government of the only God (Deut. 4:19; 10:17; Ps. 95:3; 96:4; 1 Cor. 8:5–6). As the only God, the true God is the Holy One (1 Sam. 2:2), who is unattainable by the way of natural knowledge, exalted above all sense perception, unimpeachable.

24. Gen. 1; Isa. 45:12; Matt. 11:25. That God as the absolutely free will determines himself and as the creator determines all that together makes the world is united into the statement that God is the end of the universe, or that the course of the world ministers to his glory (1 Cor. 8:6; Rom. 11:36; Eph. 4:6). The conception of the creation of the world by God lies entirely outside of all observation and ordinary experience and therefore outside of the realm

of scientific knowledge, which is limited by these. Thus, even though we are able to obtain from experience a clear idea of natural causes and effects, the creation of the world by God cannot rightly be thought of as analogous to these forms of knowledge. It can only be analogous to the original force of our will as it is directed toward a goal and comprehended in such a way that the world as a whole, and not just its individual parts, is compared to God.

25. Scientific observation of nature is directed toward the causal relationship of things. Since it regards organic beings (plants, animals) with reference to the end which they have in themselves, it denies itself the occasion to recognize them as necessarily existing for the sake of man. Such a relationship is apprehended everywhere only by the religious judgment; thus in the Old Testament everything is subservient to the world supremacy of the people of Israel.

26. [In the first edition, this paragraph reads as follows: "As with all religious interpretations of the world (cosmogonies), the biblical account of God's free creation of the world necessarily also moves to a discussion of human ends and the establishment of a religious and ethical community of men with God. This idea is given further specification in Christianity with the assertion that the world is directed toward the kingdom of God, i.e., to the ultimate end that a kingdom of created spirits should come into being whose essential nature is perfect spiritual union with God. That the world is directed toward God himself or his glory is in perfect harmony with the fact that it is directed also toward the kingdom of God so long as we understand God in terms of the concept of love." This paragraph was elucidated by the following footnote (note 12a in the original, Fabricius's edition, p. 41): "This goal of all religious cosmogonies is only a generalized statement of every particular religious view of the world. Whenever, in a religious judgment, we derive an empirical event in the world from God's dispensation, we are thinking of a purpose of God that is directed toward us, but which reaches out beyond the event itself. In the scientific understanding of certain natural entities, we conceive of a nexus of causes and their effects, also in the form of a purpose. But when we think of the purpose of an organic being (planet, animal), a purpose which it has in its own right, we conceive of that purpose being necessarily subordinated to man's purposes, although we have no scientific basis for doing so. The scientific understanding of nature, therefore, defines all phenomena as orderly effects of causes, and it defines organic beings according to their own intrinsic purposes; the religious view of the world defines all creatures according to their usefulness to man (Gen. 1:26–31)."]

27. In the majority of the inscriptions of the New Testament epistles.

28. As the end of creation (Col. 1:6; Eph. 1:10), Christ is also the central reason [Mittelgrund] for creation from the standpoint of the divine purpose (1 Cor. 8:6). As Lord over all he is the one "to whom every knee shall bow," that is, he receives divine worship (Phil. 2:9–11). But note that God the Father is placed over him (1 Cor. 3:23, 8:6).

29. Matt. 11:27. That God alone knows the Son signifies that he is set apart from all the world. God's knowledge of him, however, includes in itself a productive voluntary purpose (1 Pet. 1:20; Rom. 8:29). Thus Jesus, knowing his peculiar existence to be grounded in the love of his Father (John 10:17,

15:10), places this relation above the coherence and existence of the world (John 17:24).

30. 1 John 4:8, 16. Love is the *constant* purpose to further another spiritual being of *like* nature with oneself in the attainment of his authentic destiny [*Bestimmung*], and in such a way that the one who loves in so doing pursues his *own* proper end [*Selbstzweck*]. This appropriation of the life-purpose of another is not a weakening negation but a strengthening affirmation of one's own purpose. Thus if God is revealed as love in that he directs his purpose toward Jesus Christ his Son, the love of *God* will be revealed in proportion as this purpose encompasses even the world of which this Son is Lord, and causes it to be recognized as the means to the end, this end being Christ as the head of the community.

31. 2 Cor. 13:11, 13; Rom. 5:5–8; 8:39; 2 Thess. 2:16; 1 John 4:9–10; Heb. 12:6.

32. In the love shown by Christians to their brothers the love of God is perfected (1 John 2:5; 4:12), i.e., it finds its complete revelation.

33. Eph. 1:4–6. "God has chosen us (the Christian community) in Christ (as Lord of the same) before the foundation of the world, that we might be holy and without blame before him; having in love predestined us to the adoption of children through Jesus Christ to himself, according to the good pleasure of his will, to the praise of the glory of his grace."

34. Ps. 90:2, 4.

35. Ps. 102:25–27.

36. Ps. 24:1–2; 115:3; 135:6; 139:7–12.

37. This is the application given to these divine attributes in the theological doctrine that God as the first cause is present in all mediate causes. This doctrine consists, nevertheless, of a confused mixture of religious and scientific observation. The idea of God is not at the disposal of a scientific explanation of nature, and any such explanation would indeed offend against the content of the idea of God, if it should make him, under the concept of causation, similar to the natural causes which are intelligible by observation. The religious view of nature, however, does not limit itself to the explanation of natural phenomena as such, but subordinates their existence for the sake of man to the will of God (cf. n. 25, above), which is entirely different in kind from natural causes.

38. Ps. 139 (as a whole, culminating in verses 23, 24); 33:13–19; 104; Job 5:8–27; 11:7–20, 36, 37.

39. Ps. 145:8–9; Exod. 34:6; Ps. 103:8; Acts 14:15–17; James 5:11; Rom. 2:4; 2 Cor. 1:3.

40. Ps. 35:23–28; 31:2, 8; 48:10–12; 65:6; 143:11–12; 51:16.

41. Isa. 45:21; 46:13; 51:5–6; 56:1.

42. Hos. 2:18–21; Zech. 8:8; Ps. 143:1.

43. 1 John 1:9; Ps. 51:14; Rom. 3:25–26; John 17:25, 26; Heb. 6:10 (1 Cor. 1:8, 9; 1 Thess. 5:23–24).

44. Ps. 105; 107; 71:16–21; 86:8–17; 89:5–14; 98:1–3; 145:3–7; Job 5:8–11.

45. Miracles and signs, Ps. 135:8, 9; Exod. 3:12, 13:9.

46. Mark 5:34; 10:52; 6:5–6. We shift completely the religious conception of miracle when we begin by measuring it against the background of the scientific acceptance of the orderly coherence of all natural events. Since this scientific concept lies outside the horizon of the men of the Old and New Testaments, a miracle never signifies to them an occurrence contrary to nature nor a disruption of the laws of nature by divine arbitrariness. Hence the belief in miracle in the sense referred to above, as a gracious providence of God, is perfectly consistent with the probability of the coherence of the whole world in accordance with natural law. If, nevertheless, certain accounts of miracles in the Bible appear to be contrary to these laws, it is neither the duty of science to explain this appearance nor to confirm it as a fact, nor is it the duty of religion to recognize these narrated events as divine operations contrary to the laws of nature. Neither ought one base his religious faith in God and Christ upon a preceding judgment of this kind (John 4:48; Mark 5:11–12; 1 Cor. 1:22), especially since every experience of miracle presupposes faith. Beginning, however, with faith, everyone will meet the miraculous in his own experience; in view of this, it is entirely unnecessary to ponder over the miracles which others have experienced.

47. Matt. 5:12, 6:1, 2; 1 Cor. 3:8; 2 Thess. 1:8, 9; Heb. 10:29.

48. Job 41:3; Rom. 11:35. In general, the view of human life set forth in the biblical writings moves within the limits set by the covenant grace of God. When, therefore, the righteousness of God is appealed to for the reward of righteous men (Ps. 7:8–10; 17:3; 58:11; 139:23; 2 Thess. 1:5–7), the mutual legal relation thereby indicated is only apparent. For the righteousness of God signifies in these cases also only the consistent completion of the salvation of the righteous (par. 16), which, however, has the appearance of reward because it deals in these cases with a condition of innocence and righteousness that is already present in men. Properly, the recompense of the righteous is the work of the grace of God (Ps. 62:12); that of the wicked is their exclusion from (his grace =) righteousness (Ps. 69:24–28). Reward and punishment are not coordinated as expressions of the righteousness of God, but only as visible acts of his exercise of justice, i.e., of his government of the world (Ps. 94:1, 2; 58:10, 11).

49. Exod. 34:7; Mark 4:12; 10:29, 30. The divine punishment in its common Old Testament representation as the wrath of God, because of the nature of the emotion involved in the term wrath, excludes the idea of an exact weighing of the amount of the punishment.

50. The poets of the Old Testament find themselves completely disappointed in their natural expectation that the good would be prosperous and the wicked unhappy. They must content themselves with praying to God for the righting of the wrong condition of affairs in the future. Thus the establishment of the right order awaits the future judgment of God in the Old as well as in the New Testament.

51. Eliphaz draws this conclusion in the book of Job (4:7, 22:4–11); on the other hand, consider Job's assurance of his integrity (6:28–30; 23:10–12). As against this combination compare John 9:1–3; Luke 13:1–5.

52. Matt. 5:11; Mark 8:34, 45; Phil. 1:28. Cf. par. 32.

53. The scheme of retribution in the final judgment (Rom. 2:6–12; 2 Cor. 5:10; 2 Thess. 1:6, 7; Eph. 6:8) is surpassed by the analogy of the seed and the harvest (Gal. 6:7–8). The final result in the case of the good as in that of the evil is but the appropriate legitimate effect of the power of the good or the evil will. By comparison, the transitory temporal experiences of a contrary nature are not worthy of consideration.

54. Rom. 11:33–36. From par. 13 there follows the universal law of the divine government, maintained everywhere in the Old as well as in the New Testament, that all punishment or destruction of the wicked by God serves as a means to the complete salvation of the righteous. It is not, however, a means to the end of God's own glory or righteousness, as is set forth in Luther's and Calvin's doctrine of predestination.

55. In all folk religions the person of the founder, even when known (Zoroaster, Moses), is a matter of indifference, because the religious community, consisting of the whole race or people, is determined by nature. On the other hand, in universal religions (Buddhism, Christianity, Islam), allegiance to the founder, or worship of him, is prescribed, because only through the founder does the corresponding community exist as it is, and only by allegiance to him can it be preserved. In these cases the difference in the estimation of Mohammed and Christ is to be explained by the difference in the nature of the two religions.

56. Mark 6:4; 9:37; John 4:34; 5:23, 24; 6:44. It comes also under the prophetic conception (Exod. 33:11; Num. 12:8) that Jesus speaks what he hears from God (John 8:26, 40; 15:15) and has seen of him (John 6:46; 8:38).

57. Mark 12:1–9; 8:29; 14:61–62; John 4:25–26.

58. John 4:34; 17:4.

59. John 18:36; Mark 10:42–45.

60. The fitness of Jesus finds expression in his assertion of the mutual knowledge existing between himself and God as his Father (Matt. 11:27; John 10:15; compare Luke 2:49). He does not know God as his Father without being himself conscious that he is *the* one called of God to found the kingdom of God in a new religious community. This conviction vouches also for all the other sides of his spiritual endowment for this vocation. because all the characteristics of his life witness to his perfect spiritual soundness, and there is not the least trace in him of fanaticism or self-deception.

61. The sinlessness of Jesus (John 8:36; 1 Pet. 2:21; 1 John 3:5; 2 Cor. 5:21; Heb. 4:15) is only the negative expression for the constancy of his disposition and conduct of his vocation (obedience, Phil. 2:8; Heb. 5:8) or for the positive righteousness in which he differs from all other men (1 Pet. 3:18).

62. Heb. 2:18; 4:15; Mark 14:33–36; 1:13.

63. The principle of Matt. 11:28–30. The two Greek words *praüs kai tapeinos* ("gentle and lowly") point to the use of one Hebrew or Aramaic word, *anav*, which indicates the regular characteristics of the righteous in their suffering under the persecution of the godless (Pss. 9:12; 10:12–17; 25:9; 37:11;

69:32). The addition of *te kardia* ("in heart") denotes that Jesus in his righteousness is ready to endure all the undeserved sufferings which follow from the reaction against his activity in his vocation. Thereby, however, he makes a distinction in kind between himself and the righteous of the Old Testament, who always seek to be delivered from their undeserved suffering.

64. John 4:34.

65. John 10:28–30, 38; 14:10; 17:21–23.

66. John 15:9, 10; 17:24, 26; 10:17; 12:49, 50.

67. John 1:14; Exod. 34:6, 7; compare par. 16.

68. Matt. 11:27.

69. Matt. 17:24–27; 8:11, 12; Mark 12:9.

70. Matt. 11:28–30. Compare n. 63, above.

71. John 71:1, 4, 5; 16:16, 33. Accordingly, the view of Jesus' life given by Paul in Phil. 2:6–8 is not complete. The path of obedience even to death is for Jesus only apparently a degradation beneath his dignity. It is in truth the form of his self-exaltation above the world and above its usual standards (Mark 10:42–45). That is to say, one *becomes* great through degradation in service only because one *is* already great in unselfish obedience (Phil. 2:1–5).

72. In apostolic usage, the Old Testament name of God, "Lord," is applied only to the risen Christ, exalted to the right hand of God (Phil. 2:9–11). Yet this conception can only be understood on the condition that this attribute is discernible also as an actual characteristic in the historical life of Christ (par. 23). But this dominion of Christ over the world has no other sphere of activity save such as is maintained through the power of a will concentrated upon God's supramundane purpose of love. Also the apostles regard Christ as creator only in this respect, that because he comprises typically in himself the goal of the world, i.e., the kingdom of God and the glory of God, he furnishes in the divine creative will the means for the creation of the world (Col. 1:15–18; 1 Cor. 8:6; Heb. 1:1–3). This line of thought, however, leads over into the territory of theology proper and has no direct and practical significance for religious belief in Jesus Christ.

73. Melanchthon, Loci (1535, CR XXI, 366): "The scriptures teach us the divinity of the son not only speculatively, but practically, i.e., they command us to pray to Christ and to trust in Christ, for thus is the honor and divinity truly accorded to him."

74. There is a complete misconception of the problem, and the understanding desired is rendered impossible, if the principle is followed that historical knowledge of Christ is possible only insofar as one is divested of religious devotion to him.

75. Accordingly, his death will be regarded, not as a just punishment for blasphemy as his enemies intended it, nor as the result of fanatic daring, but as the completion of the work of his vocation, which he accepted with dutiful determination because he recognized in it God's purpose for him. This significance of the death of Christ, set forth by the apostles, marks also the right and complete understanding of Christ's obedience in life, as it was completed in his death. (Cf. n. 110, below.)

76. Gal. 2:20; 3:27; Rom. 6:5, 11; 8:2, 10; 12:4, 5; 1 Cor. 12:12.

77. Rom. 10:9; 1 Cor. 15:3–20; 1 Pet. 1:3; 3:21, 22; Heb. 13:20, 21.

78. Mark 14:62; John 10:17, 18; 17:4, 5.

79. It is impossible to arrive at the view of sin which is in accordance with Christianity before arriving at the knowledge of what Christianity regards as good. Therefore it is a peculiarly inconsiderate demand, that one should recognize his own and universal sin in their full extent, in order from this alone to derive a longing for a redemption such as is promised in Christianity.

80. Augustine's doctrine of original sin, i.e., the original inclination to evil transmitted in procreation which is for everyone both personal guilt and subject to the divine sentence of eternal punishment, is not confirmed by any New Testament author. Paul draws from his scholastic exegesis of the account of the fall only the conviction that the universal decree of death for man was the consequence of the sin of the first human beings, and the conclusion that their descendants have sinned since that fate was theirs also (Rom. 5:12–19). Neither Jesus nor any of the New Testament writers either indicate or presuppose that sin is universal merely through natural generation. The expressions in the Old Testament which approach this view (Ps. 51:5; Job 14:4; 15:14) are not didactic in character and not suited to determine the Christian conception.

81. Gen. 8:21; Matt. 5:28; Gal. 5:16–21; 1 Cor. 6:9, 10; Titus 3:3; 1 Thess. 4:3–8; Luke 15:21; 1 Cor. 6:18–20; 8:12; 1 John 3:4.

82. CA II, 1: "Since the fall of Adam all men who are propagated according to nature are born in sin. That is to say, they are without fear of God, are without trust in God, and are concupiscent."

83. Therefore the sinlessness of Jesus (cf. n. 61, above) does not contradict his human nature.

84. This gradation is indicated in 1 John 5:16, 17. It is also signified when Jesus represents sin or the world as an object of redemption on the one hand (Mark 2:17; Luke 13:2–5; 15:7, 10, 24, 32; 18:13) and incapable of salvation on the other (Mark 8:38; Matt. 8:22; 12:39–45; 13:49; 16:4). In the same way with reference to Num. 15:27–31, a distinction is made between sins arising from ignorance or mistake and therefore receiving forgiveness (1 Pet. 1:14; Eph. 4:17–19; Acts 17:30; 1 Tim. 1:13; James 5:19, 20) and those which are committed freely or with firm resolution and bring destruction in their train (Col. 3:5, 6; Eph. 5:5, 6; Rev. 21:8).

85. James 1:14, 15 and Mark 9:43–47 represent individual impulses and their bodily organs as causes of the temptation to sin, insofar as the impulses are directed to worldly good and the organs mediate that attraction. Along with this, the power of social custom as well as the authority and example of others furnish seductive occasion to sin (Mark 4:17; 9:42; 1 Cor. 8:13, 21; Rom. 14:13, 21; Rev. 2:14). But also the suffering of the good, when not understood, works in the same way (Mark 14:27, 29; 1 Cor. 1:23; 1 Pet. 2:8).

86. James 4:4; 1 John 2:15–17. The expression "the kingdom of sin," to be sure, is not directly biblical; yet it is indicated in the representation of the devil as the prince of this world (1 John 5:18, 19; John 12:31; 16:11). Of

course this nexus of sin is unlike the kingdom of God, in that it is controlled by no positive purpose.

87. Rom. 3:9; 5:20, 21; 6:12–23.

88. The absolute inability to good, which the reformers wish to find expressed in the sinfulness of every individual, is not asserted in the New Testament and is limited even in the reformers themselves by the recognition of *justitia civilis* as the work of sinners.

89. The manifestation of conscience in involuntary self-condemnation for a deed done is to be understood as an exercise of freedom, i.e., of self-determination to good, but this of course takes place only on the presupposition that one is brought up in a moral fellowship. An evil conscience is a positive manifestation, a so-called good conscience the absence of the same. In the New Testament the former is referred to in Heb. 10:2, 22; and the latter in Acts 23:1; 2 Cor. 1:12; Heb. 13:18; 1 Pet. 3:16; and both together in Rom. 2:15. That a good conscience has only a relative value in proving a mode of action to be right is shown in 1 Cor. 4:3, 4. As to the conception of the positive law-giving conscience, cf. n. 177, below.

90. John 9:1–3; Luke 13:1–5; compare n. 51, above.

91. Luther, for instance, failed to exercise this tenderness of feeling when he declared Zwingli's tragic end a divine punishment for his heresies (*WA, BR,* IV, 332, 352).

92. Rom. 5:12.

93. Rom. 14:7, 8; Phil. 1:21–24; Rom. 8:35–39.

94. The deliverance of the people of Israel from Egyptian bondage into an independent national life and the establishment of their own true religion (Exod. 15:13; 20:2), is the type by which all similar expectations of the prophets are governed, in each recurring subjugation of the people to foreign nations (Ps. 111:9; Isa. 35:10; 45:17; 51:11). The conversion or the spiritual renewing of the people is, to be sure, included in this conception as well (Isa. 10:21; 32:15–18; Ezek. 36:24–30; Ps. 130:8).

95. This is not even the definite meaning of such passages as Rom. 11:26, 27; 1 Pet. 1:18, 19; 2:24; they depend rather upon being made clear by the line of thought which follows.

96. Redemption is like forgiveness of sins (Col. 1:14; Eph. 1:7; Heb. 9:15; 10:16–18) and justification or acquittal (Rom. 3:24–26); this latter again is also forgiveness of sins (Rom. 4:5–8). The figure of the forgetting or covering of sins by God does not mean that God commits an intentional self-deception as to the existence of human sin, but it has the meaning expressed in the conception of pardon, that the result of transgression, namely, the interruption of intercourse between the guilty individual and the representative of moral authority, is purposely brought to an end by the latter. This meaning follows from the comparison of the divine forgiveness with the human (Luke 11:4; Matt. 11:25).

97. It is utterly purposeless to compare the catholic and the protestant conceptions of justification [*Rechtfertigung*, to be declared just], since they stand in relations which are completely indifferent to one another. That is to say, the

catholic conception of justification [*Gerechtmachung*, to be made just] through the imparting of love to the will is intended to explain how sinners are made capable of good works. This thought has therefore a different purpose from that of the protestant formula referred to above; in themselves both might be true at the same time and in force side by side without conflicting with one another. Yet the catholic formula sets forth a spiritual occurrence in a mechanical and materialistic way and is not consonant with the normative biblical conception. The conception of *dikaioun* ("righteous") adopted by Paul (Rom. 3:26, 30) follows the meaning of a Hebrew verbal form (*hizdik*), which denotes the pronouncing of one as righteous by the sentence of a judge (Rom. 4:11).

98. The justification established by God's gracious judgment (*dikaiosune theou*, "righteousness of God") depends on faith (Rom. 1:17; 3:22, 26; 9:30; Phil. 3:9).

99. 2 Cor. 5:18, 19; Rom. 5:10; Col. 1:21.

100. Matt. 17:26; 1 John 3:1; Gal. 4:4–7; Rom. 8:14–17. Luther's *Large Catechism*, III, "God will lead us to believe that he is our real father, and we are his real children, to the end that we, in all boldness and confidence, may ask of him as dear children of a dear father."

101. Since the Christian life is only complete in the fulfillment of both of these conditions—assurance of reconciliation (or adoption) and the seeking of the kingdom of God and its righteousness—these two lines serve as a mutual proof of their rightness and genuineness, or mutually condition one another. This appears in the following propositions: (1) Assurance of reconciliation is not justified when the life is either directly sinful or marred by a predominating form of self-seeking. (2) A life directed by a constant good purpose fails of its end when the assurance of reconciliation is marred by a predominating self-righteousness. (3) Insofar as the moral life must be judged incomplete in general, and also because of sin's interruptions, this lack is balanced not only by the assurance of divine forgiveness but also by the purpose to make greater effort and improvement and by the carrying out of this purpose. The commonly received idea opposed to this rests upon the error that in Christianity forgiveness of sins is a substitute for what is supposedly the original arrangement, wherein one might attain the right relation to God by mechanically fulfilling the law.

102. This is evident from the fact that Christ, in the institution of the Lord's Supper (Mark 14:24), refers back to Jeremiah's prophecy (31:31–34) of the new covenant, whose foundation is the forgiveness of sins. As the prophet holds out the prospect of this covenant only to the whole of the people Israel as the continuing community of the true God, so Christ in agreement with this thinks of the community as existing in the twelve, for whom he makes the covenant of forgiveness efficacious by the sacrifice of his life—cf. Luther's *Small Catechism*, second part, third article, "in which church God daily and abundantly forgives all my sins and the sins of all believers." See also *Large Catechism*, II, 40–42 and *CA* I, 5 and "Treatise on the Power and Primacy of the Pope," 24 (Tappert, p. 324).

103. In the catholic system the idea of forgiveness of sins is made clearly

efficacious only in the ceremony of the priestly absolution of the individual in the sacrament of confession. A similar procedure is maintained in the Lutheran confessional, without there being any reference in their liturgy to the specific principle of the reformation, namely, that in consequence of the redemption mediated through Christ we belong to the community founded upon the forgiveness of sins and accordingly we do not make confession of past sins, in the sense that we have lost the state of grace and therefore receive forgiveness as something new. This confessional practice rather furthers the fateful error (cf. n. 100, above) that churchly forgiveness of sins is a substitute for a defective striving after the good.

104. Although the love of God has been occasionally construed as the ground of a reasonable leniency on God's part toward the weakness of men, yet it does not furnish the datum for a so-called natural religion, which indeed does not exist. But even were it otherwise, leniency toward the imperfections of human conduct is an entirely different thing from Christian forgiveness of sins. Such leniency accepted as a divine substitute for human weakness would sacrifice the seriousness of moral obligation and would utterly fail to assure a fellowship of men with God, in which the task of the kingdom of God calls forth the constant effort of the will.

105. The instruction to pray for the forgiveness of sins (Luke 11:4) and the command to exercise a forgiving spirit (Mark 11:25) apply to the community as existing already in the twelve disciples and express the thought that in this community one cannot appropriate to himself the forgiveness of sins without at the same time giving proof by a forgiving spirit, or the love of one's enemies, that one is engaged in the ethical work of the kingdom of God. (Cf. n. 101, above.)

106. Mark 14:24 refers to sacrifice in the covenant (Exod. 24:3–8). Insofar as the Israelites entered by this act upon their vocation as the possession of God and as a kingdom of priests (Exod. 19:5, 6), compare Acts 20:28; Rev. 1:5, 6; Titus 2:14. Rom. 3:25, 26 and Heb. 9:11–14 refer to the type of the general annual sin-offering (Lev. 16). 1 Pet. 1:18, 19 refers to the passover, which belongs to the deliverance from Egypt. Eph. 5:2 makes no distinction between these various kinds of sacrifice.

107. The sacrifices prescribed in the Mosaic law, as well as the sacrifice concluding the covenant, signify that by these acts the covenant community approaches its God; the sacrifices depend therefore upon the certainty of his covenant grace. This is also true of the sin-offering which has reference only to such transgressions as do not involve a breach of the covenant (Num. 15: 27–31).

108. John 10:17, 18; 14:31; 15:13, 14; 17:19; Rom. 5:19; Phil. 2:8; Eph. 5:2; Heb. 5:8, 9. Compare n. 75, above.

109. The combination in the epistle to the Hebrews, especially in 2:17; 4: 14–16; 6:20; 9:11, 24–26.

110. It is remarkable that the epistles have so few reminiscences of the life of Christ. Hence it appears as if the emphasizing of his death as the act of redemption counted upon an interpretation of this act which is in complete contrast to the assessment of his life. Yet it is plain that the apostles under-

stood the divinely purposed death of Christ to be a sacrifice only as it was connected with his obedience in his life's vocation. This highest proof of the obedience of Christ serves thus as a redemptive sacrifice, because 'it can be understood as summing up in itself the value of his life given in the service of God and of the community to be established. Mark 10:45: "For verily the son of man came not to be ministered unto, but to minister, and to give his life a ransom for many."

111. John 15:10; 10:17, 18; compare n. 66, above.

112. John 17:20–26.

113. The view that Christ, by the vicarious endurance of the punishment deserved by sinful men, propitiated the justice or wrath of God and thus made possible the grace of God, is not founded on any clear and distinct passage in the New Testament. It rests, rather, on a presupposition of natural theology, clearly of Pharasaic and Greek origin. This presupposition is that justice is the fundamental relation between God and man to which religion is subordinate. And along with this a principle is accepted which is contrary to every judicial system, namely, that on the whole justice may be maintained as well by vicarious punishment as by the regular course of law. But these two ideas cannot be coordinated. For the object of justice is the universal well-being of a people or a company of men, and punishment is comprehensible only as a subordinate means to this end (par. 18). Now all law is binding only because the lawgiver shows himself a benefactor, a maintainer of the public weal. Thus the goodness of such a benefactor is the motive for the recognition of his law by the society he founds. Applied to God, this principle shows that the experience of God's goodness or grace is precedent to every law which gives expression to mutual rights between God and man. Therefore the "covenant of works" cannot be regarded as the fundamental relation between the two, and hence the "covenant of works" cannot rationally be transformed into the "covenant of grace" by Christ's fulfilling the conditions of the former and so doing away with it.

114. 1 Pet. 3:18; compare Eph. 2:16–18; Heb. 7:19; 10:19–22. The same thought is expressed in saying that the community is sanctified by the sacrifice of Christ (John 17:19; Heb. 10:14), for "to sanctify," "to make his possession," and "to cause to come near" all mean the same thing (Num. 16:5).

115. The symbolism of all lawful animal sacrifice in the Old Testament has the following content: The ministering priest, who is authorized, in the place of the people or of the individual Israelites, to bring their gifts (*corban,* that which is brought near) into God's presence, fulfills this purpose in sprinkling the blood containing the life of the animal upon the altar where God meets with the people (Exod. 20:24) and in burning the animal, or certain parts of it, in the fire, where God is present (Lev. 9:24). By these actions, which present the gift to God, the priest "shields" the people or the individuals from the God there present. This accords with the presupposition that no living being can come *uncalled* into God's presence without being destroyed. But the gift, brought according to the divine order, is the covering or protection under which those in covenant with God are ideally brought into his presence. In the sin-offering there is no rite prescribed which would signify any different

conception from that of the burnt-offering and the peace-offering. In the annual general sin-offering only the blood of the goat is sprinkled on the cover of the ark of testimony (ark of the covenant), because this is a higher symbol of the gracious presence of God than the altar of sacrifice. When God thus suffers the national community, who are conscious of sin, to draw near him in prescribed ways, then in these acts the relative separation from him resulting from sin is done away with. This bringing near to a gracious God, thus accomplished, is the ground of the fact that sins are forgiven, i.e., that they no longer separate men from God.

116. [In the first edition, this paragraph reads as follows: "Since the particular kind of communion with God that a religion embodies is linked with a corresponding stance of men toward the world, dominion over the world has been referred to Christ as an attribute which was incorporated into his distinctiveness as the Son of God and became efficacious in the obedience to his vocation which was directed toward establishing the kingdom of God (par. 23). Overcoming the world through patience in suffering was also incorporated into his obedience to his vocation to the extent that that obedience displays his role as priestly representative of the community which he is to lead to God. From this it follows, however, that for this community also, the calling to spiritual dominion over the world is inseparable from its complete reconciliation with God. Conversely, the hostility toward God which one abandons when he is reconciled with God, must be seen as servitude to the world. It is inconceivable that the man who is reconciled with God would be indifferent to the world. Therefore, spiritual dominion over the world belongs necessarily with reconciliation to God or sonship to God."]

117. Heb. 3:1; 9:15; 12:24.

118. [In the first edition, this paragraph reads as follows: "The same scope of Christ's vocational obedience which filled his life and came to fulfillment in his death is conceived under the two contrasting viewpoints of the office of royal prophet and the royal priesthood, the representing of God to men and of men (in the community) before God. In this double significance of his life, Christ appears as the mediator of the highest conceivable communion between God and man. For this reason, the community established by Christ fulfills this communion with God as its father and assures to every individual membership in this community as well as forgiveness of sins or justification and his position as child of God through faith in Jesus Christ. In relation to the world, this religious faith is the state of Christian freedom, not simply negative freedom from guilt and the power of sin, but rather the positive freedom and dominion over the world in which that negative freedom also comes into our experience."]

119. Thus the idea of Athanasius, that the positive result of redemption through Christ is the deification of the human race, is untenable.

120. Mark 8:29; James 2:1; 1 Pet. 1:7, 8; 1 John 5:1; Heb. 2:3; Rom. 3:21, 22; Acts 4:10–12.

121. John 10:15–18.

122. Mark 9:23; 11:23; Rom. 4:13; 8:31–39; 1 Cor. 3:21–23; James 1:9; 1 John 2:25; 4:9; Rom. 5:1, 2, 17; 1 Cor. 4:8.

123. John 8:36; Gal. 5:1; Luther, "The Freedom of a Christian," *LW* 31: "Now just as Christ by his birthright obtained these two prerogatives, so he imparts them to and shares them with everyone who believes in him according to the law of the above-mentioned marriage, . . . Hence all of us who believe in Christ are priests and kings in Christ, as 1 Pet. 2:9 says" (p. 354). "First, with respect to the kingship, every Christian is by faith so exalted above all things without exception, that nothing can do him any harm. As a matter of fact, all things are made subject to him and are compelled to serve him in obtaining salvation" (Rom. 8:28; 1 Cor. 3:21-33) (Ibid.). "The power of which we speak is spiritual. It rules in the midst of enemies and is powerful in the midst of oppression . . . Lo, this is the inestimable power and liberty of Christians. Not only are we the freest of kings, we are also priests forever . . . , we are worthy to appear before God to pray for others and to teach one another divine things" (p. 355). "From this anyone can clearly see how a Christian is free from all things and over all things so that he needs no works to make him righteous and save him since faith alone abundantly confers all these things" (p. 356). In this interpretation of the freedom founded on faith we find the specific difference between catholicism and protestantism. Catholicism prescribes in its place the *timor filialis* ["filial fear"], the continued anxiety lest one offend God by transgression of the law. This anxious fear before the lawgiver conforms to the whole catholic system and holds men in slavery beneath the structure of supposed guarantees of salvation, which reach their culmination in an infallible pope. The protestant, on the other hand, lives in reverent trust in God our Father, a trust which imparts courage to strive after the righteousness of God, and he needs no other guarantee than the grace of God revealed in the man Christ Jesus (Rom. 5:15).

124. 1 Pet. 1:15; 1 Thess. 4:7. The opposite condition is abnormal (2 Cor. 6:1).

125. Phil. 2:12, 13; Heb. 13:20, 21.

126. 1 Pet. 1:2; 1 John 3:24; 4:13; Heb. 6:4; 10:29; 1 Thess. 4:7, 8; Gal. 5:5, 6, 22-25; 1 Cor. 3:16, 17; Rom. 8:4, 13.

127. 1 Cor. 2:10-12; Gal. 4:6; Rom. 8:15, 16. Melanchthon, *Loci* of 1535, *CR*, XXI, 366, 367: "Scripture desires us to know the divinity of the Holy Spirit in consolation and renewing. It is useful to consider these the offices of the Holy Spirit. In this invoking of the Son in these exertions of faith, we get to know the Trinity better than in useless speculations which argue over what the persons of the Trinity do among themselves not what they do for us."

128. 1 Pet. 1:3, 22, 23; James 1:18; Gal. 6:15; Eph. 2:10; Rom. 6:4, 6; 12:2; Col. 3:9-11; Eph. 4:22-24. New birth, the usual expression for the ideal beginnings of the Christian life, corresponds to none of the expressions used in these passages. It is necessary to be on one's guard against wishing to make certain of this foundation of one's own Christian life by direct experience or at a definite time. Objectively, the new birth or new begetting by God or admission into the relation of sonship with God coincides with justification, as well as with the bestowal of the Holy Spirit. This again is the same as admission into the community. Thus for the one who attains to the independence of his Christian life through the innumerable means of education belonging to

the Christian community, it is quite impossible as well as unnecessary to mark the beginning of this result. What individuals regard as the beginning is at best to be considered only a step in their Christian development.

129. Rom. 5:1–4; 8:31–39; 14:17, 18; James 1:2–4, 9, 25; 1 Pet. 1:3–9; Phil. 4:4.

130. James 1:4; 3:2; 1 Cor. 2:6; Phil. 3:15; Col. 1:28; 4:12; Rom. 12:2; Heb. 5:14; 6:1; 1 John 4:18; Matt. 5:48.

131. 1 John 1:8.

132. Not individual good works, but a complete consistent life-work, is the duty set forth in the chief writings of the apostles (James 1:4; 1 Pet. 1:17; Heb. 6:10; 1 Thess. 5:13; Gal. 6:4; 1 Cor. 3:13–15). Good works are to be considered only as the manifestation of a consistent state of life (James 3:13; 2 Cor. 9:8; Col. 1:10).

133. In James under the name *sophia* ("wisdom") (1:5; 3:17), in Paul and elsewhere under the name of *hagiasmos* ("holiness") (1 Thess. 4:3–7; 1 Cor. 1:30; Rom. 6:19, 22; Heb. 12:14; 1 John 3:3).

134. This is clear in the case of Paul, who grounds his expectation of the completion of his salvation upon that which he accomplished in his calling (1 Thess. 2:19; Phil. 2:16; 2 Tim. 4:8; 1 Cor. 3:5–9). Cf. par. 57.

135. [Ritschl uses the term *sittlicher Beruf* frequently in the paragraphs that follow. The term is translated here as "ethical vocation." As Ritschl says clearly in paragraph 57, he is referring to the ordinary vocation or occupation in which a man carries out his daily work, by which he earns his livelihood, contributes to society, and fulfills his own personal destiny. To refer to this as one's ethical vocation may be misleading, because it could imply that an *ethical* vocation is a different vocation from the regular occupation in which one lives his life, or that it is an additional vocation. By describing the vocation as *ethical*, however, Ritschl is speaking about the attitude which a man holds toward his regular occupation and the status it assumes for him. The attitude should be a very serious one, because the occupation must be carried out in high ethical responsibility, precisely because one's daily occupation carries a very high status as the vehicle in which a man fulfills his destiny as a son of God who contributes his own labor to the work of God's kingdom. An *ethical vocation*, therefore, is an ordinary, worldly vocation which is entered into and carried out with high ethical resolve and religious understanding.]

136. James 4:8–10; 1 Pet. 2:11, 12; Rom. 8:13; 13:12–14; Col. 3:5–10.

137. The exercise of righteousness serves for sanctification (Rom. 6:19, 22; compare Heb. 12:14), i.e., for the attainment of a godly character.

138. Rom. 6:11. It is analogous to this that the perfect no longer look upon that part of their career which is behind, but on that which is ahead (Phil. 3:12–15).

139. 1 John 1:8.

140. Mark 1:15; 2 Cor. 7:9, 10. Luther's first thesis of Oct. 31, 1517 (in "Explanation of the Ninety-Five Theses," *LW*, 31, 83): "When our Lord and Master Jesus Christ said, 'Repent,' he willed the entire life of believers to be one of repentance."

141. The example of Christ, it is true, is only appealed to in the New Testament in particular respects, as love (Eph. 5:2), devotion to the public good (1 Cor. 10:33; 11:1; Phil. 2:2–5), patience in suffering (1 Pet. 2:21).

142. *CA* XXVII, 49–50: "For this is Christian perfection: honestly to fear God and at the same time to have great faith and to trust that for Christ's sake we have a gracious God; to ask of God, and assuredly to expect from him, help in all things which are to be borne in connection with our callings; meanwhile to be diligent in the performance of good works for others and to attend to our calling. True perfection and true service of God consist of these things and not celibacy, mendicancy, or humble attire" (contrast to the catholic conception of Christian perfection as attained only in monasticism). This contrasted conception of perfection corresponds to the conception of sin in *CA* II, 1 (see also n. 82, above).

143. Mark 8:35–37: "Whosoever shall lose his life for my sake and the gospel's the same shall save it. For what shall it profit a man if he shall gain the whole world and lose his own life? Or what shall a man give in exchange for his life?" The valuing of life as an incomparable good, superior for us therefore to the value of the whole world, is here presupposed as a universal conviction. But at the same time, a truth is also presupposed which is in direct opposition to this conviction, namely, that the loss of life, which awaits every man, proves the insignificance of life in the presence of the regular order of the world. But if one assures his life through union with Christ, even though it be by losing it according to the order of the world, then, on this special condition, the correctness of the claim felt by every human being to have a value surpassing that of the world is established, and any experience of an opposite nature is rendered invalid.

144. 1 Cor. 3:21, 22.

145. *CA* XX, 24: "Whoever knows that he has a Father reconciled to him through Christ . . . knows that God cares for him." The goal and the test of justification by faith in Christ are reverence toward God and trust in his help in all times of need. Compare *Apology*, XX. This reciprocal relation between a special trust in providence and the certainty of reconciliation with God is not rendered less valid by the fact that Seneca also says (*De providentia*, 2): "The brave man is more powerful than all external circumstances. I do not say that he does not suffer, but he conquers. . . . He ponders the actions that are appropriate for all things. . . . The god of the fatherland gives his attention to brave men." For in the first place, these sentences do not signify that trust in God's providence is a datum of the so-called natural or rational religion that all men are said to possess. Instead, it is a special mark of the Stoic philosopher and not common to paganism as a whole, since *natural religion* can attain to this idea neither in its polytheistic form, nor in tragic poetry, nor in the course of philosophy as a whole. But these sentences from Seneca are also not at all like the Christian expressions which they resemble, because they stand in connection with all the hardness of the Stoic sense of self and consciousness of power. [Here Ritschl cites further passages from chapters 2 and 4 of Seneca's work, taking issue with Seneca's admiration of heroic suicide.] According to the Christian standard, suicide is only conceivable as a result of an utter lack of faith in the providence of God.

146. Rom. 11:33–36. Cf. n. 54, above.

147. This knowledge breaks through occasionally even in the Old Testament (Jer. 30:11; Prov. 3:11, 12; Ps. 118:18). In Christianity this knowledge follows from the necessary explanation of the sufferings of Christ the righteous one (Mark 8:34, 35; James 1:2, 3; 1 Pet. 1:6, 7; Heb. 12:4–11; Rom. 5:3, 4; 8:28).

148. 1 Thess. 5:16–18. Thankfulness to God is in general the motive for joy, which is expected to be the pervading tone of the Christian life. Cf. also Rom. 14:17; 15:13; Phil. 4:4.

149. Humility is most clearly expressed in the "fear of God" (1 Pet. 1:17; 3:2; Phil. 2:12; Rom. 11:20; 2 Cor. 5:11; 7:1), which is the "beginning of wisdom" (Prov. 9:10), i.e., godly righteousness.

150. "Humility is like an eye, which sees everything else, but not itself; real humility does not know that it exists." (Scriver) Here the line is drawn against the self-conscious pride of virtue in Stoicism, and the self-conscious pride of religion in all kinds of Pharisaism. The healthy emotional life, expressive of constant harmony with one's self or with the world and with God, moves along under the escort of unclear conceptions. Thus religious experiences of conscious and hence heightened happiness are always infrequent and of dubious value, since their discontinuance is usually experienced with dissatisfaction. We must judge in accordance with this the cases of conscious religious happiness and the universal desire for religious enjoyment.

151. Humility will, it is true, usually be accompanied by modesty toward others (both meanings meet in *tapeinos* ["lowly"], Phil. 2:8; Matt. 23:12; Col. 3:12; Eph. 4:2; Phil. 2:3; 1 Pet. 5:5), but also, on occasion, by anger and zeal against the wicked (Mark 3:5).

152. Such a case is judged as "false humility" in Col. 3:20–23. Jesus judges as hypocrisy (Matt. 23—*hypokrites*, "actor") the ceremonial legal exhibition by the Pharisees of humility as a special devotion to God. The zeal which seeks to impose upon others this or similar ceremonial legal forms of humility, or to put them into effect by force, is fanaticism.

153. James 1:3; 5:10, 11; 2 Cor. 6:4; Rom. 5:3; 12:12. Calvin's *Institutes*, (McNeill, 708): "Yet such a cheerfulness is not required of us as to remove all feeling of bitterness and pain. Otherwise, in the cross there would be no forbearance of the saints unless they were tormented by pain and anguished by trouble."

154. Peter Martyr Vermilius: "This is the character of the sons of God, that they frequently take time for prayers; for that is what it means to perceive the providence of God."

155. Matt. 7:7–11.

156. Mark 14:36; 1 John 5:14.

157. 1 John 3:21, 22.

158. 1 John 5:15. That is, the certainty of God's care in general is not disturbed by the fact that many petitions for individual blessings are not directly answered, but rather it furnishes a compensation for the fact that certain petitions are not answered with exact literalness.

159. This is the error of the catholic view that monasticism implements real Christian virtue or the ideal of the supramundane angelic existence just because it is outside of the natural forms of morality. The giving up of family, private property, complete independence and personal dignity (in obedience to superiors) does not in itself assure a more positive and a richer development of the moral nature, but rather threatens it. For these blessings are absolutely essential conditions of moral health and the formation of character. Pietistic inclination approaches the error of the catholic system in this matter.

160. 1 Cor. 7:20–24. If here even the condition of slavery is viewed in the light of an ethical vocation and so made morally endurable (1 Pet. 2:18, 19) this is certainly true of all kinds of free labor. As to labor, 1 Thess. 4:11; 2 Thess. 3:10–12; as to public spirit, Phil. 2:2–4; Rom. 12:3–5; Cf. *Apology*, XV, 25–26. The demand of Christ in Mark 10:21 has reference to the condition on which the calling of the disciples was to be exercised at that time and does not prescribe monasticism for all times.

161. *Apology*, XXVII, 48–50. (As to the conversation of Christ with the rich young man, Matt. 19:21): "Perfection consists in that which Christ adds, 'Follow me.' This sets forth the example of obedience in a calling. . . . Callings are personal, but the example of obedience is universal. It would have been perfection for this young man to believe and obey this calling. So it is perfection for each of us with true faith to obey his own calling."

162. The ethical blessings of family, station, and patriotism can be perverted into a narrow-minded pride of family, pride of station, and national vanity.

163. Luther, "To the German Nobility," *LW*, 44: "Just as those whom we call clergy (*die Geistlichen*) are distinguished from other Christians only by the fact that they are to administer the word of God and the sacraments—this is their work and office, in the same way secular officials hold the sword to punish the wicked and to protect the pious. A shoemaker, a smith, a peasant, each one has the work and office of his own craft, and yet they are all at the same time consecrated priests and bishops, i.e., spiritual persons [*geistliche Personen*], and each one ought to be useful and serviceable to the other in his office or his work." From "Concerning Monastic Vows": "The obedience of sons, wives, servants, and captives is more perfect that the obedience of monks. Therefore, if we are to move from the imperfect to the perfect, we must go from the obedience of monks to that of parents, masters, tyrants, enemies, and all others."

164. Mark 10:6–8; Gen. 2:24. *Apology*, XXIII, 11–13: "The union of man and woman is by natural right. Natural right is really divine right, because it is an ordinance divinely stamped on nature." Therefore the positive institution of the legal marriage contract falls under the control of the state. Christian marriage is legal marriage between Christians, and does not, therefore, first derive its Christian character through consecration by the church.

165. Mark 10:9–12; 12:25; 1 Pet. 3:7. Exceptions to the indissolubility of marriage appear early, Matt. 19:9; 5:32; 1 Cor. 7:15.

166. Eph. 5:25–29.

167. Col. 3:18, 19; Eph. 5:33; 1 Pet. 3:1.

168. 1 Cor. 7:14.

169. Col. 3:20; Eph. 6:1-3.

170. The view of the Middle Ages, shared even by Luther, that we could get along without legal ordinances were it not for sin, because then everyone would do what is right from love, is false. This view does not take into account the necessary organization and gradation of the ethical principles for the different spheres of life, whereby we are spared a waste of energy. The use of legal enactment thus makes active life an easier matter than would be possible if at every step it were necessary to consider the highest possible standards and their application to ordinary civic duties.

171. Mark 12:17.

172. 1 Pet. 2:13-17; Rom. 13:1-7.

173. Society, when unorganized into a state, whether in a revolutionary or nomadic condition, is an absolute hindrance to the Christian task of the kingdom of God. Even the Israelites were obliged to abandon the nomadic life in order to perform the duties of their religion, whose fundamental promise was that they should acquire a permanent dwelling place (Gen. 12:1-3).

174. CA XVI, 6: "Therefore Christians are necessarily bound to obey their magistrates and laws except when commanded to sin, for then they ought to obey God rather than men (Acts 5:29)." This limitation of the duty of obedience to the state deals with a very distant possibility. The expression of Peter referred to asserts rather the duty of Christian confession in direct opposition to unjustifiable limitations proceeding from a churchly authority.

175. Paul clearly recognized this (Rom. 12:2; Phil. 1:9-11; cf. Rom. 2:18). This proving of what is different, the good and the bad, denotes the finding out of duty, i.e., of what is necessary to do in a particular case. Col. 1:9, 10 refers further to the reciprocal relation, that by wisdom we recognize what God's will is as to a particular course of action, while by the performance of the recognized duties the ability to recognize duty is increased.

176. This table of virtues is complete. All others referred to in ordinary discourse are either synonyms (as faithfulness with conscientiousness or kindliness) or subspecies of self-control (chastity, frugality, moderation) or principles of duty which correspond to the virtue of kindliness (modesty, uprightness, readiness to serve, etc.). This may be seen in the fact that kindliness is to be present always, while these special activities cannot be exercised in all cases, since they must be suspended in intercourse with certain persons.

177. The exalted importance of conscientiousness (Luke 16:10; 1 Cor. 4:2) appears in the fact that it serves as an abbreviated standard of right for the actions of one's regular vocation. It does not, it is true, serve to determine the necessary manner of conduct outside of the regular calling. It is, however, often enough applied as a rule in this realm, through a belief in the authority of conscience as a trustworthy and final standard for all ethical conduct. But the correctness of such a belief is confuted by the fact that there exists also an erring or weak conscience (1 Cor. 8:7-12; 10:28-31; Rom. 14:1-4), which is to be respected in the person of its possessor but is also to be recognized as a tribunal needing correction by higher standards. Still less can the conscientiousness of individuals determined for themselves by false judgment be accepted as a general law for others. When one, for instance, not only erro-

neously makes ascetic rules a part of his own Christian vocation but also wishes to judge others by his own conscientiousness so determined, his conscience is spotted or scarred (Titus 1:15; 1 Tim. 4:2, 3), because he must have suppressed his doubt as to the rightfulness of his proceeding.

178. Wisdom: 1 Cor. 3:10; 6:5; Luke 21:15; Matt. 23:45; 25:2. Discretion, soberness: 1 Pet. 1:13; 5:8; 1 Thess. 5:6, 8. Determination: Rom. 14:22, 23; Col. 4:15; Eph. 5:15, 16. Constancy: Luke 8:15; Heb. 10:36; 12:1; Rev. 2:2; Rom. 2:7.

179. Matt. 10:16; Luke 16:8.

180. 1 Cor. 13:4, 5; Gal. 5:22; Col. 3:12; Eph. 4:32; Phil. 4:5.

181. The moral peculiarity of individuals depends upon the different degrees in which the several groups of virtues are developed, and the various combinations thus arising. At the same time it is also conditioned by the nature of one's vocation, the grade of intelligence and the kind and grade of artistic ability which belongs to each one in general and affects his own moral self-expression.

182. This principle decides against Jesuitic morality, which, because the general moral law does not extend to definite actions, treats the conception of obligation as itself indefinite; it accordingly withdraws the individual possible actions from any definite determination and teaches that they are to be decided according to the authority or assurance of individuals in harmony with the precept that "the end justifies the means."

183. This appears clearly in Christ's Sermon on the Mount (Matt. 5–7), the particular precepts of which are sometimes applicable only by analogy, and sometimes have reference to intercourse with brethren, i.e., with men of like moral disposition. Thus they always take for granted the free judgment of circumstances which cannot be enumerated in the rule.

184. James 1:25.

185. Because the duty of one's vocation is the regular and ordinary form of the duty of love, its fulfillment is rightfully recognized as a part of Christian perfection (see n. 142, above). For the determination of the duties belonging to one's vocation, the virtue of conscientiousness which corresponds to the vocation is, in the formula of the authoritative conscience, the ordinarily sufficient subjective standard. Hence conscientiousness seems to extend also to the judgment as to whether one is called to the performance of certain extraordinary duties of love. Yet this is the very realm where the erring conscience (see n. 177, above) has full play, when one forgets that his own vocation has its limitations, and that some actions are really less analogous to it than one easily imagines.

186. Calvin, *Institutes*, III, 10, 2 [McNeill, 720–21]: "Now if we ponder to what end God created food, we shall find that he meant not only to provide for necessity but also for delight and good cheer. . . . Did he not, in short, render many things attractive to us, apart from their necessary use?"

187. This is the underlying principle of the second table of the commandments (see n. 13, above).

188. The right conception of modesty must always be distinguished from such a false ascetic conception as that which Thomas á Kempis expressed (*De Imita-*

tione Christi, I. 7): "If you possess anything good, then believe the better of other people, so that you may preserve humility. It does no harm for you to subordinate yourselves to others; but it does great harm for you to place yourself above others." This rule contradicts the natural impression of many experiences and involves a constant reflective self-scrutiny in comparing ourselves with others, and it is even more unwholesome, since the result sought after can often enough be reached only by ignoring the truth. For in modesty the important thing cannot be that one regards an immature man as more mature than himself, etc.; but the important thing is that one subordinate himself as an individual to the worth of the fellowship which is sought, in that he puts himself both in speech and action in relation to another. When we are forbidden to judge [*richten*] others (Matt. 7:1–5), the giving up of all moral judgment [*Beurteilung*] of others is not demanded of us. It appears rather from a comparison of that rule with James 4:11, 12 and Rom. 14:4, that such judging of others is wrong when it elevates itself indirectly above the lawgiver or ignores the value of another in God's sight. For thereby the significance of this one for our fellowship would be denied also; but the necessity of such fellowship is established by the law of Christ and by the common dependence of all upon God. One can thus, for instance, make clear to himself the lower moral grade of another in accordance with the truth and yet show him modesty, i.e., the loving regard for his personality which makes one care for his education or improvement.

189. The sincerity which duty demands of us is not the same as natural frankness, though it is made easier by frankness, and the material of individual self-communication is contained in them both. But frankness cannot come to its full expression in sincerity without a restriction by the common end which one is seeking in contact with others. This limitation of natural frankness in sincerity varies according to the character of those with whom one has to do—the two negatives, immodesty and insincerity, denote direct and positive violations of regard for others, the latter as falsity under the guise of sincerity. Non-sincerity or reserve is to be distinguished from these as a purely negative manifestation.

190. Therefore rectitude is possible apart from the disposition of love, as is the negative regard for the person and property of others (see n. 187, above). Both are included in the conception of civil justice which according to the doctrine of the reformers is possible even in the sinful state. It is, however, to be remarked that even in this conception of rectitude the standard is found not in the positive law but in the idea of justice. For this rectitude also excludes such forms of fraud as under certain circumstances are not subject to punishment by the letter of the law and the administration of justice connected with it, for instance, usury, i.e., using another's distress to one's own profit under the form of a legal contract.

191. These three principles have a common opposite in the fundamental unwillingness to please which refuses personal services, gifts and information (in disobliging taciturnity or reserve). Truthfulness has, however, a more distinct opposite in lying, or in a fundamental mendacity. Not every untrue statement is a lie. In the realm of art, in jest, in the deception of children or the sick or enemies, an untrue statement is occasionally permissible or even

desirable. But a lie is an untruth told with the purpose of injuring another or of gaining an unwarrantable advantage for one's self, or both. Mendacity is the habitual inclination to untruthfulness, arising either from such a purpose, or from such an indifference to truth as excludes the purpose of being of service to others through truthfulness.

192. Matt. 5:23, 24.

193. Matt. 7:6.

194. [In the first edition, this paragraph stands as follows: "Perfection, which consists in the exercise of religious and moral virtues and in the performance of the duties of love regulated by our ethical vocation, is necessarily accompanied by a feeling of blessedness. In the present worldly existence, only a few persons succeed in attaining this pinnacle of Christian character-formation and in asserting it in the struggle with their own sin and in patience in the face of external restraints, since ethical sensitivity only throws stronger light on all the defects and faults which present themselves to that sensitivity. Moreover, it is not possible to create a community of the perfect as such, so as to establish a smaller circle, so to speak, within the larger community of those who worship God. For men's striving after the kingdom of God is never evident to the observation of others in such a way as to allow us to enter into a particular alliance for the purpose of advancing that effort. Furthermore, the task of education which is implied in the imperative of the kingdom of God would be hindered rather than advanced if Christians of highest character isolated themselves from the rest of the community as a particular, more restricted group. Nevertheless, the communal concern of the Christian religion is not satisfied by the confidence that a few persons will always be able to scale the heights of Christian perfection. For this reason, this communal concern engenders the hope that those Christians who have attained their own personal form of perfection will attain the higher communal goal of life and blessedness under conditions of existence other than those that prevail in this world of experience."]

195. Such an order appeared originally in Buddhism, then in Manichaeism, then was applied in the estimate of Christian monasticism, and finally appears again in pietistic circles. In all these similar manifestations, there is prominent a religious bias toward an abstract denial of the world, which in varying degrees is common to these religions and tendencies. At the same time it is true, a separation of the *perfecti* from the *auditores* (as they are classified in Manichaeism) only appears when at bottom there is a strong tendency toward a ceremonial-legal conception of religion.

196. [In the first edition, this paragraph reads as follows: "Eternal life grows out of the common destiny which Christians possess by virtue of reconciliation through Christ and therefore is a result of God's grace; but, since this eternal life belongs to the Christian as the distinctive goal that is to be attained within the community, it is conditioned by the exercise of justification and by sanctification. Furthermore, as the supranatural and supramundane consummation of the humanity which is uniting itself in the kingdom of God, this eternal life is only conceivable under circumstances in which the natural conditions to which our spiritual life is bound in this present world will either be removed

or altered in the future. Christ and the apostles expected the appearance of this consummation and these circumstances to come more quickly than actually was the case, and they did so in terms of the dramatic images of God's judgment over the world, which had been utilized by the Old Testament prophets. Natural science also sets forth, by its methods, the end of the present world order, particularly the dissolution of the solar system, by which the earth processes are determined. In contrast, the religious estimate of our spiritual and ethical life that arises in Christianity provides the basis for hope that that spiritual and ethical life will be maintained and strengthened in communion with God and in the kingdom of perfected spirits. As decisive as the subjective certainty of this consummation may be in our own feeling regarding the significance of our lives—formed as they are by Christian influences—there remains necessarily a lack of clarity in our concrete vision of the means by which this consummation will be actualized and shaped in the hereafter, because our present experience cannot touch upon those things. For this reason, all of the forms set forth in the New Testament concerning the last things possess a symbolic significance. Similarly, those structures of thought which we have to acknowledge as the framework for religious hope cannot be filled out with a content that is directly perceivable."]

197. Mark 8:38; 9:1; 1 Pet. 4:7; James 5:8, 9; 1 John 2:28; 1 Thess. 4:15; 1 Cor. 10:11; 15:52; Heb. 10:35–37. Compare, on the other hand, 2 Pet. 3:4–9; Rev. 19:11–22; 1 Pet. 4:5; Heb. 10:30, 31; 2 Cor. 5:10; Matt. 25:31–46.

198. 1 Thess. 4:16, 17.

199. *CA* XVII, 1: ". . . at the consummation of the world Christ will appear for judgment and will raise up all the dead. To the godly and elect he will give eternal life and endless joy, but ungodly men and devils he will condemn to be tormented without end."

200. Here belongs the expectation of continued existence in a body corresponding fully to the spirit (1 Cor. 15:35–53; 2 Cor. 5:1; Phil. 3:20, 21); as well as the destiny of those who are not saved, of whom it seems uncertain whether they shall suffer endless punishment or be annihilated (Mark 9:43–48; Rev. 19:20; Rom. 2:9, 12; 9:22; Phil. 3:19; Rev. 17:8, 11; Matt. 7:13).

201. The same community which, in mutual moral action, forms the kingdom of God is through reconciliation with God at the same time destined to unite itself in public worship (see n. 18, above).

202. The fruit of lips which confess God's name is the sacrifice of praise (Heb. 13:15; cf. 1 Pet. 2:5), a sacrifice which occasionally, even in the Old Testament, is recognized as the opposite of, and the most complete substitute for, material sacrifice (Hos. 14:2; Ps. 50:14, 23; 51:15–17; 116:17; Isa. 57:19).

203. The word "prayer" is a real hindrance to the recognition of this fact, since the first thought it suggests is that of petition. But one only needs to look through the Psalms, which in Hebrew are called *tehillim* (songs of praise), to recognize the norm of the matter in the statement above.

204. The calling upon God as our Father through Jesus Christ (par. 12) distinguishes Christianity from all other religions, including that of the Old Testament. For although God stands in the Old Testament as the father of the chosen

people Israel, which is his son (Exod. 4:22; Hos. 11:1), the right is first given to the members of his community by Christ to regard themselves individually as sons or children of God, while he designates the Israelites as strangers, i.e., as servants of God (Matt. 17:24–27). Accordingly, it is characteristic that Paul, in the opening of his epistles, identifies himself with the community he addresses by giving thanks to God as our Father and as the Father of our Lord Jesus Christ and does so on the ground of the existence of the Christian religion in that community (1 Thess. 1:2–5; 2 Thess. 1:3, 4; Gal. 1:3–5; 1 Cor. 1:4–9; 2 Cor. 1:3–7; Rom. 1:8; Col. 1:3–6; Eph. 1:3–6; Phil. 1:3–7; cf. Acts 2:11, 47).

205. Phil. 4:6; 1 Thess. 5:16–18.

206. John 14:13, 14; 15:16; 16:23, 34.

207. For various reasons the text of this prayer and the occasion for it as given in Luke 11:1–3 are to be preferred to the text and the context in Matt. 6:9–13. In the former the prayer consists of five petitions [Here Ritschl includes the Greek text of the Lord's Prayer]. What is added in Matthew proves to be only an enlargement of the second and fifth petitions. For the coming of the kingdom of God consists in God's will being done on earth as in heaven (Ps. 103:21), and being delivered from evil is identical with being kept from temptation.

208. This is the meaning of the "name of God" (Ps. 9:10; 69:36; Deut. 28:58; 32:3; Isa. 30:27; 50:10).

209. Isa. 29:23; Ezek. 36:23.

210. Matt. 6:31, 32.

211. Priests are those who are permitted to draw near to God (Num. 16:5). In this sense the Israelites were originally a kingdom of priests (Exod. 19:6). The exercise of this right was then limited in being restricted to the mediation by the sacrifice of the official Levitic priests. In Christianity this condition is done away with, since in its community only the sacrifice of prayer is offered; thus all Christians are priests (1 Pet. 2:5, 9; Rev. 1:9; 5:10; Heb. 7:19; 10:22; 13:15).

212. Matt. 10:32, 33; Rom. 10:9; 1 Cor. 12:3; Phil. 2:11. This confession of the church corresponds both to its historical peculiarity and to its universal human destiny. By this confession Christians are to be distinguished from all other religious communities, but at the same time they are to extend their community until it embraces humanity.

213. Mark 4:14; John 5:24, 38; 8:31; 14:23, 24; Luke 10:16; Acts 4:29; 1 Pet. 1:23–25; Rom. 1:1; 1 Cor. 14:36; Col. 1:25; 1 Thess. 2:13.

214. Eph. 4:4–6; 1 Cor. 10:17.

215. 1 Cor. 11:26; Matt. 28:19. The marks of the unity of the church are not similar in nature to one another, and no one of them ought to be emphasized in a one-sided manner. The preaching of the divine word in the church must be evaluated with reference to its goal, namely, that the church may be united in the prayer-confession of God through their Lord Jesus Christ, and the two acts instituted by Christ fully attain their divine sacramental significance only when they are performed as acts of worship on the part of the com-

munity. Thus the definition of the church in the *CA* VII, 1: "The assembly of all believers among whom the Gospel is preached in its purity and the holy sacraments are administered according to the Gospel," is incomplete, because it lacks the characteristic of uniform prayer. But further, a right understanding of the matter would not be reached if the word of God, prayer, sacraments, were only enumerated side by side as similar characteristics of the church. For the contrast must be maintained between the word *of God* and the prayer *of the community*, in order to recognize the reciprocal relation between the two, and it must be made clear, in the case of baptism and the Lord's Supper, that the reciprocal relation between the *act of the community* and the *gracious gift of God* is expressed in one and the same act.

216. Belief here has reference to the church as the union of believers in the Holy Spirit and as the sphere designated by the forgiveness of sins (see n. 102, above). This belief recognizes these determinations of value as belonging to the church and recognizes the church in these relations as a reality whose existence is assured by God. Legal forms, however, are not definitions of value for religious faith, and thus it ignores them in establishing the religious significance of the church.

217. Acts. 2:1–11.

218. 1 Thess. 5:12, 13; 1 Cor. 16:15, 16; 1 Pet. 5:1–5; Heb. 13:17.

219. 1 Cor. 6:1–6; 7:10–17.

220. *CA* V, 1. The fact is overlooked here that the preachers of the divine word are at the same time the liturgists, i.e., those who offer prayer for the congregation. Now as prayer is an activity in whose exercise all Christians are priests (see n. 211, above), there can be no objection to designating those who offer the public liturgical prayers as official priests. In so doing the right of the catholics to limit this title to the sacrifice of the mass is denied, since in the protestant sense no other kind of sacrifice belongs to the priest than that which belongs to all, the sacrifice of the lips—prayer.

221. John 10:16.

222. Baptism and the Lord's Supper, in spite of their original intent (see n. 214, above), unfortunately can no longer be called actual characteristics of the unity of the church. The Lord's Supper is almost everywhere without hesitation made the confessional sign of churchly schism. Baptism also is no longer what Luther considered it, a common characteristic of all sects. In the Greek church, which practices a threefold immersion, the sprinkling of the western church is not so fully recognized that Latin Christians may not be baptized at the option of the individual priest. The numberless sects of Baptists do not recognize infant sprinkling as baptism at all. And lately the Roman Catholics have been departing from the former recognition of heretical baptism and occasionally rebaptize converts from protestantism.

223. The earliest document of the kind, the so-called Apostles' Creed, cannot rightly be regarded as the uniform confession of the *whole* church. For in the Greek church it is neither in official use, nor is it generally known, since there its place is occupied by the Nicene-Constantinopolitan formula of the rule of faith.

224. *CA* XXVIII, 12, 21: "Therefore, ecclesiastical and civil power are not to be confused. . . . Hence according to the Gospel (or, as they say, by divine right) no jurisdiction belongs to the bishops as bishops (that is, to those to whom has been committed the ministry of Word and sacraments) except to forgive sins, to reject doctrine which is contrary to the Gospel, and to exclude from the fellowship of the church ungodly persons whose wickedness is known, doing all this without human power, simply by the Word."

225. Luther, "To the German Nobility," *LW*, 44: "Since secular authority is ordained by God, to punish the wicked and to protect the good, they shall be suffered to exercise their office unhindered throughout the whole body of Christendom, regardless as to whom it may affect, be it pope, bishops, priests, monks, nuns, or whomsoever it may."

226. Acts 2:38; 8:16; 10:48; 19:5; Rom. 6:3; Gal. 3:27; Matt. 28:19.

227. Acts 2:38. Many passages of the New Testament which are generally understood as referring to the Christian baptism of the *individual*, do not have reference to this, but to the *general* renewing of man by the Spirit of God, which is symbolically referred to in the Prophets as cleansing and quickening through water (John 3:5; Titus 3:5; cf. Ezek. 36:25, 26; Isa. 32:15; Joel 3:1).

228. *CA*, IX, 2: ". . . children offered to God through Baptism are received into his grace." Here the baptism of children is rightly represented as a consecrating of them by the community, an action which is effective because of the relation of the community to God.

229. 1 Cor. 10:16, 17; 11:23–26; Mark 14:22–24; Matt. 26:26–28; Luke 22: 19, 20.

230. Luther's *Large Catechism*, V, 32: "Now, the whole Gospel and the article of the Creed, 'I believe in the holy Christian church, the forgiveness of sins,' are embodied in this sacrament and offered to us through the Word."

INDEX

Index